CW00870993

Shaping Postwar Europe

Shaping Postwar Europe

European Unity and Disunity
1945–1957

Edited by Peter M. R. Stirk and David Willis

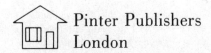
Pinter Publishers
London

© Peter Stirk, David Willis and contributors, 1991

First published in Great Britain in 1991 by
Pinter Publishers Limited
25 Floral Street, London WC2E 9DS

All rights reserved. No part of this publication may be reproduced, stored in a retrieval system, or transmitted by any other means without the prior written permission of the copyright holder. Please direct all enquiries to the publishers.

British Library Cataloguing in Publication Data

A CIP catalogue record for this book is available from the British Library

ISBN 0 86187 161 8

Typeset by Witwell Ltd, Southport
Printed and bound in Great Britain by Biddles Ltd., Guildford and Kings Lynn

Contents

List of contributors

Peter M. R. Stirk – Lecturer in Politics, Sunderland Polytechnic.
David Willis – Lecturer, Department of European Studies, University of Hull.
Michael Burgess – Lecturer in Politics, Department of American Studies, University of Keele.
David Ellwood – Professor of History, Department of History, University of Bologna.
P. P. D'Attorre – Department of History, University of Bologna.
R. N. Berki – Professor, Department of European Studies, University of Hull.
Mihály Fülöp – Hungarian Institute of International Affairs, Budapest.
Stuart Croft – Graduate School of International Studies, University of Birmingham.
David Weigall – Senior Lecturer, School of History, Anglia Polytechnic.
Antonio Varsori – Department of Politics, University of Florence.
Ruggero Ranieri – Department of Economic History, London School of Economics and Political Science.
Vicki L. Golich – Department of Political Science, Pennsylvania State University.
G. Izik-Hedri – Director, European Cooperation Foundation, Budapest.

Acknowledgements

It is a pleasant duty to record that this volume is the product of a research project, *European Unity in Context*, which was funded by a substantial grant from the Leverhulme Trust. As well as providing for a full-time Research Fellow the grant facilitated the holding of three conferences at the University of Hull. Help towards the expenses of some overseas delegates was also received from the Great Britain/East Europe Centre.

Thanks are also due to Professor R. N. Berki without whose vision and effort the research project and associated conferences would not have existed. Finally, Jacky Peters, Secretary of the Department of European Studies, not only ensured that the administration of the conferences progressed smoothly but also that the enterprise was agreeable.

PMRS
DW

1 Introduction: Shaping Postwar Europe

Peter M. R. Stirk and David Willis

The articles in this volume arose from a conference held in September 1989, when the collapse of the forty-year-old cold war divisions was still in the future. They deal with the shaping of Europe into a political, economic and cultural structure and the birth of an era whose end is now being celebrated. Yet much survives from the postwar shaping of Europe, most evidently the broad pattern of territorial delimitation – with the notable exception of German reunification – and the European Community, whose founding treaties mark the end of the period under consideration. The solidity of the territorial settlement and the success of the European Community exemplify the successes of the shaping of Europe in the postwar world. Nor can other survivals be ignored. The repressed nationalism of eastern European states has resurfaced to compound the immense difficulties of reconstruction in central and eastern Europe. The current period of reconstruction is not a purely European affair. It is taking place in a world context, itself shaped by institutions and patterns of cooperation whose foundations were laid in the postwar period of reconstruction. For while the postwar superpower conflict developed and maintained divisions within Europe as well as 'artificial' patterns of cooperation (notably the Council for Mutual Economic Assistance), a broader vision was also consolidated. A 'raft' of international agreements and institutions emerged, dedicated to the promotion of economic and political cooperation: the General Agreement on Tarrifs and Trade (GATT), the International Monetary Fund (IMF), the International Bank for Reconstruction and Development (IBRD) and the United Nations. Although they were all embroiled in the conflict of the cold war, they had been envisaged as strategies for global cooperation. Their survival, like the eventual success of the European Community, is as striking as their failure to realize wartime hopes. To a great extent, then, the current transformation takes us back to the immediate postwar era. The failure to secure Pan-European integration and to maintain superpower cooperation in the wake of 1945 is the legacy of the postwar shaping of Europe, a legacy that must now be resolved. Only an incorrigible optimist would imagine that the solution will be rapid or easy.

The articles assembled below illuminate some of the difficulties encountered in managing a process of reconstruction and integration. From the perspective of the federalists, whose vision of a postwar Europe was forged in resistance to the Nazi New Order, the immediate postwar years were often ones of bitter disillusion. As Burgess shows in chapter two, the radical hopes for the creation of European polity, facilitated by the great powers and borne forth by a popular movement committed to the replacement of the nation-state, ran aground on the realities of postwar politics. The postwar era soon looked like a 'false dawn'. Restoration, not transformation, was the order of the day. In the wake of the Second World War, however, restoration was a major undertaking and entailed its own novelties. Chief among the latter was the American involvement in Europe to an extent hitherto unknown. The United States, like many of its Allies and ex-enemies, was committed to the reintegration of Europe into a world economy and, for the first time, came to see some kind of European federation as part and parcel of the wider process of reconstruction. The United States, once suspicious of European federation, became an active proponent of federation and soon found itself in the position of trying to drag recalcitrant European governments towards a goal it had once opposed.[1]

The impact of the United States in shaping the postwar world, and maintaining it, has been rivalled only by that of the Soviet Union. The two superpowers have been credited, in retrospect, with creating a kind of stability, albeit one based upon the division of Europe, which the Europeans had been incapable of achieving on their own account.[2] The role of the United States grows even more prominent: it outpaces that of its superpower rival when it is placed within a wider context. For the United States presided over the restoration of a global economy. It has been argued that the role of the United States was a veritable precondition of the global economy. So vital has American hegemony come to be seen that the faltering of its supremacy in recent years is now cited as a threat to, or more optimistically, a challenge to the ability of others to maintain international economic cooperation.[3] At the end of the Second World War there was little doubt that the United States was the pre-eminent nation. Untouched by the ravages of war, secure in the possession of vast raw material resources, in possession of the most advanced and horrendous weapons of war, the United States presented an image of unprecedented power. The challenge of America was a multifaceted one. As an ally it could offer military protection, though fears of a return to isolation meant there was no guarantee that protection would be forthcoming. As a banker and a source of raw materials, foodstuffs and goods, it could play a vital role in economic reconstruction, though the abrupt ending of the wartime Lend-Lease agreements cast doubt on its willingness to play its role. Uncertainty about the intentions of the United States was to persist for differing periods depending upon the particular facet of the complex phenomenon of the United States that was at issue.

Clarity about the United States' economic commitment to Europe began to crystalize in 1947. Postwar recovery had proved to be more problematic than expected; by the end of 1946 the severity of Europe's problems were beginning to impress themselves upon American policy-makers. The Marshall Plan, following on from the announcement of the Truman doctrine, is a seminal turning point in the shaping of postwar Europe.[4] The American offer of aid to Europe, named after the Secretary of State, George C. Marshall, turned out to mark the division of Europe. As the states of Europe that fell under the Soviet sphere of influence refused to participate, in some cases against their initial inclinations, an economic division was added to the political and military division. The Marshall Plan, as Ellwood describes here in chapter three was itself a highly complex process. In part it was a package of economic aid, the significance of which continues to be disputed, bolstered by a commitment to free trade. It also became an attempt to transform the expectations and behaviour of Europeans on a wide front. The 'politics of growth' that the Marshall Plan administrators sought to export to Europe operated on a different timescale from the more prosaic matters of meeting immediate shortages or even securing agreement to free-trade policies. It is this aspect, the transformation of 'wants, needs, attitudes and aspirations', to which Ellwood draws attention.

The 'politics of growth' was not an invention of the postwar era. Nor were the responses of Europeans to the Marshall Plan any the less rooted in national histories. Stirk explores the responses of two different groups, British and German trade unionists and socialists. In neither case was there a blind or supine acceptance of the American prescription. Attempts were made to interpret and adapt the promise of the Marshall Plan to the interests and histories of the British and German labour movements. In the British case this meant that some aspects of the Marshall Plan, the drive for increased productivity, were turned against other aspects of the Plan, the idea of European integration. In the occupied Western zones of Germany the constraints were more severe. Yet even there socialists had recourse to arguments similar to those used by British socialists, and to other arguments used by their ideological opponents at home. D'Attorre describes the response of another type of society, Italy, recalling the novelty of the American presence in Europe. Before the invasion of Italy by Allied forces the United States had been a land of myth, reflected through the prism of Hollywood. After the war Italy bore the brunt of the American attempt to shape European society, yet proved no less resistant or recalcitrant – and, more importantly, no less adept at using the Marshall Plan ideology as an instrument in older, indigenous disputes, than the northern European countries.

In eastern Europe the problems were different. It was not merely that the Soviet Union's veto on participation in the Marshall Plan precluded the participation of the east European states in the OEEC and excluded them from the benefits and challenge of American aid and ideas. Nor was it just that Stalin vetoed the attempts of some east European leaders to bring about regional integration. According to Berki (chapter six) there were far deeper obstacles to integration in the region. In the works of the Hungarian István Bibó, Berki finds a scepticism about the ability of these states to contemplate integration. Lacking any secure and democratic consensus they thereby lacked the basis of successful integration. The problem, as Fülöp (chapter seven) details, was scarcely helped by the great powers. Whatever the intractability of resolving the ethnic mix of eastern Europe, the great powers refused to provide mechanisms for dealing with the minorities they consigned to different states. Despite the better judgement of Ernest Bevin, the great powers, including Britain, refused to make any specific provision for the protection of minorities in the peace treaties, offering only the guarantee of universal human rights by the United Nations and ultimately washing their hands off the affair by telling the Hungarians to negotiate a suitable settlement of the problem themselves.

The burden of national histories had an effect in the West, too. The drive towards European integration, or rather western European integration, had been successfully stalled by the European states in the OEEC. The partisans of European federation, to be sure, had helped to push the governments towards the creation of the Council of Europe, but the governments had ensured that the Council would remain within their own control. A unique position was held by Britain, the only sizeable European power to escape defeat and occupation: a fact to which British politicians of all political persuasions were only too willing to point. Britain, despite its underlying economic weakness, consciously sought to manipulate the European question in order to enhance its unique status. Croft (chapter eight) explains how this culminated in support for European integration – as an appendage of an Anglo-American Alliance. The signing of the North Atlantic Treaty in 1949 seemed to confirm the viability of the British strategy. The following year, however, European integration was relaunched by two French initiatives and Britain found herself responding to the lead of others. The transformation could scarcely have been greater. At the end of the Second World War, advocates of European integration across the continent had looked to and expected British leadership. Now, in 1950, France emerged as the forerunner and received the backing of the United States. Having lost the battle to contain potential German economic and military power by other means, France turned to European integration, with the Schuman Plan and the Pleven Plan.

The Pleven Plan looked as if it would succeed when the EDF Treaty was signed. Yet, as Weigall shows in chapter nine, both Britain and France refused to recognize the limits of their new role in the world. Faced with the choice of operating within NATO or within a new European framework, they refused to be constrained within either and sought to continue to play an independent military role. Italy's response to the EDF was both more ambiguous and more ambitious. The EDF itself appeared as a threat to Italy, for it was feared the EDF would detract from the NATO within which Italy was enjoying a good relationship with the United States and, most importantly, gaining readmission to the ranks of the great powers. Unable to oppose the EDF, for fear of offending both France and the United States, Italy, under the guidance of pro-European ministers and at the instigation of Altiero Spinelli, sought a more radical solution by suggesting the inclusion of an Article committing the participant states to a form of EPC. In the end this gambit was undermined by the refusal of the French National Assembly to ratify the Treaty.

By the time the EDF Treaty was rejected the European Coal and Steel Community (ECSC) was already functioning. The ECSC, like all the institutions of western European integration, was launched out of a mixture of motives: commitment to the goal of a supranational European organization was blended with longstanding attempts to organize west European heavy industry, whose first success occurred in 1926 with the International Steel Cartel, and French concern that a revived Ruhr would sweep French industry from the market and doom plans for the modernization of France. The ECSC was also significant as an attempt to move forward without seeing British participation as a condition of progress. As Ranieri explains in chapter eleven, the British position was dogged by many old and increasingly dubious assumptions. The belief that the Commonwealth offered a way out persisted, despite the fact that British steel was being driven from Commonwealth markets and was being deprived of the preferential treatment it had enjoyed.

Civil aviation presents a different picture. Still the industry of the future it lacked the tradition of elaborate cartels that characterized the steel industry. Moreover, European governments sought to promote their 'national champions', guaranteeing their survival by purchases for national airlines at a time when European firms lagged behind American concerns. The economic logic of increased research and development costs, the American challenge and the persistent failure of European firms to produce viable sales all pointed in the same direction: transnational cooperation, facilitated and if necessary enforced by governments. The failure to grasp this strategy in the 1940s and 1950s was not purely a product of the relative novelty of the industry. After all, the most modern of all, atomic power, became the focus of EURATOM.

Despite their military and economic weakness the western European states had proved able to exert an influence on the evolution of European integration that exceeded their resources. Their success in promoting or obstructing European integration, in seeking to resist, aid or divert the flanking superpowers varied enormously, as did their ability to grasp the extent of the changes bequeathed by the Second World War and the need to respond to them. Historic claims to prestige, especially with Britain and France, or claims to territory, even if populated by other nationalities, proved to be especially hard to undermine. Other changes such as the impact of Americanism could be resisted more easily, in the short term. As both Ellwood and D'Attorre point out the transformation of attitudes and aspirations would take longer.

There is, then, a series of discrepancies between the different dimensions of European unity and disunity.[5] Changes at the level of high politics, the formation of alliances, could be achieved relatively rapidly. Changes of fundamental political structures, of the extent desired by the wartime federalists or of the extent prescribed as a precondition of integration by Bibo were to take longer, and in the former case at least are still outstanding. There is, moreover, a difference in the rate of change and timescale between the regions of Europe. For western Europe 1957 does, in retrospect at least, mark a significant turning point. The Rome Treaties, establishing the EEC and the EURATOM, were, to be sure, not the only landmark. The Council of Europe, the ECSC, Western European Union and NATO were also forms of European integration, which were to have lasting effect upon the postwar order. Yet of these only NATO can be argued to have had an equivalent effect, at least until recent events called its purpose into question. The EEC, periodically strengthened and expanded, may still be far from the hopes of federalist Europeans at the end of the Second World War, yet it has unquestionably outpaced the other organizations of western Europe. European unity can in no way be reduced to the EEC, as most of the contributions to this volume make clear, but the Rome Treaties did mean that henceforth even the other forms of western European organization would be constrained by their relationship to the EEC. In the history of east European integration, as

Izik-Hedri reminds us in chapter thirteen, 1957 does not have the same significance. Despite parallels between the EEC, the CMEA and the EFTA – a common commitment to increasing intra-regional trade as a proportion of total trade and the denial that they were forming closed economic blocs – there was a difference in the inherent chronology of developments in East and West.

West European chronology was affected, as Willis demonstrates in chapter fourteen, by the existence of a host of other international régimes: most prominently GATT, IMF and COCOM. The potential tension between these Western dominated, global régimes – global that is in regulating the 'world economy' – and European integration was played down in the shaping of the postwar world. Yet, as Willis emphasizes, these régimes were themselves to become a source of division in Europe, and consequently a cause of instability and inequality within the international system as a whole. Indeed, the very strengths of the United States and the initial weakness of the European states contributed to anti-Americanism and helped to push western European economies in the direction of European integration. Both the American dominated 'global' régimes and European integration within the framework of the EEC promoted the emergence of countervailing regional trading blocs, most notably EFTA and the CMEA. Pan-Europeanism and internationalism had, indeed, been seen as antagonistic for much of the period before the end of the Second World War. Yet, in the shaping of postwar Europe, the United States, at the height of its power, promoted régimes, including European institutions, which were to give a greater freedom of manoeuvre not only to the united Europeans but also to individual states. Willis suggests that smaller states typically gained a greater voice within the international régimes of the postwar world than they would have had without them; in this he is supported by Varsori's account in chapter ten of the Italian decision to resolve their dilemma over the EDF by accelerating and expanding the organization.

The articles in this volume are clearly not intended to give an account of the specific origins of the institutions of European integration. Rather, they are intended to indicate that the shaping of postwar Europe was a multi-dimensional process, marked by failure, misperception and unresolved problems as well as by the achievement of stability and partial unity. This fact has much to do with the ability of European states and societies to influence the outcome at a time of weakness. The hindsight won from observations of previous patterns of international conflict has often overstated the consistency and competence of superpowers in shaping the process of European integration, while underestimating the national and European interests and identities that have continued to work against the grain of imposed geopolitical settlements.

2 Innocents Abroad: Federalism and the Resistance Between Party and Movement 1945-47

M. Burgess

Recent research has firmly underlined the crucial links between the basic political ideas that lay at the root of Resistance thought and the emergence of federalism as the guiding principle for Europe's future.[1] The appeal of federalism to the intellectual Resistance across war-ravaged Europe lay in its offer of a double guarantee: it furnished the prospect of effectively reconciling freedom and authority which in turn promised a new Europe at peace with itself. Leading from the individual as an assertive autonomous human being to the complex network of human relations characteristic of the new postwar European society, federalism appeared at once as a means and an end to be attained. In postwar Europe it became a political strategy that sought consciously and purposively to formalize the political links both *within* and *between* European states. Only in this way would postwar Europe be given a new meaning as a unified whole while simultaneously preserving important local and national diversities.

The new attitudes towards, and the changed perceptions of, freedom and authority which were rooted in the Resistance experience prompted many Resistance élites to champion federalism as a veritable panacea for all the outstanding problems it was believed would confront postwar statesmen. Here we must emphasize the true character of the Resistance movements. As Lipgens observed, they constituted an *intellectual* Resistance: the members of the Resistance fought not only *against* totalitarian rule, but even more, in their view, *for* something. In their quest for a better and peaceful society they fought Hitler not for the old national states but rather for a new European society.[2] One Italian Resistance veteran summed up this crucial distinction succinctly: 'we continue to call the movement of liberation in Italy a "resistance"; but let us not forget that it was not a resistance but an attack, an initiative, an ideal innovation, not an attempt to preserve something'.[3] The consensus of opinion that emerged among Resistance groups throughout Europe was that the unequivocal defeat of totalitarianism and the creation of a 'United States of Europe' in its place went hand-in-hand. To allow the old nation-states to recover and regain their former position in a world of international rivalry would be to recreate the conditions for war and totalitarian rule.

Domestic state federalism, then, was only part of what was construed as a larger process. By itself it was deemed inadequate to guard against the possible recurrence of future totalitarian pretensions. It had to be buttressed by and within a wider supranational federal system of interlocking states to safeguard peace, democracy and human rights. Federalism would effectively curb the excesses of the belligerent state and extinguish the dangers of nationalism. It was best represented as a sort of seamless web stretching from the individual to European society and back again, overcoming the obstacle to natural human cooperation traditionally associated with the old artificial nation-state.

Resistance thought in many senses may have been ideologically ambiguous, but it nonetheless contained certain consistent and unshakeable beliefs germane to the reconstruction of Europe. Perhaps the most persistent of these was the need for the state to be effectively held in check by a strong international authority. Federalism converted the essentially negative propositions of Resistance thought – anti-totalitarianism, the basic distrust of the state, fear of exaggerated nationalism and the aversion to war – to positive prescriptive action for postwar Europe. But once the Second World War had ended, how could federalism be translated into practical action? In the radically changed circumstances of postwar Europe was not the very idea of the Resistance itself a contradiction? How could its political ideals and experience, nourished by the war itself, be effectively preserved and persistently promoted after 1945? The critical issue confronting Resistance intellectuals at this time was that of political strategy. Let us look briefly at the two main choices with which they were faced.

Leaving aside the most obvious and simplistic differences between political parties and political movements, the literature of political science makes few clear-cut analytical distinctions in respect of these two phenomena. Organization, recruitment, finance and leadership pertain to both. Similarly, both popular participation and mass mobilization are eagerly sought by parties and movements alike. Yet a 'movement' is not synonymous with a 'party'. Parties are by definition partisan. They convey a sense of ideological exclusivity; they breed sectionalism, self-interest and division. To those in a movement the word 'party' often has unpleasant connotations that include *inter alia* fossilized bureaucratic structures and élite-directed hierarchies remote from the membership.[4]

It is instructive here to recognize the importance of self-designation. It is significant that Resistance activists, whether they were among the intellectual élite or the military combatants, perceived themselves as part of a movement and used the term to describe themselves. The Movimento Federalista Europeo (MFE), founded in August 1943, illustrates the conundrum of 'movement versus party' that confronted political strategists in Italy.[5] Among leaders of the first group of Resistance members to elaborate a clear, systematic approach to the goal of a federal Europe were Altiero Spinelli, Ernesto Rossi and Eugenio Colorni. In the first half of 1941 a statement based partly on a reading of the Marxist classics on the one hand and partly on the Federalist Papers of Hamilton, Madison and Jay on the other was compiled and in July 1941 smuggled to Rome. Written by Spinelli and Rossi, it was entitled the 'Manifesto for a Free and United Europe' but quickly found fame as the 'Ventotene Manifesto' after the island of Ventotene on which Spinelli and his fellow conspirators were confined.[6] This Resistance group constituted what was the first unmistakably federalist group to organize itself on Italian soil; the Ventotene Manifesto which provoked considerable debate among the programme drafters of the re-emerging Italian parties, became 'one of the basic documents of the European federalist movement'.[7]

But in July 1943 Colorni had advised against the founding of a specifically 'European Party' because the anti-Fascist groups had already acknowledged the need for a European federation.[8] Indeed the new programmes of all the re-emerging Italian parties, except the Communists, incorporated the general aim of European unification.

The founding conference of the MFE decided that it was 'not just an alternative political party . . . the MFE aims at being the movement above parties which within every party rejects the persistent error that the important thing is first to establish national independence, democratic freedom and social justice, and in the end the fraternisation of peoples will come about of its own accord. It sees this as an illusion and the priority of aims to be just the opposite.'[9] Postwar international events were to impel a major strategic rethinking among the federalists during 1945–7 but in 1944 the logic of the MFE's central committee was nonetheless clear:

We cannot consider forming a federalist party at the moment because it would have no prospect of attracting enough popular support with an understanding of the actual priority of European problems over national problems. A party, that is to say an organisation created by democratic means to win power in the state presupposes the existence of a state. So long as there is no federal state and consequently no federalist democratic political struggle, there can be no federalist party.[10]

This interpretation of the MFE's predicament towards the end of the war was subsequently reaffirmed by Spinelli. In June 1945 he drew up a balance-sheet of the prevailing circumstances that impinged directly upon the MFE's political strategy: 'Our vision of a Europe in which all state structures would have collapsed, but the peoples would be free to decide their destiny in freedom, has not materialised . . . The troops of the superpowers have occupied the defeated countries and placed them in tutelage.'[11]

The Resistance predictions of the immediate postwar circumstances first outlined in the Ventotene Manifesto of 1941 simply failed to occur. The victorious superpowers did not arrive, as the Resistance hoped they would, as supporters in the fight against nationalism and the recovery of the nation-state. Indeed they flatly opposed the goal of a European federal union. Moreover, many federalists underestimated the rapidity by which people reaccustomed themselves to thinking in terms of nation-states. This prompted a minority of federalists, including Spinelli, to recognize the need for a studied campaign of relentless attrition to be conducted inside the states and national parties in order gradually to undermine old modes of thought. The main problem for federalists in the early postwar years was to avoid illusions sustained largely by their own self-deception, itself born of a refusal to admit that their European ideal was, temporarily at least, quite impracticable.

The question of political strategy split the MFE during 1945–7. Should it campaign for the European peoples to be mobilized as a genuine popular opposition movement dedicated to forcing the hands of governments or should it channel its energies into supporting parties and governments known to be in favour of federalist solutions? Spinelli's realistic and sober assessments of the postwar situation drove him to defend the latter course of action. He explained why in characteristically candid terms:

As it was impossible to put federalist ideas into practice for the time being, they should not try to mobilise the masses, for once we had won their backing we should not be able to find anything for them to do right away. Rather our main task is to win over the leaders of the progressive parties for the federalist programme by co-operating with their commissions for foreign affairs and, in due course, with the Consultative and Constituent Assemblies.[12]

It is not surprising that the rank and file of an association like the MFE should dislike such a strategic reappraisal. To many it meant the collapse of a long-cherished Resistance dream. It also meant admitting to a mistake.

Spinelli appealed in an 'open letter' to the majority of those who attended the MFE conference in Florence in January 1946 to come to terms with the new postwar realities: 'if we do not want to become a small clique of people with our heads in the clouds, we must frankly acknowledge that our prediction and consequently our programme have proved to be mistaken'.[13] This brief survey of the MFE's strategic dilemma in postwar Europe underlines the fundamental difficulties that confronted the various Resistance movements when they sought to translate their federalist vision into reality. The Europe of 1945–6 did not provide conditions for either a mass movement against governments and parties or a supranational European federalist party. For federalists it was a period of re-evaluation and reassessment. It was also a time of confusion and impotence. Given the configuration of international power politics, the conservative restoration at home and the overriding priority of economic reconstruction, former members of the underground who championed a federal Europe found themselves operating in a vacuum.

These unpropitious circumstances were to change dramatically during 1947 when external events in particular propelled the federalists into concerted action at a European level. Meanwhile the twilight zone between party and movement was temporarily explored in the immediate postwar years in Italy. During June–November 1945 Italy alone among the countries of western Europe was governed by a Resistance leader who shared the ideals of the non-Communist Left. We shall now turn our attention to the *Partito d'Azione* (Action Party) as the only case-study of a Resistance party that attempted to put Resistance thought into practice.

What would a Resistance party look like? As a national political party rather than a national movement, like the MFE, the Action Party's record in office, albeit very brief, epitomized the moral strength and political limits of Resistance ideas. Led by the Milan Professor Ferruccio Parri, a former military chief of the Resistance forces in the North, the Action Party had 'a brilliant intellectual leadership but no mass base'.[14] Founded in January 1943 it comprised remnants of the former party known as *Giustizia e Libertà* (Justice and Liberty) dating from 1929, university groups anxious to combine socialism and political liberalism and radical anti-clerical republicans from the Northern Italian cities.[15] Primarily a party of intellectuals, its composition certainly seemed to fulfil Spinelli's desire for a new party embodying the principles of the Resistance. It was essentially a vehicle – a political experiment – to facilitate the rise of a new élite to positions of real influence.

As individuals the Action Party's original group of leaders were to make important contributions to Italy's postwar development: Manlio Rossi-Doria as an agrarian reformer; Riccardo Lombardi as the economic theorist of the Socialist Party; Ugo La Malfa as the Republican minister responsible for trade liberalization and the later proposals for national economic planning; Altiero Spinelli as the Secretary-General of the MFE and later member of the Italian and European Parliaments; and Ferruccio Parri as the first postwar prime minister who for over twenty years was President of the group of European federalist parliamentarians in the Italian Senate. Aware that the Italian Resistance, as with other Resistance movements in occupied Europe, was ideologically heterogeneous – having been created and led by established political parties – the federalists were successful in persuading every political group except the Communists to accept the idea of a federal Europe. But it was the Action Party that was by far the most vigorous supporter of their views. Already at the foundation conference in 1943 the final version of its programme spelled out this European goal:

the bringing about of a European federation of free democratic countries . . . which decisively rejects the principle of absolute state sovereignty, advocates the renunciation of all purely territorial claims, and favours the creation of a legal community of states with the necessary institutions and the means to establish a regime of collectively organised security.[16]

By 1945 it was no surprise to discover that many leading federalists had joined the Action Party's ranks. Apart from Spinelli, who was for a short while head of the party's North Italian secretariat, Ernesto Rossi and Aldo Garosci became members with the specific aim of moulding and shaping it into a party of revolutionary leadership.[17]

In what James Wilkinson called 'a season of hope' [18] the Action Party, led by the 'idealistic' Parri,[19] formed a government in June 1945. Parri's five-party cabinet was dominated by the left-wing parties (Socialists, Communists and the Action Party) but the coexistence of the Christian Democrats, led by Alcide De Gasperi, underlined the expedient nature of his administration. Parri was in reality a compromise choice between the Left, who proposed Pietro Nenni, and the Christian Democrats, the largest single party, who supported De Gasperi. Nonetheless Parri himself was a forceful leader, genuinely dedicated to achieving fundamental social and political reform. His very accession to office possessed a double significance: he symbolized both 'the Resistance continuity with prewar anti-Fascism and the innovations possible in the postwar climate of experiment and change'.[20] Derek Urwin claimed that Parri's own lack of political experience contributed to his speedy failure,[21] but in June 1945 'his very lack of political experience seemed a virtue, he owed no political debts (and) was tied to no financial interests'.[22]

Parri's policy programme reflected his Resistance ideas and experience. He opposed the Italian monarchy and favoured a republic. Opinion on this throughout Italy was divided. But it was Parri's determination to carry through his proposals for agrarian reform, land redistribution and the socialization of industry that provoked hostility from among the powerful established conservative forces in postwar Italy. Parri symbolized the *vento del nord* (wind from the north) – the spirit of social and political renovation – which derived its sustenance from the committees of liberation that had sprouted during the brief period of hope and confusion between Mussolini's downfall and Badoglio's armistice in 1943. Those that had been formed in the North, the *Comitati di Liberazione Nationale d'Alta Italia* (CLNAI), rapidly formed a structure of parallel governments and were active in nominating local officials and assuming administrative responsibilities. They saw themselves as a prefiguration of a future Italian government.

Coming from this social and political milieu, Parri sympathized with proposals to decentralize Italian government. Indeed he advocated domestic and European federalism. The practical experience of the CLNAI urged him to support increased worker participation in the management of industry along the lines of the management councils created by these committees of liberation in the factories of Milan and Turin in April 1945. The logical corollary of this industrial policy also meant plans to break up monopolies and a redistribution of power from large concentrations of capital like *Confindustria*, which united Italy's most powerful enterprises, to small and medium-sized businesses. If we add the goal of currency reform and the moral determination to resume and accelerate the programme of purges initiated a year earlier by the Bonomi government, but subsequently allowed to lapse, it becomes clear why the Resistance-based drive for radical reform should have raised countervailing forces against it.

Walter Lipgens described the domestic programme of peacetime Resistance parties as 'combining humanist and Christian traditions with Socialism', some-thing which, he argued, 'struck people as a somewhat incongruous mixture'.[23] F. Roy Willis alluded to Parri's brief tenure of office as 'a six-month period of confusion' and referred to his policies as 'vague and impractical'.[24] The direct cause of his fall was a realignment of political parties but Parri had from the outset lacked the support of the ruling groups, determined to retain their privileges acquired under Mussolini's régime, and the populace at large. Rather than heralding a permanent change in Italian political culture and behaviour, Parri's premiership seems in retrospect to have been merely an interregnum. James Wilkinson described it as 'a brief burst of innovation favoured by the uncertainty of the first months following the Liberation': it was 'an aberration not a precedent'.[25]

How, then, should we assess the role and record of the Action Party? Derek Urwin claimed that its death-knell could be taken as 'the final indication that the ideals of the Resistance movements could not be directly implemented, not just in Italy, but in the whole of liberated Europe'.[26] And F. Roy Willis asserted that 'the failure of the Action Party was the failure of the federalists'.[27] Clearly the Action Party represented a political experiment with a significance far wider than just Italy. Let us therefore briefly examine the reasons for its failure and the extent to which it was 'the failure of the federalists'.

Parri, as we have seen, represented the new political élite that derived its prominence from a heroism and selfless defiance rooted in the anti-Fascist Resistance. His political beliefs were simultaneously grounded in the liberal socialism associated with the *Giustizia e Liberta* movement of the 1930s. In the short run, Wilkinson has argued, this 'policy of mediation' placed Parri midway between Marxism and its liberal critics and made him acceptable to both.[28] The very ambiguity of the Action Party's position proved to be strategically advantageous. But once Parri attempted to implement his policies of renewal and moral regeneration, the fragile consensus that had supported him quickly collapsed. Lacking a strong mass base, support among the ruling groups for a party of intellectuals simply evaporated.

The political experiment launched in June 1945 succeeded in alienating virtually every major social and political group in Italy. Parri's critics attacked him paradoxically both for inaction and excessive rigour. Faced with the overwhelming task of reconstruction and growing unrest among the unemployed and homeless, the Parri government appeared to some to be moving too slowly toward its stated goals. To others, principally on the Right, his policies were far too ambitious. They threatened powerful vested interests. The lower middle class, especially a large group of minor functionaries entrenched in the Italian administration, felt vulnerable to proposals for extending the purges while the upper echelons of the middle class viewed Parri's economic reforms with great anxiety. The widespread sense of menace has been accurately summarized by James Wilkinson and is worth quoting at length:

The government's plan to break up the large industrial combines was resisted by the Liberals as a direct attack on free enterprise. Many small producers, who would have benefited from this plan, interpreted it as a conspiracy against private property . . . The management councils created in the North further alienated many businessmen, who considered them but the first stage of a Communist campaign to capture the 'commanding heights' of industry. The prospect of monetary reform stirred passionate opposition from those who feared that their bank assets would be frozen or confiscated. The result was a tacit alliance among Liberals, Christian Democrats and the Confindustria that shattered the unity of the Resistance by dividing the middle and working classes on the issue of personal liberty versus social justice.[29]

There is, then, a consensus of opinion among interested scholars concerning the failure of the Action party as a peacetime Resistance party. But is it also correct to regard it as 'the failure of the federalists'? In one particular sense this was certainly true: none of their hopes had been realized. Both internal and international circumstances had been against them. Parri could expect support neither from the central administration that feared his reforms nor from the Allied Military Government that continued to exercise control over the Italian North where he could have anticipated most support. But there is another sense in which the federalists can be said to have failed. Here we return to the question of political strategy: was it wise to make European unification the single goal of their foreign policy?

On this question Walter Lipgens was unequivocal: such a strategy was not enough to establish a viable party.[30] In the absence of a mass groundswell of support for the notion of a federal Europe the Action Party was forced to rely upon the goodwill of their main party rivals. Unless there was a broad base of

agreement among the majority of parties not only upon the goal of a federal
Europe but also upon the means necessary to achieve it, then the only possible
outcome would be failure and disappointment. According to F. Roy Willis, the
federalists were doomed from the beginning because they failed to realize that the
idea of a federal Europe 'had to grow from internal forces inside Italy and could
not be imposed upon Italy from without'.[31]

In retrospect it is tempting to regard the Resistance leaders in postwar Europe
as innocents abroad. They appear as naive and impractical. Parri himself
epitomized the valiant Resistance warrior floundering in an alien peacetime
environment – 'an idealist adrift in the savage world of politics'.[32] With one or
two exceptions, like Einaudi's Liberals, most political parties in reality paid only
lip-service to the idea of a federal Europe. Both the Communists and the Christian
Democrats were aware that the real battle to be fought was over control of the
postwar Italian state. Unlike the Action Party, foreign policy for them was tied
inextricably to their own respective internal aims. And in the end few people were
prepared to risk a journey towards an unknown destination; they returned instead
to their old familiar traditional values where they felt safe.

During the crucial years following the end of the War, the period that the
federalists had looked to as their golden opportunity for uniting Europe, it is clear
that 1945–7 was a false dawn. These years were not a prologue to European
unification but an epilogue to a failed political strategy. Yet if these were years of
disappointment and despair for the federalists the picture was not one of total
abject failure. In Italy they succeeded in securing the insertion of Article 11 into
the new constitution (finally ratified in 1948) which committed the state to
specific limitations of sovereignty in the event of membership of some future, if
undefined, European organization of states. And in the wider European context
the shift from reform to restoration marked only the end of the first postwar
phase in the struggle to unite Europe. The quest for a federal Europe would
continue along different routes.

The year 1947 proved to be a major turning-point in postwar Europe with the
advent of the Marshall Plan and its subsequent rejection by the Soviet Union
which also torpedoed the possibility of participation by the east European states.
For the plethora of federalist associations that had sprung up across western
Europe and were united in the *Union Européenne des Fédéralistes* (UEF), officially
founded in December 1946 in Paris, these developments created an entirely new
situation. American approval of European union meant that federalist endeavours
would perforce be organized without, but not against, eastern Europe. Postwar
realities, as always, imposed themselves upon federalist strategy. Existing
relations between Europe and the two superpowers and the nationalistic attitudes
of European governments would remain the major obstacles to a federal Europe.
Nonetheless, if doubts continued to exist about the appeal of the federal idea as an
effective mobilizing force, the federalists' experience during 1945–7 suggested
that this was not the beginning of the end but on the contrary only the end of the
beginning.

3 The Marshall Plan and the Politics of Growth

D. W. Ellwood

In the first part of this tentative historical exploration of the concept of growth it was suggested that the Second World War era saw a revolution in the idea held by Western governments and ruling groups of their responsibilities towards society.[1] Full employment and higher standards of living became the declared objectives of politicians, bureaucrats, employers, and moderate reformers of all shades on both sides of the Atlantic. These were people who saw themselves engaged in a dramatic effort to reconquer the fundamental bases of that legitimacy and credibility inevitably compromised by two World Wars and the upheaval of the Great Depression. Hugely encouraged by the technological and organizational feats of the war machines, the new and not-so-new leaders in Europe and America made unprecedented promises of economic security and progress, enshrining them in the Charter of the United Nations. In so doing all paid tribute to the supreme role they expected America to play in the postwar world; all expected to renounce some degree of sovereignty; all foresaw the importance of the United States in supporting (i.e. financing) their own national visions for the future, and all feared chaos and the rise of the revolutionary Left should America fail them. Few understood the force of America's own will to power, the urge to project the presumed lessons of America's own historical experience for the presumed benefit of all Europe and all mankind. Even fewer guessed the gap between the grand Rooseveltian plans for world reconstruction and the ability to intervene practically and knowledgeably on the ground.

This gap was only closed definitively with the Marshall Plan. Its discovery had been even more painful in the European capitals than in Washington. As the Truman administration thrashed around in the chaos produced by putting off political choices until the end of the War and assuming America's wishes were the world's commands, desperate appeals were coming from London, Paris, Rome, the Allied command in Germany and elsewhere for aid to buy food and fuel, aid to begin reconstruction, aid to prop up currencies, to restart trade and to keep fragile national coalitions in business. Nothing the World Bank, the National Advisory Council, the Army or even the United Nations Relief and Rehabilitation Administration could do was nearly enough to face the conditions, as the Europeans saw them; only a comprehensive response to the emergency – as each country lived it – would enable democracy to survive and prevent revolutionary turmoil bringing a repetition of the aftermath of the First World War.

The Truman Doctrine was a hastily improvised response to these pressures, confirming Europeans and the Washington administration in their new-found belief that by far the most effective way to get the results desired was to insist on the red threat above everything. Whether the eventual end results of the Truman Doctrine ever corresponded to the intentions seems to be unknown: only the origins and expression of the initiatives have attracted historical attention, not what subsequently developed on the ground.

On a much grander scale, the same is true of the Marshall Plan itself. While great effort has gone into researching the origins of the Plan and its diplomacy, extraordinarily little is known of its effective application country-by-country from 1948 to 1951, when it became indistinguishable from Mutual Security. Substantial macroeconomic studies have brought new knowledge of the Plan's overall results in western Europe, and specifically in Germany, Denmark, Britain and now Italy.[2] But the European Recovery Programme (ERP) was much more than a device for raising output quickly, revitalizing economic activity and balancing the transatlantic current account. With the ERP the grand Rooseveltian objectives of free trade and higher living standards everywhere returned to the forefront of America's policies in Europe: it could even be said that with the addition of the Mutual Security project, the third of the grand visions of wartime had been reinstated: collective security, now seen not in the utopian conception of the UN, but in the much narrower and more concrete terms of the Mutual Defense Assistance Program (MDAP) and NATO.

The Marshall Plan was clearly a mighty weapon in the Cold War: Ambassador Harriman, its head in Europe, went so far as to characterize it as 'a fire-fighting operation' in a private meeting of American Ambassadors in Paris in 1949.[3] But its many other dimensions were no less important: to create a new framework of interdependence in the industrialized world, to promote European harmonization and integration in the context of expanding world commerce and to promote global trade and payments' liberalization . . . all in the name of eradicating the presumed causes of war and revolution by bringing the force of the American example to bear on European chaos and backwardness. So a grand effort of modernization was implied, not dissimilar to the one Herbert Hoover and his private-sector allies had sketched out in the 1920s, but now with the full weight of America's new economic strength and organizational techniques behind it.

Whether the Europeans expected or desired such treatment when they so anxiously signed on for the ERP in the summer of 1947 is another matter. Each country had its own renewal plans or methods, usually revolving around the construction of a variant of the welfare state in which collective goods and social security received top priority, far higher than all but the most basic forms of personal consumption. That was why the few wartime joint declarations of purpose – such as the Atlantic Charter or the UN Charter itself – had always referred to full employment and higher standards of living jointly but separately.

All the Europeans knew that production and exports would have to increase significantly to pay for the new scheme of things, and some, such as the British and the French, were clearly braced to face the task. As much recent research has shown, all had benefited from the technological progress accompanying the war; some, usually thought of as quite backward at the time – such as Italy – were considerably further ahead on the path to full industrialization than appeared from the outside.[4] But in 1947 none of them were economically or politically strong enough to resist any of the American propositions, though they would fight to the end against the Washington idea of European integration aimed at the creation of a single market.[5]

In no way were the Europeans singly or together able to stop or even condition the dramatic radicalization of the American–Russian rift that gathered pace in 1947 and evolved into full-scale Cold War by the spring of 1948. Unequipped for this new kind of ideological confrontation, non-aligned west European governments were expected to get on the team as quickly as possible, leaving them barely time to wonder why they had had to exert themselves so in 1945-6 to alert America to the danger. The Czech coup and the Italian elections, both in the spring of 1948, helped the passage of the Marshall Plan through Congress (far from certain until that time). Both guaranteed that when it began work on the ground, the ideological and psychological dimensions of the effort would be just as significant as its economic inputs. These additional facets of the Plan would aim to change attitudes and outlooks, aspirations and mentalities. For the sake of votes first: to stop the rise in support for Communist parties and Left trade unions. But in the longer term it aimed to bring about a renewal of Europe's 'spiritual vigor',[6] which came to mean a radical shift in the priorities and expectations of individuals towards ideals of personal progress that could be defined in the language of income and consumption.

America was at the height of its power in the twentieth century, economically, politically and ideologically. Much of Europe still lay in ruins and showed few signs of healthy recovery in 1947-8. Everywhere there was evidence of the ideological exhaustion and demoralization of the European ruling classes and their governments: 'Who hasn't heard remarks,' asked an ERP Information Officer in Paris in 1950, 'Such as "Why rebuild when the Russians will tear it all down again?" or "Why should I stick my neck out by taking sides?" When the Commies take over, it won't be healthy to have it on my record.' [7] It was into this void that the Marshall Plan message stepped so effectively, providing a 'return of hope', a 'psychological blood transfusion', as the Plan's overall Administrator Paul Hoffmann said in the course of the twentieth anniversary celebrations in 1967. To achieve this result, propaganda, termed 'information', was seen from the beginning as a fundamental part of the entire operation. Because the problem was not just to raise production but to raise productivity, not just to bail out bankrupt governments but to modernize the state, not just to encourage international cooperation but to push for the single integrated European market, not simply to save ailing industries but to change the war between reactionary capitalists and revolutionary workers into a dynamic relationship between enlightened producers and contented consumers. America triumphant showed how all this could be done; projecting this example into Europe was the job of the ERP 'Information Program'. If the Europeans were not interested, then Stalin's peace-loving hordes would be happy to liberate them from the yoke of war-mongering, capitalist imperialism: that was the choice by 1951.

The result was the largest international propaganda operation ever seen in peacetime. Opposing it was the Cominform, the Soviet-bloc bureau set up in November 1947 with the explicit aim of generating a massive propaganda counter-offensive against the Marshall Plan in western Europe as well as in the eastern sphere. European Recovery Program's effort in this area got under way in the Spring of 1948 when one of America's leading journalists and broadcasters, Al Friendly Jnr., was appointed to head the new Information Division. What the planners in the ERP's head-quarters (the European Cooperation Administration (ECA)) wanted was 'an effective means for countering Communist propaganda against us and at the same time building positive support for us and our policies throughout the world'. Giving assistance alone would not automatically produce goodwill, they noted, referring to the experience of the Greek-Turkish aid effort. Instead:

The aim would be to help the people of Racine and Muncie know where the things they produce have gone, what use is being made of them and what the people are like who are on the receiving end of their help. Vice-versa the workers of France and the farmers of Denmark must be told where the goods they receive come from, what the people are like behind the aid provided and what their motives are in providing help.[8]

To this end the European Cooperation Masterplan signed by each participating country contained a special section entitled 'Publicity', authorizing 'that wide dissemination of information on the progress of the program is desirable in order to develop the sense of common effort and mutual aid which are essential to the accomplishment of the objectives of the program'.[9] Publicity divisions were set up in each country mission soon after the effective start of the ERP in June 1948. The key countries were considered to be France, the Bi-Zone and Italy, followed by a second band containing Greece, Turkey, Austria, Trieste and the French Zone of Germany, a third including England and Sweden and a fourth grouping the rest.[10] But it was in Italy that the largest campaign emerged, the one considered 'tops' in the Paris field headquarters of the programme.

Heading the effort in Italy was Andrew Berding, an energetic former head of the Rome bureau of Associated Press, co-author of Cordell Hull's memoirs and a future assistant Secretary of State for Public Affairs. Berding and his small staff were extraordinarily active and inventive. In the first month alone they established a daily survey of the Italian press, made contacts with radio, film, press and news-agency offices, prepared a three-room exhibition with accompanying booklets, postcards and photos, set up documentary film production arrangements and agreed with the Italian national radio network on an eight-language weekly shortwave broadcast and a fifteen-minute weekly programme in Italian.[11] They came to think in terms of tens of documentary films, hundreds of radio programmes, thousands of mobile film shows, millions of copies of their pamphlets and tens of millions of spectators for their exhibitions and films.

There is no mystery about the operating principles Berding and his staff applied in their campaign. These approaches were arrived at fairly quickly and changed little up to the outbreak of the Korean War. They were similar to the methods used in the other ERP countries but were probably applied more intensively in Italy, taking their cue from the frantic propaganda battle of the April 1948 elections. A January 1950 report by Berding explained: 'Carry the message of the Marshall Plan to the people. Carry it to them directly – it won't permeate down. And give it to them so that they can understand it'.[12] The basic thrust then was for a truly mass programme using 'every method possible . . . to reach Giuseppe in the factory and Giovanni in the fields', or as the Paris office put it, 'slugging it out way down among the masses'.[13]

In his January 1950 summary prepared for a Congressional presentation, Berding also listed the other key operating principles: 1) to convince the Italians 'that the Plan is his as well as Mr Marshall's': in other words to increase the sense of national identification with the Plan and encourage a personal stake in its outcome; 2) to demonstrate the depth and seriousness of Italian-American cooperation: 'Thus the signs which the Mission has induced the Italian Government to put up by the many hundreds over the ERP Counterpart fund projects carry the color of both countries, side by side on the same shield'; 3) to make use of local identities, particularly regional ones, by demonstrating the work done in each area; 4) to direct special attention to key 'target groups', particularly trade unions, Communist and non-Communist; agricultural workers; housewives, as runners of 'the economics of the household'; management in business and industry, 'in whose hands lie the guidelines of productivity', and finally children, following the example of the Church, which 'has always maintained that the best way to win and retain followers is to convince them while they are young'; and 5) to avoid direct confrontation with the massive waves of Communist propaganda directed against the Plan. Thus 'when the Communists said the Marshall Plan was a plan of war, the Mission never said it was not a plan of war but over and over again, in thousands of inhabited centres, with every means at its disposal, the Mission put across the slogan: 'ERP means peace and work'. Korea could not have been a more unfortunate event from this point of view.

The sixth key operating principle was to avoid accusation of interference in Italian internal affairs. Not surprisingly this was the principle that gave the publicity men most difficulty, especially since they were under pressure in Congress to step up their labelling of goods and services originating in the US with American flags.[14] When applied on the ground these principles proved extremely flexible and no idea seemed too large or too daring for the Information Program in its heyday. Ideas such as Counterpart, the dollar gap, productivity and European integration were not only quite new to European ears but difficult to communicate in the best of circumstances. Little wonder that the ERP information directors in Washington felt that 'we have become in surprising measure . . . the principal fount for education about the big economic problems and developments disturbing the world today', a challenge that no information service had ever faced.[15]

Opening up an ERP pamphlet or visiting a Marshall Plan exhibition in the months down to June 1950: what were the themes one would always find? What was the message? A booklet distributed at the Venice exhibition on ERP in July–September 1949 opens with a dramatic quantification of the dimensions of American aid: three ships a day, $1000 a minute, two weeks' salary from every worker. The goal was a 'higher standard of living'. The text explains:

By utilising American free supplies of foodstuffs and raw materials, Italy and the other nations included in the ERP plan hope to attain by the year 1952: – A higher standard of living for the entire nation, – Maximum employment for workers and farmers, – Greater production, through exploiting all their energies and by a close economic collaboration with all the other ERP countries.

The essential mechanisms of the Plan are then outlined: how supplies of wheat and raw materials from the US turn into lira deposited in a special fund at the Bank of Italy, which is then used for public works and other 'productive improvements aiming to diminish unemployment'. The details follow, under-lining how new machinery has modernized factories and how greater output needed to be integrated Europe-wide to facilitate emigration and stabilize economic life on a continental scale. The concluding message states that:

ERP is a unique chance offered to European nations toward reconstructing their economy, raising the standard of living among the masses, and attaining by the year 1952 an economic stability which is the foundation of political independence . . . Every worker, every citizen is bound up in this rebirth. The future and the peace of Italy and of Europe, the general well-being of all, depend on the will and the work of each single one of us.[16]

The reference to the masses and to workers illustrates the crucial importance the ERP as a whole attached to changing the balance of power, the structures and above all the attitude prevalent in the world of trade unionism. Here information activities were only part of a vast operation directly aided by the American trade unions that actively sought to organize non-Communist unions where, as in France and Italy, hardly any had existed before. Without entering into the merits of this still-controversial undertaking, which was largely part of the ERP as a fire-fighting operation, it is worth noting that the entire thrust of the effort was to create trade unions with different ideological objectives than those dominated by the Left parties that had emerged after the fall of Fascism. The creation of a single 'non-political organization devoted to the economic improvement of the job-holder' was to be the aim; a furious propaganda and political battle developed on this front from 1949 onwards.[17] In Britain, too, a major campaign was launched to modernize union practices and attitudes, involving the Labour government, the TUC and the leadership of the major industrial unions. With conferences, seminars, publications and team visits to the US, the Mission men were convinced by 1952 that they had done a remarkable job in changing attitudes to work and its modernization, in a situation that had appalled the Americans on their arrival.[18] Whether directed at workers or employers the key words were always mass production, scientific management and above all productivity. A typical portable exhibition on the subject would explain what productivity was, 'how it has given the United States a high standard of living, how increased per man output can result in better-ment of living conditions, social progress, strength and ability to defend democratic institutions'. In each country there were specialized reviews on the subject, joint committees, trips to inspect American factories, conferences, and eventually in some countries even 'productivity villages' where model factories and workers' communities could be seen in action.[19]

The Anglo-American Productivity Council was seen as a model of its kind, sponsoring no less than 66 team visits to America, covering most of the heavy industries, but also the retail sector and universities, to discover the secret of their successful links with industry. The results were summed up in a book-length presentation by the economist Graham Hutton entitled *We Too Can Prosper*. Its message was clear: 'Higher productivity is the brightest hope for every man, woman and child that the standard of living can be maintained and improved. Its importance and the universal concern in its achievement therefore cannot be exaggerated.' And for Hutton that meant changing attitudes first and last: individual attitudes especially, but also 'the climate of opinion, the social environment and the morale of a people'.[20]

For the first anniversary of the Marshall Plan Raymond Aron paid eloquent tribute in *Le Figaro* and over the radio to the results of the American gesture: and it was the psychological effects the eminent French philosopher chose to emphasize. He spoke of the return of 'a sense of hope and confidence', of 'restored courage and reawakened energy', transforming 'almost at once, the psychological atmosphere of the "cold war" '. A new sense of solidarity had emerged, said Aron, providing 'an occasion without precedent to bring about what has been the centuries-old dream of philosophers, and what is today an imperious necessity of history – the unity of Europe'. It was up to the Europeans themselves, he concluded, 'not to lose this unique opportunity'.[21]

But the Americans were not satisfied with the progress achieved in these directions. The great information-effort itself had been set up in part because, as Al Friendly put it in April 1948, not only did the Europeans not know about American aid, 'they don't even know their own countries are cooperating with each other'.[22] A few months' experience on the ground convinced the ECA men that if the basic problems were to be tackled, they had better stop diagnosing and start prescribing, because 'the Europeans are not going to do it by themselves, at least not soon enough', as one of them put it. But the ERP was intended especially to promote European self-help, stimulating cooperation and coordination without outside interference: that was the whole point of the OEEC, in which the US did not sit.

Thus a basic tension emerged in the effort that sometimes worked creatively but usually did not. Referring to the strains it put on the propaganda front, the director of the Industrial Division in Holland said pithily: 'the United States was paying the piper and it was always a great problem how loudly we could call the tune'.[23] In the search for 'a real tool for manoeuvering the Europeans into a frontal attack on the basic problem'[24] the obvious device was the OEEC itself. By 1949 the publicity people had agreed to get 'OEEC on top – and ECA underneath – all our major projects', even such obviously American spectaculars as the international friendship trains and the string of barges that carried a vast ERP exhibit up the Rhine.[25] But by August 1950 only one joint OEEC-ECA film had been produced compared to 50 ECA-only documentaries and, as a conference of top-level information officers was told, it was impossible to do more when you needed the approval of all 19 OEEC members for 'every shot, comma, semi-colon'. Full-scale nationalism was what went on inside the OEEC, the meeting was told, with Spaak and Marjolin the only genuine Europeans in it.[26]

Nevertheless west European economic and political integration as soon as possible was always a key ECA objective, as the propaganda people were constantly reminded, and much of their material reflects it. Films with stories on Norwegian-Italian interdependence, or why Lampedusa needed Trieste, or the arrival of ships bringing life and work throughout Europe in the form of a chain-reaction, all testify to the urgency of the integration priority in American eyes.[27] Only in the third and fourth year did the recognition come that adapting the messages and the media to local circumstances would help their effectiveness. In the early stages the ideal was to have press articles, radio shows, films and exhibitions that could be sent anywhere in Europe and be shown in the United States, including on television. For film news the ECA used the March of Time organization and Fox-Movietone. But for the material aimed to carry the message to the masses, a system of local subcontracting was used whereby local writers, producers and directors would take the basic scheme and work it up in the required format using their own language and local resources – all paid for with national Counterpart funds. The American origins of the operation would thus appear in a national disguise, but one which unsurprisingly left few deceived or satisfied. As a *Newsweek* correspondent put it after visiting Italy: 'even the most sincere friends of the United States sometimes find it hard to appreciate what they are getting'.[28]

The self-evident rightness of the Marshall Plan's goals and methods turned out to be harder to project than expected, and the regular meetings of the Mission information officers in Paris reflect a steady growth in awareness of the difficulties of applying abstract principles and concepts to complex and chaotic local situations. The outcome was disappointment with the short-term results, especially when measured in terms of the rise or fall of support for Left parties and unions. 'The European workman listens listlessly while we tell him we are saving Europe, unconvinced that it is his Europe we are saving', complained a senior staff member in Paris in February 1949.[29] Some of the ECA men felt that practical, meat-and-potatoes results from the Plan would win over the workers. All of them believed that facts in this area were the best form of propaganda: hence the publicity in newsreels of ships arriving, railwagons unloading and factories working.

In the early days it was possible to believe that the working man of Europe was not particularly interested in the Marshall Plan battle against Communism, but sought rather 'a promise of a larger stake in his country's economy – enough income to enjoy better food, a new suit, a picnic or the movies, less cramped living quarters, a chance to retire when he is old'.[30] But by the end of 1949 experience and extensive opinion-polling had brought a significant shift in outlook, to the point that the Director of Information in Paris was told by his Research and Analysis Section that 'the underlying concern of the majority of Europeans today is security . . . (meaning) employment, health and old-age benefits . . . (or further), that a man's life, when begun, contains the reasonable assurance and expectation of a rational progress toward a reasonable conclusion'. The Director of Information must have been shocked to learn from this paper that the concept of higher standards of living was 'rapidly becoming anathematic to Europeans', but he must have been reassured to hear that the basic ERP objectives of higher productivity and European economic unification would not be affected in any way, since only by these means, felt the writer, could the Europeans in fact achieve the social security they so anxiously sought. But in the meantime the Marshall Plan would have to recognize the legitimacy of welfare capitalism, insisting simply that it be applied, as doctrine and reality, without restriction in all Europe. The writer concluded:

The question is always either asked or implied 'What does America get out of the Marshall Plan?' Here we have the answer: America and a unified Europe, partners in the Atlantic Community, derive increased security from heightened productivity.[31]

Although by the end of 1949 the top people in ECA were convinced that the European socialization wave had come to an end, the search began in earnest at this time for means to convince Europeans that America was in favour of social reconstruction and was not intent on defending the ways of the old ruling classes. While some looked to democratic ideology and tried to persuade themselves that 'free enterprise as practised in America is not really very different from Socialism as practised in Western Europe',[32] others sought to dispel the suspicions provoked by ERP's obvious lack of enthusiasm for the land-reform programmes emerging in Italy, the tax reforms mooted in France and British nationalizations.[33] But scepticism persisted to the end over America's motives in launching the Marshall Plan; any discussion of its impact must take into account the substantial opinion-poll evidence and commentary of the time on what Europeans of all social and political groupings made of the great project.

A November 1948 poll carried out on its own initiative by the *Daily Express* found that 80 per cent of those interviewed knew what the Plan was (an unusually high number by European standards at this date). Of these 54 per cent thought it would work, 7 per cent did not, while 39 per cent did not know. In favour of the Plan were 60 per cent of the interviewees; 11 per cent were against it while the rest did not know. But in an editorial comment, the paper 'frankly regretted' that the majority favoured the Plan, since the *Express* was convinced that 'Britain with the Empire can and should seek the means of recovery in her own resources.'[34] In a much larger-scale private effort, the Common Council for American Unity, an élite liberal organization dedicated to interracial and international understanding, found European opinion in 1949 to be largely in favour of the ERP and overwhelmingly on America's side in the Cold War. But their letter-poll of 100 opinion-makers in all walks of life in the 16 ERP countries discovered significant dismay over certain aspects of the projection of American power, from Hollywood to ideological dogmatism, from advertising to the general materialism of American life. Majorities of 80 to 85 per cent on the key issues were not enough for the Council: the percentage remaining was people whose faith and understanding of the Marshall Plan, America's role in the Cold War and the way of life America was offering to the rest of the world was considered inadequate.[35]

The ECA's own pollsters surveyed approximately 2000 people in the middle of 1950, covering France, Norway, Denmark, Holland, Austria, Italy and Trieste. In Paris only 35 per cent declared they had even heard of the Plan; in France as a whole 64 per cent of those who had heard of it felt it was bad for the country.[36] But France was a special case, the only country with opposition on this scale, and the one in which a November 1950 poll found the Government's rating on economic policy down to 3 per cent in favour. When Frenchmen were asked on this occasion 'which political party they felt was looking out for the interests of the working man, 21 per cent named the Communist party and 13 per cent named the Socialists. In a sample of over 2,000 people, no respondent ever mentioned any other party.'[37]

In the earlier survey of 1950 the results were usually more encouraging. An average of 80 per cent of those polled knew of the Plan and 75 per cent approved of it (55 per cent was the minimum), with 25 to 40 per cent having a detailed knowledge of how it worked. But as commentators at an Information Officers' meeting in London in August remarked, it was among the minorities not 'on the team' that the key targets were to be found: the workers and peasants. They were the ones most seriously doubting America's motives, just as Communist propaganda encouraged them to do.[38] In a top-level analysis of two and a half years of effort, carried out for Ambassador Harriman's deputy, Milton Katz, it was admitted that knowledge of the Marshall Plan and its popularity were by that time – November 1950 – stagnant. While the percentage of the population opposing the Plan in countries such as France and Italy was smaller than the Communist vote, the doubts still persisted in 'much too great a segment of the European population' around the question of 'whether US policy was aimed at progressive improvement in general living standards or was designed more to shore up economic and social systems which are not popular and to restore to power reactionary and conservative vested interests'.[39] Even in the ruling groups, morale and attitudes were considered unsatisfactory, with 'neutralism, pacifism, we-don't-want-to be-occupiedism' spreading, according to the head of the Information Division of the London Mission. Restoring self-esteem was the key priority, he insisted, which meant 'helping them regain dignity and influence in an (international) community which perhaps is changed but in which they can continue to play a useful part'. In this context 'European economic and political unification' (the phrase was standard) had a useful part to play, even if it meant running the risk of encouraging the Third Force idea that challenged 'the drive for the military unification of the North Atlantic'.[40] At this point it would be easy to portray the Marshall Plan as in deep political crisis by the middle of 1950, unable to bring about the fundamental shifts in attitudes, expectations and behaviour which, as we have seen, had made up such a strong component of the whole operation from the beginning. Even in Italy, where so much effort had been spent, government, industry and labour 'persist in taking a very dim view of productivity', a Labor Division inspector from Paris reported in June. According to this observer the fundamental economic and political context of the Marshall Plan effort there had to be changed, since it was up against 'the prime flaw of Italian industry . . . its parasitic nature, its monopolistic structure,, practices and outlook', and its distribution system, 'an heirloom of the 13th century'.[41]

But to depict the fate of the ERP as a failure by its own lights would be to ignore the contradiction mentioned at the beginning of this analysis between the short- and long-term aims of the plan. The ERP men were under immense pressure to get instant results, overnight increases in production, immediately visible improvements in housing, transport, energy, industry, agriculture, downturns in Communist votes by the next election and enthusiastic endorsement of everything America stood for by the next Congressional budget-hearing. What happened was rather different. To take a prominent contemporary reference, we may say that something modestly approaching the ECA vision of European 'unification' in 1952 will now take place in 1992. At the time it was quite impossible to demand a drop in support for the Italian Communist party in the 1951 elections when not a penny had been spent of the 1949 investment budget by the beginning of 1950. It was equally idle to expect a quantum leap in British exports to America when United States trade barriers remained unchanged and Britain was unable to satisfy demand at home or in the rest of the world.[42] The fundamental contradiction was only overcome with the fullscale emergency of the Korean War from June 1950 onwards. But the Marshall Plan was radically changed in nature by this development, becoming more and more overshadowed by military priorities and the great push for rearmament. Governments trembled before the new demands made on their budgets (NATO promises notwithstanding); throughout ECA it was recognized that the strains could produce 'internal security crises' in countries such as France and Italy, or at best sceptical neutralism of the kind evident in Britain. Nevertheless, insisted Washington:

We must recognize that goal of placing Europe in posture own immediate self-defence is an objective which overrides in immediate importance any one of the economic goals we and European leaders have established in the past two years.[43]

But the ECA men on the ground had already decided there was no conflict between the defence and the ERP objectives: it was just a matter of 'bending' the existing policy goals to the new requirements. An August 1950 staff paper produced in Paris noted that there were three existing policy themes:

1 The Marshall Plan is good for you: i.e. Marshall aid shipments give people more to eat, more jobs, better houses, etc.
2 Europe should 'integrate'.
3 Productivity must increase if Europe is to have a better living standard and sell in world markets.

In order to increase European 'stability, self-confidence and, therefore, self-respect', the three themes would now be transposed:

1 Marshall aid and military assistance are good for you because they give you – as Europeans – a fighting chance to make Europe strong enough to discourage any aggression.
2 *But* – this strength can only be achieved through unity. As separate, rival powers, the nations of Free Europe *are* weak, *are* dangerously exposed.
3 Productivity must increase because more food, more machines, more of nearly everything is needed to make Europe so strong it will be unassailable.[44]

In the following years each of these themes received dramatic new emphasis, but none more than the productivity drive, the subject of a pan-European accord in 1952, and the Moody and Benton amendments to the original ERP act in 1951 and 1952, which provided another $400m for this purpose alone. But by this time the publicity and information programme had long since changed its self-image: full-scale 'psychological warfare' was now the order of the day. 'You Too Can Be Like Us': that was the original message of the Marshall Plan, and it was the task of the Information Program to bring it home to Europeans everywhere: 'They learned,' wrote Administrator Hoffmann in his memoirs, 'that this is the land of full shelves and bulging shops, made possible by high productivity and good wages, and that its prosperity may be emulated elsewhere by those who will work towards it.' [45] 'Prosperity Makes You Free' proclaimed the slogans on the Marshall Plan Freedom Trains as they brought aid and comfort in the dark days of the late 1940s. But there was more then prosperity, there was the concept of growth: it enters the language of economics and politics at this time, by way of the Truman administration's Council of Economic Advisers of 1949. Then came the so-called 'revolution of rising expectations', identified by a senior ECA man, Harlan Cleveland, as early as 1954, possibly the first sighting of the so-called 'economic miracles' in Europe.[46] The 'miracles' – quite unforeseen in 1952 – seemed heaven-sent to justify everything the Marshall Plan had stood for and certainly allowed European and American politicians to claim that this was what they had intended all along.

In 1960 the OEEC became the OECD, with the United States a full member; as its founding convention stated, the OECD's purpose was 'to achieve the highest sustainable economic growth and employment and a rising standard of living'.[47] The Marshall Plan aimed at much more than 'viability' – the balancing of transatlantic payments accounts – or the restoration of living standards to their 1938 levels. It came to seek a comprehensive modernization of market relationships within Europe and between Europe and the United States. In 1949 a *New York Times* correspondent lamented that a country like Italy still had not developed its own capitalism or mass-market: 'The idea,' he wrote, 'of persuading the low-income consumer to feel the need for something he has never had, using advertising, and then to give it to him at a price he can afford, could be the Marshall Plan's biggest contribution to Italy – if it gets anywhere.' [48]

Looking back in 1978 on the era of the 1950s, W. W. Rostow – author of the bible of the growth system *The Stages of Economic Growth* (sub-title *A Non-Communist Manifesto*) – declared that there was nothing invented by the Europeans in their new era of high mass-consumption that had not been seen already in the high points of America's development in the twentieth century. Cars, chemicals, communications, consumer durables: the American model had been transferred to Europe.[49] It was the spirit moving the extraordinary expansion of the 1950s that was unprecedented, in the view of the economic historian, Michael Postan, writing in the late 1960s: 'What was really remarkable . . . was that economic growth was so powerfully propelled by public sentiments and policies. In all European countries economic growth became a universal creed and a common expectation to which governments were expected to conform.' And, Postan insisted, this had come about through the projection of America's influence: what America gave, what she preached and what she was.[50] In reality the economic Marshall Plan so well-known to history and now so scaled-down by economic historiography worked on the supply side of the market equation. But there was another ERP, perhaps even more enduring in its results, seeking to change wants, needs, attitudes and aspirations, powerfully at work on the demand side of the same equation.

4 Americanism and Anti-Americanism in British and German Responses to the Marshall Plan

Peter M. R. Stirk

The American attempt to promote European recovery that bore the name of Secretary of State George C. Marshall is one of the most disputed events of recent European history. Its origins, coherence, intent and effects have all been questioned. Its original status as an act by which Europe, or at least western Europe, was saved from the ravages of stagnation, autarky, poverty and Communism has been qualified and diminished or subtly reaffirmed. At its boldest the American vision combined perceptions about both America and Europe as types of economy, polity and culture, with Europe's future salvation being seen as lying in its imitation of America. The prescription for Europe was integration, preferably under the aegis of a supranational authority, free trade, increased productivity, anti-Communism and a new model of social organization that would displace the old class conflicts of European society. Merely to list the different facets of the Plan indicates its complexity. That complexity is in turn compounded by the fact that the Plan was no mere utopian sketch of a future Europe but was to provide relatively immediate solutions to urgent and pressing problems, most notably the vexed problem of the restoration of industrial activity in Germany and the so-called dollar gap between the United States and Europe as a whole. At the visionary level, high productivity stood out as the key to success. At the practical level the restoration of trade, throttled by the autarkic order of the 1930s and early 1940s and in ruins in the wake of the War, stood out as the most pressing concern. Both came together in the prescription of a united Europe. High productivity, seen as the solution to distributional conflicts and the threat of 'belly-Communism', was to be promoted by the abolition of Europe's internal barriers to trade. Just as the large internal market of the United States was seen as the historic precondition of high productivity in the USA so too Europe's lagging productivity was to be rectified by economic union.

The shortcomings of the Marshall Plan, especially the successful resistance of most European governments to the imperatives of integration and the associated loss of national sovereignty, have been emphasized recently.[1] Yet a more general process, namely the 'Americanization' of Europe, has also received revived attention.[2] As might be expected, the challenge presented to Europeans by this 'Americanization' appears particularly acute for European Socialists. For all the similarities between the two continents, one simple difference had long been unmistakable and provoked the query made famous by Werner Sombart's *Why is there no Socialism in the United States*? The distinction was reaffirmed in the postwar era by the German Socialist, Richard Lowenthal (Paul Sering) in his influential *Jenseits des Kapitalismus*.[3] The problem, for Socialists and Europe, can easily be summarized: if Europe imitates the American model then what place would there be for that most distinctively European phenomenon, Socialism? The point was not lost on either American or European contemporaries of the Marshall Plan. Benton, a member of the Committee for Economic Development, whose ideas and personnel pervaded the offices of the Marshall Planners, was unequivocal. The neo-capitalist ideology formulated by the Committee was, he said, the American 'answer to the European brands of socialism'.[4] In Europe reaction against the Marshall Plan as the spearhead of a capitalist restoration was led by the Communist parties.[5] Alongside the theme of capitalist restoration ran fears of US competition, injured national pride and catalogues of the depravity of American civilization. Communist-party antipathy to the Marshall Plan naturally aided the contrary sentiment among the non-Communist Left as each made attitudes to the Plan a symbol of loyalty in their broader and more deep-rooted disputes. Yet Communist criticism evidently struck a chord among the members of Europe's Socialist parties, as is attested by the frequency with which Socialist defenders of America sought to counteract the image of 'the Americans' as an undifferentiated and rapacious mass.[6]

In retrospect it is easy to see the force of a suggestion made in a recent work on the impact of the Marshall Plan, that 'Marshall aid and the American influence in Britain . . . certainly contributed to that mix of forces that was leading Labour to lose its sense of socialist purpose and self-confidence as a radical reforming party in the late 1940s.'[7] Similar judgements have been made on the response of the German Socialists. In both cases Socialists are seen as succumbing to an American ideology of increasing productivity and growth whose long-term consequences, inimical to the Socialist enterprise, they were almost wilfully unaware of. From a Socialist stance then, one could retrospectively construct a vicious circle analogous to the virtuous circle perceived by the American Marshall Planners. According to the vicious circle, the orientation towards economic growth goes hand-in-hand with the dissipation of Socialist planning, while the redistribution of wealth and integration into an American-dominated global trading-system goes hand-in-hand with the failure to establish European unity on the basis of a 'third way' between the Communism of the Soviet Union and the Capitalism of the United States.[8]

The danger inherent in viewing the postwar era in terms of this vicious circle is that European Socialists appear as dupes or at best as unwitting pawns whose failures of judgement and perception are the more pronounced the more they are counterposed to the purpose and coherence of the American Marshall Planners. It is, therefore, worth reflecting upon the European, predominantly European Socialist, response to the Marshall Plan and especially to the idea of increasing

productivity and the new order of trade. As will be shown there was no shortage
of anti-Americanism among British and, albeit to a lesser extent, German
Socialists. Their basic criticisms resembled those of the Communists. There is no
reason why they should have differed, for both drew upon the same stock of
images and arguments common to European political culture as a whole.[9] This
paper, however, will suggest that most British and German Socialist leaders took a
less-jaundiced view of the United States, not because they succumbed to an
American ideology, but as Socialists and as British or German Socialists.

As is well-known Ernest Bevin was one of the first to react positively to
Marshall's Harvard speech of 5 June 1947. The prompt and more or less
consistent support of the Foreign Secretary for the Marshall Plan did much to
ensure that the Labour Party and the broader Labour movement would endorse
the Plan. His roots in the trade-union movement consolidated his ability to speak
as a member of *their* government.[10] This moral leverage in no way provided
immunity from criticism. When Bevin enjoyed an easy passage at the Labour
Party Annual Conference in 1949, the break with what was becoming a tradition
of critical resolutions drew comment from Hugh Dalton.[11] The criticisms of the
Marshall Plan and relations with the United States invoked images that formed
part of the European perception of the United States in the interwar years. The
United States appeared above all as the source of the Depression and as an
economic competitor. In the first Labour Party Annual Conference after the
announcement of the Marshall Plan, one delegate combined both fears in his
rhetorical question:

Who is taking our export trade away? Who has tied strings to the loan to prevent our
Dominions and us from defending ourselves? I suggest that the answer is the United
States. The only way we can maintain our standard is, as our Foreign Secretary has just
started doing, to make arrangements with the planned economy countries where there will
be no slumps at all.[12]

The leading left-wing MP and critic of government foreign policy, Koni
Zilliacus, moved a composite resolution, which was defeated, along similar lines.[13]
Implicit, and sometimes explicit, in such sentiments was the exaggerated belief
that the United Kingdom already enjoyed a planned economy.[14] Thereby the
United States appeared even more strongly as the land of unregulated capitalism,
and hence as the source of a potential slump. While a depressed American
economy would threaten to drag down countries tied to it, a prosperous America
figured as an unfair competitor whose surplus production was being dumped
through the Marshall Plan. Thus R. Silk proclaimed bluntly at the Annual Trade
Union Congress of 1948 that 'It is also clear that the aid is of a kind not so much
as to what we want but as to what America wants to get rid of'.[15] Speaking in the
wake of the Economic Cooperation Act of April 1948 and the Economic
Cooperation Agreement between the United States and the United Kingdom of
July 1948, the USDAW delegate had little difficulty in pointing to the restrictions
privileging American shipping and to the vague provisions enjoining the United
Kingdom to supply indeterminate materials to the United States 'for stock-piling
or other purposes', in order to bolster the suggestion that the intentions of the
United States were less than benign.

Injured pride also played a prominent part. The first series of shocks had followed closely upon the end of the War with the abrupt ending of Lend-Lease, the difficulties over negotiating an American loan and the refusal of the Americans to share information about atomic weapons. Further developments did little to ease the problem and Bevin turned on his critics in 1947 with the pointed reminder that the role of supplicant was not an enjoyable one. Injured pride was also part of the response in the debate over the implications of superior American productivity. The notion that Europe could learn from the American experience here found its first transnational institutional expression in the Anglo-American Council on Productivity. The Council was the product of a meeting in June 1948 between Stafford Cripps and European Cooperation Administrator Paul Hoffmann. Both men were of a technocratic disposition and they discovered a common enthusiasm for the promotion of industrial productivity. The Council, involving both businessmen and trade unionists from both sides of the Atlantic, was to acquaint the British with American methods and techniques supposed to underly the American advantage in this area. It was to become the model for analogous organizations across Europe as the European Cooperation Administration developed a technical assistance programme from December 1948.[16] The initial response at the TUC Congress of 1948 is well-summarized in the President's Address:

If American practice is held up to us as a pattern for us to follow, and when the mechanical equipment of our factories is contrasted with those of America, we are not being conservative or obstructive in saying that the productive techniques which have been carried further in other countries, we invented.[17]

Pride had been evident in the reassurance given by an early report, 'Can Americans Help Our Industries?' in the TUC publication Labour to the effect that the 'traffic in ideas' would be two-way. A more pragmatic observation was that Britons did not need any advice to work harder. Subsequent reports reiterated this point but with changing emphasis. For Labour could report in March 1949 that the Americans did not work harder at all. In a report published in August, which seems to have forgotten about the idea of two-way traffic, entitled 'Round-Up Report of Industrial Teams Seeking Ideas in USA', Labour pointed to the common result of all the investigations: namely that there was a consistently greater use of machines rather than men to move equipment and material. The March 1949 issue had discerned greater productivity even where no new machinery was introduced but where there was greater cooperation between management and labour.[18] As Anthony Carew has shown, such cooperation was by no means the norm and British trade-union leaders were well-aware of the fact.[19]

The facts, however, mattered less than the implications. If the much-vaunted US superiority could be ascribed even in part to labour-management cooperation in areas of production then there was a good argument for challenging the jealously guarded privileges of British employers. Somewhat different was the enthusiasm for the highly indeterminate phenomenon of 'productivity consciousness', which was supposed to enthuse American workers and management alike. It is easy to see why this ethos might appeal to the employers, for it is easily bent in the direction of injunctions to work harder and distracts attention from organization within the factory, let alone issues of ownership.[20] More understandable was support in November 1949 for the 'Three Big S's in SucceSS': that is, simplification, standardization and specialization. These virtuous practices were achieved, *Labour* noted, by collaboration between American firms. For Socialists accustomed to looking for the incipient traits of the new social order in the old, the step from interfirm collaboration to Socialist planning was not necessarily a great one.[21] This desire to discern the new in the old was compounded by some curious judgements about the import of the new international agreements and institutions. Kenneth Younger, after referring to the proclamations of full-employment policies, the European Coal and Transport Organizations and the activities of the United Nations Relief and Rehabilitation Agency, declared, 'These are acts of international Socialism and not less Socialist because Capitalist America has taken a lead.' In a similar vein, George Catlin, at the same Labour Party Annual Conference of 1947, cited the Bretton Woods agreements and the proposed International Trade Organization as 'the proper way to internationalize and Socialize American capital'.[22]

Consideration of the broader debate on productivity helps to explain why the TUC publication became such a rapid convert to the productivity campaign and points to what was perceived as the Socialist dimension of it. There was, in the first place, little new in the basic concerns of the Anglo-American Council. Increased production had been a priority during the War; in times of manpower shortages that meant, in part, increased productivity. The same imperative was carried over into peacetime in the interests of economic recovery. *Labour* was, indeed, reporting on the Industrial Organization Bill in February 1947 and noted that the purpose of the proposed Development Councils was to increase efficiency and productivity in essential industries. The May 1947 issue referred to a Working Party Report on the clothing industry in similar terms, replete with emphasis upon tripartite cooperation and comparisons with American conditions.[23] The emphasis upon tripartite cooperation points to the Socialist dimension. Charles Dukes' Address to the 1946 Annual Trades Unions Congress made it quite clear. The trades unions, he said, had an interest in improving the efficiency of industry:

in improving their techniques, and insisting upon the highest attainable standards of mechanisation and modern scientific methods.
Implicit in this view is the realisation that industrial efficiency is not the exclusive concern of management, and not solely the responsibility of the employers' side of industry.[24]

In brief, the common pursuit of improved industrial production entailed the erosion of managerial prerogative. Yet the affirmation of efficiency was no mere tactical move. It had long been a standard thesis of Socialist literature that Capitalists restrained production for the sake of their profits.[25] More specifically, members of the British Labour Party and trade-union movement liked to regard the employers as the source of attachment to outdated traditions. The future, which meant a more prosperous future, belonged to the Labour movement. It is therefore no surprise to find Herbert Morrison submitting a report to the 1948 Labour Party Annual Conference entitled *Production the Bridge to Socialism*. Speaking in its support he declared that:

Socialism has always aimed at an abundance of goods and services, but past Socialists have
sometimes been so preoccupied with the immense problems of securing a fair distribution
that they have not tackled in detail the equally immense problem of securing full
production.[26]

The commitment to production was also a guard against the recurrence of past
evils. Bevin put the matter forcefully when he suggested to delegates to the 1947
Annual Trades Union Congress that the choice facing the UK was between the
'old method of starvation' or salvation by production. Increased production was
to prevent a recurrence of the unemployment and misery of the 1930s and to
secure British independence.[27] The two goals were put together with a polemical
twist at the Labour Party Annual Conference the following year:

If the Tories were in power they would try to solve our economic difficulties by creating
unemployment and then welcoming American capital into this country in order to get
dollars. We, on the other hand, have decided that we are going to follow a policy of
national independence; that we are going to fight our way through by earning and by
producing the goods that we require.[28]

In so far as Marshall Plan ideologues were promoting increased production and
productivity they were knocking at an open door in the case of the British Labour
movement. Precisely for this reason, however, it is worth recalling that British
Socialists had, at the least, what they perceived to be good Socialist reasons for
their enthusiasm. They also clearly had some more nationalistic reasons. Both the
dislike of being told what to do by Americans, be it within the factory or as a
nation, and the aim of securing autonomy through production were as much
questions of national pride as anything else. There was, however, one aspect of
the Marshall-Plan package that was not particularly welcome, in whatever guise:
the association between productivity and an enlarged European market. Few
indeed were the Socialists who took up this idea with the enthusiasm of the
Frenchman André Philip, but the British Labour movement noted the idea only to
sidestep it.[29] Thus, the Labour Party memorandum to the Socialist Conference of
21–22 March 1948 duly recorded the standard argument that productive
efficiency in the United States was related to the existence of a large internal
market and then promptly seized upon the sections of the Committee for
European Economic Cooperation Report that emphasized the limitations and
difficulties confronting a European Customs Union.[30]

Most critics of official policy called not for a European commitment but for
trade with 'other' planned economies, most notably the Soviet Union. With the
exception of this increasingly marginalized alternative the most prevalent
preference was for strengthening trading links with the Commonwealth and
sterling area: this was seen as a source of raw materials, which could be paid for in
sterling, and as a market for Britain's industrial goods. That is, it was consonant
with government policy and with the existing distribution of British trade.
Perhaps equally important, it was consistent with prevailing sentiment. As is well-
known the Labour-Party document, *European Unity*, affirmed that:

In every respect except distance we in Britain are closer to our kinsmen in Australia and
New Zealand on the far side of the world, than we are to Europe. We are closer in language

and in origins, in social habits and institutions, in political outlook and in economic interest.[31]

The German response to the Marshall Plan was bound to be more diffuse, given the fragmentation of policy formulation in an occupied country divided into four zones and the uncertainty about Germany's future integrity as well as its economic and political constitution. This confusion was compounded by the fact that Germans – that is Germans in the western zones – were often belatedly and incompletely informed of developments of the Marshall Plan. Typical of the initial position was that the *Länderrat* of the American zone was not even sure whether it would be allowed to discuss the Plan with the military governors. A summary of a meeting with the Herter-Committee, one of the American commissions involved in the Plan, recorded that the Germans would be grateful if they received access to the data collected by the Paris Conference that was officially formulating the European response to Marshall's offer. As late as 30 July 1948 *Oberdirektor* Pünder, then head of the *Verwaltungsrat*, was obliged to reserve judgement on the agreement, which incorporated the Bizone into the Marshall Plan, signed on 14 July between the USA and the USA-UK Occupied Areas, on the grounds that the text of the agreement was not yet known to the Germans.[32]

Germans in general, including German Socialists, were not necessarily in a good position to judge the long-term consequences of the Marshall Plan. Nevertheless, it was quickly welcomed by Kurt Schumacher and Hans Böckler, the most important leaders of German Socialism and trade unionism. Their positive reponse was hardly surprising. Any Allied gesture that promised material aid or marked a step away from the Carthaginian peace promised by the Morgenthau Plan was apt to be seized upon. Nevertheless, German Socialists were no more uncritical than their British counterparts. They had emerged from the War with the conviction that a new Socialist order was on the agenda; they were equally convinced that as one of the prime targets of the National Socialist régime they had a moral right to inaugurate the new society. At least from 1946, the new social and economic order was associated with the idea that Europe's, and especially Germany's, future lay in being a Third Force that could mitigate the growing tension between the superpowers and provide a model which, by virtue of exhibiting features of both socioeconomic systems, would mediate between the two types of society represented by the superpowers. The idea that the Marshall Plan might prove incompatible with both elements of this vision was expressed in the same breath that welcomed the Plan.

The immediate concern for the German Left was the significance of the Marshall Plan for the socialization of basic industries in Germany. This concern was expressed at the beginning of August 1947 by the *Deutsche Gewerkschaftsbund* (DGB) of the British zone. The DGB wished 'to express the affirmation of the Marshall Plan by the trade unions but also to express the clear will of the trade unions to hold fast, now as before, to their demands for the reorganization of the economy'.[33] Depsite these worries, Hans Böckler, the DGB leader, consistently moved to bolster the commitment to the Marshall Plan; he met with some criticism on his return from the 1947 TUC Congress at Southport where, it was charged, he had sacrificed the commitment to socialization for the sake of the

Marshall Plan. Böckler was not alone in his willingness to back the Plan. Only one of the seven trade-union federations rejected it, and even then the rejection, by the executive, was subsequently revoked. At an Extraordinary Congress, held at Recklinghausen in June 1948, called to discuss the Marshall Plan, Böckler's position was supported, albeit after a cursory debate.[34] Assessment of this decision was not, and is not, easy. In retrospect Böckler was probably right when he replied to his critics with the rhetorical question, 'Does not America have the ability to work towards the preservation of large capital even without the inclusion [in the Marshall Plan] of the western zones?'[35] Indeed, when the Americans did hinder German socialization plans – plans that were not always pursued with great enthusiasm by the Socialists themselves – they relied quite simply upon their authority as an occupying power, bolstered by the justification that decisions concerning ownership of such significant industries could only be taken by representatives of the German people as a whole. Such representatives, they maintained, did not as yet exist.

The possibility that the Marshall Plan might divide Europe, and hence undermine the Third Way, was evident from the rejection of the Marshall Plan by the Soviet Union. But the issue was far from settled, or so it appeared, for the idea of the Third Way continued to flourish and even grew in its appeal. One leading socialist advocate of European unity and the Third Way, Carlo Schmid, saw the Plan as an opportunity for Europe to begin the process towards recovery and integration, albeit without Germany. Paradoxically the initial exclusion of Germany was to have a dual benefit: for Germany and for Europe. In the first place Europe, as a Third Force, would mediate between East and West, contribute to a reduction of superpower tension and thereby open up the way for a reunification of all four zones of Germany. The reunified Germany, and here came the second advantage, could then join the rest of Europe which, as a unified body, would then have no need to fear German predominance within Europe. Though Schmid clung to this option for as long as possible, the summer of 1948 effectively ended any plausible hopes for his scheme. Pressure for the formation of a western state came in the shape of the London Recommendations which were communicated to the Germans at the beginning of July. By then, currency reform, the extension of the new currency to Berlin and the ensuing blockade had taken place. While Schmid was able to persuade other German leaders of the virtue of his strategy at a meeting in Koblenz (8–10 July), the western state was accepted later in the same month, with Schmid's fellow Socialist, Ernst Reuter, entering an impassioned plea for the western state on behalf of Berlin.[36]

In the wake of this decision the Marshall Plan acquired even greater significance as a confession of faith and as an instrument whereby the Germans, or at least those in the western zones, might more rapidly gain some measure of sovereignty and freedom of action. The rhetorical role of the Plan, which goes a long way to explaining the exaggeration of its practical effect, crystallized in May 1949 amid the final preparations for the foundation of the Federal Republic. The American view, or at least that of General Clay, was recorded by Pünder when they met prior to Clay's departure from Germany. In Pünder's words, 'The western Allies demanded above all a clear avowal of *their* ideology as embodied in the ideas of the Marshall Plan.' The Socialists scarcely disagreed and were positively eager to exploit the propaganda value of the Plan, fearing only lest the

United States might make concessions to the Soviet Union. Thus, *Senator Präsident* Kaisen of Bremen 'warned against a restoration of the previous interzonal trade with the Soviet Union, for thereby the Soviets would be freed from their embarrassment . . . The prospect, however, of including the eastern zone was the most important propaganda instrument'.[37]

Responses to the Marshall Plan were complicated by other considerations arising from more general judgements about America and Americans. Prominent among these was the early contact with American trade unionists, especially of the American Federation of Labour (AFL). As Werner Link has shown these contacts consolidated into a veritable transnational coalition, with the AFL providing strong support for the re-establishment of the German unions and for their policies, albeit with some qualification. The attitude of Georg Reuter of the *Bayerische Gewekschaftsbund* is certainly understandable in this context. For he argued that the involvement of the AFL and Congress of Industrial Organizations (CIO) in the Marshall Plan Administration would, of itself, lead to adequate German trade-union participation in the Plan.[38] The alliance with the American trade unionists also appears in the response of the SPD. Schumacher had expressed his support for the Plan at the Nürnberg Parteitag in June–July 1947, though it does not appear to have been until April 1948 that there was any substantial discussion within the SPD – and even then the debate focused on Germany's share in Marshall-Plan aid. The claim submitted by Pünder was found wanting and the ensuing recommendation was that the German trade unionists should ask the AFL–CIO to lobby for an increase.[39]

Alongside the exigencies of occupation and transnational alliances amid the emergent Cold War were judgements about long-term trends within the United States. Appropriately enough they proved relatively resistant to considerations of the day. Among the most prominent critics of the United States was Fritz Sternberg. His book *The Coming Crisis*, completed in the spring of 1946, saw the prodigious increase in American production as the source of a new and even more severe world crisis. America's position among the Capitalist states was so paramount that the coming American crisis threatened to shake the rest of the world even more severely than its predecessor.[40] *The Coming Crisis* was reviewed in November 1947 by Peter Blachstein in *Geist und Tat* and this review was, according to Hans-Peter Schwarz, the source of economic arguments for Socialist anti-American sentiment.[41] Sternberg himself expressed opposition to the Marshall Plan in October 1948, in *Neuer Vorwärts*. He still saw the United States as a crisis-ridden land, which was now trying to resolve its domestic difficulties by rebuilding Europe on the basis of private capitalism. Sternberg confidently expected that German and other European workers would resist when they saw the German economy being re-established under the industrialists who had collaborated with the Nazis.[42]

In almost total contrast to Sternberg were the views of Otto Bach. His article of March 1948 noted that German capitalists would seek to exploit the Recovery Programme for their own purposes but also emphasized more positive features. The recovery of western Europe could lead to the revival of trade with the east: that is, with western Europe's natural market for industrial goods and its natural source of raw materials. Contrary to the hope of the German capitalists, the Marshall Plan was not an affirmation of the search for profit, but was rather expressive of welfare-state policies. Furthermore, this fact reflected the underlying realities of the age:

The fact that governments, parliaments and organizations are engaged in this plan – even if they often place excessive emphasis upon national economic interests – is clear proof that not only is the concept of a European economy gradually emerging but also that recognition of the fact that this economy can only develop within the framework of economic planning is growing from day to day . . . As a socialist I can only applaud the fact that this development involves the pressure to plan and that it is precisely the representatives of a distinctly capitalist world who are having to point the European countries to the road to planning. The idea that socialists must be on their guard against a plan that comes from a capitalist country and whose purpose is the well-being of capitalist society, completely fails to grasp the law of social development which is already finding expression in the pressure to plan.[43]

In retrospect such affirmation have been judged as naive or at best self-deceiving; they often appear as little more than window-dressing behind which lay a politically motivated acceptance of a commitment to integration with the West, with all that entailed. Yet, if such they were, they were remarkably widespread, being similar, as has been indicated, to views expressed in the United Kingdom. The United States did in fact enjoy a not-inconsiderable reputation as both a symbol of democratic government and as a symbol of progressive, if not quite socialistic, policies. Roosevelt's New Deal had laid the foundations of this image of a socially progressive America and had an immense impact upon European Socialists in the 1930s. Truman's Fair Deal appeared to be a continuation of the same theme. His election with the support of American trade unions as well as his veto of the Taft-Hartley Act, which restricted the role of American unions, did much to confirm this progressive image. Typical of the enthusiasm for America's new direction was Max Biehl's *Die Vereinigten Staaten als Wirtschaftsmacht*, published in 1949. In Biehl's words: 'Truman's programme far surpasses everything that has previously existed and if only a part of it becomes law America will scarcely be behind the most recent conditions of England.'[44]

For German Socialists the other aspect of the United States, its image as the symbol of democratic and republican government, was of peculiar importance. They had been accustomed to regard the Socialist movement as the heir to a failed bourgeois revolution in Germany. The experience of the Third Reich confirmed this self-estimation, for, the argument went, did not the bourgeoisie cast aside the virtues of democracy, parliamentary government and the rule of law as their economic interests were threatened? From this perspective the prime task of the Socialists was to re-establish, on a firmer and more thorough basis, those bourgeois forms of government; in this the United States was the obvious ally.[45] Such general sentiments were prone to being revoked as the Americans failed to live up to their radical image. Schumacher had been disillusioned as early as the spring of 1946. But like so many facets of the ideological map of the early postwar years these sentiments confounded the simple dichotomies that had once held sway.[46]

It is worth recalling that the ideological opponents of the German Socialists, the so-called ordo-liberals, who shared the American goal of a private Capitalist order and lauded the virtues of competition, also had doubts about the United

States. Their worries are of some interest in themselves and also serve to indicate that, for contemporaries at least, the Socialist supposition that America was now a progressive land was not implausible. The United States, it appears, was not an unequivocal model for the German prophets of a competitive market. These worries were clearly expressed in a substantial article reviewing policy on competition, entitled 'Die Politik des Wettbewerbs in den USA'.[47] Its author, Heinrich Kronstein, upheld the original stance of the ordo-liberals to the effect that the maintenance of the Capitalist order could not be left to the free-functioning of the market but required the active coordination of political and economic strategies. Surveying the history of the United States from its inception he could discern only two periods when the requisite insight into the integration of political and economic strategies had been evident. Unfortunately, both periods, associated with the names of Hamilton and Roosevelt, revealed opposition to a competitive order. The ambitions of the latter had, it was true, induced a counter-move that pointed in the right direction but was now being dissipated; and the would-be planners were on the march again, with both the Marshall Plan and the supposed fears of a European cartel providing welcome pretexts.

The ideas of the virtuous circle, of increasing productivity facilitated by new machinery and techniques of production combined with European cooperation and the establishment of a 'viable' trading pattern, naturally had different connotations in Germany. As with all participants in the European Recovery Programme there was a commitment to the 'Production Effort' as the Report of the Committee for European Economic Cooperation called it.[48] But above all in Germany this initially meant no more than the restoration of the disrupted production of the pre-war era. The package of measures offering a prosperous future based upon continual growth had little meaning when an apocalyptic crisis appeared to be on the agenda. As has been emphasized by Klemm and Trittel this was the predominant concern of leading German politicians until well into the spring of 1948.[49]

An attempt has been made to see early efforts to increase production in the Ruhr mining areas as foreshadowing the Marshall Plan. The miners' leaders had tried to associate claims for socialisation and workers' control, as well as improved food supplies, with agreements to increase production, mainly through increased shifts. By the late summer of 1947 production had increased and food supplies had improved, but without the desired gains in terms of ownership and control. Thus it is claimed, 'The increase of production took place – not with socialization – but with *Speck*,'[50] If the Marshall Plan is seen as entailing improved consumption for the workers in return for the retention of the capitalist order, and this was indeed one of its elements, then the argument has some force. However, there was much more to the virtuous circle than this. It was supposed to entail a radical change in attitudes and prospects for Capitalism. From this more visionary, but nevertheless decisive, perspective 'Speck' is hardly sufficient.

As the Marshall Plan unfolded, much the same impressions were created in the minds of German trade-union visitors to the United States as in the minds of their British colleagues. After the visit of a delegation in October and November 1948 Markus Schleicher reported to the *Bayerische Gewerkschaftsbund* that:

The trade unionists were extremely impressed, not only by the size of the country and the productivity of the American economy but especially by the high living standards of the workers and the strength of the American trade unions as well as by the interest – even in government offices – shown in the cooperation of German trade unions in the decisive programme of reconstruction.[51]

Yet the German equivalent of the Anglo-American Council on Productivity, the *Rationalisierungs-Kuratorium der deutschen Wirtschaft*, did not emerge until later, in 1950. Interestingly, the German Ministry for the Marshall Plan went out of its way to emphasize the German roots of the enterprise. The joint Fifth and Sixth Report noted the American input in the context of the Marshall Plan but then added, 'The earlier *Reichskuratorium für Wirtschaftlichkeit* also serves as a model'.[52] As Volker Berghahn has shown German managers were proud of their autochthonous traditions and there were signs of tiredness with the prodigious output of American-inspired literature.[53] Even more important than this are the twelve reports of the Federal Ministry. Although it is not difficult to find statements consonant with the Marshall-Plan vision that place the appropriate emphasis upon productivity, these are not predominant. In the concluding report the productivity campaign, though dealt with but ten pages earlier, was not included in a list of four factors that had, it was claimed, decisively influenced industrial recovery. These were:

1 the currency reform;
2 the abolition of the controlled economy;
3 the rehabilitation of constitutional authority in the form of the federal government;
4 the change in the attitude of the Western World, especially of the United States, to the 'German Problem'.[54]

If anything should be added to this list in the light of other summative statements in the reports it is trade liberalization, which was seen in any case as part and parcel of the abolition of the controlled economy.

This does not mean that the image of American productivity was without effect, though it does seem that the more exalted ambitions of the Americans for transferring American 'know-how' and managerial attitudes took much longer to achieve (to the extent that they ever were) than envisaged. In the period under consideration here it may well have been more long-standing assumptions that were effective. The decisive document here is a brief article published in 1953 by a leading Socialist, Viktor Agartz, by that time head of the Research Institute of the DGB. The article, 'Beiträge zur wirtschaftliche Entwicklung 1953', proclaimed:

Wages policy cannot simply be dynamic, it must also be expansive. It is not enough to subsequently bring real wages up to the level of development of the national economy. Wages policy must itself seek to force expansion, in order, by consciously increasing purchasing power, to call forth the extension of production. The USA is, here, a most instructive example. An expansive wages policy is also the most effective means of continually spurring enterprises to higher rationality, to increasing productivity and thereby to underpinning the expansion of wages.[55]

It is worth noting that a German trade-union delegation to America in 1926 had come to much the same conclusion. Expansive wages were *the* cause of high productivity which in turn provided the basis for higher wages.[56] German Socialists had long been disposed towards an underconsumptionist theory of economic crises and the notion that American levels of productivity could be achieved by the same measures used to avoid crises was too good to miss. Agartz, then, could draw on a substantial tradition in promoting his 'expansive wages' policy.

Trading patterns were important for the German Socialists, too, as indeed they were for the British Labour movement. The British had seen the goal as the strengthening of traditional trading links with commonwealth and colonial or ex-colonial states within the sterling bloc. Their commitment to improved productivity and production was to secure their independence from the Americans by consolidating trade in this area. The productivity campaign, consonant with but different in meaning to the Marshall Plan, pointed away from European integration, another goal of the Marshall Plan. An analogous option was not open to the German socialists, at least not for long.

Whereas the British could look to the sterling bloc as the safe haven from the vagaries of the international, American-dominated, world market, the Germans were obliged to look to Europe. This was the option favoured by Gerhard Kreyssig in a text completed in 1942 but first published in April 1946.[57] Kreyssig drew a distinction between intra-European trade and extra-European trade, arguing that the former would be much more important than before the war. It had to be more important, for Europe could no longer rely upon its prewar experience of using services and interest and capital repayments to cover trade deficits. The answer lay in achieving better coordination of trade within Europe and hence reducing its entwinement with the non-European world economy. To explain how this would work Kreyssig turned to the relation between the industrial and agricultural sectors of Europe. Intra-European trade was to be enlarged by increasing the percentage of Europe's agricultural production which was taken by the industrialized regions of Europe. This already stood at 75 per cent but an increase in the figure would not only secure markets for the agricultural sector but would also boost its purchasing power and hence the market for the products of the industrial sector. The whole process was to be managed by a European Trading Corporation, modelled on British wartime authorities, which would act as a clearing centre for intra-European trade as well as intervening in European and world markets to, *inter alia*, stabilize price levels and regulate extra-European trade.[58] Kreyssig stressed that his Trading Corporation was not to be a trading monopoly but it is not difficult to see the incompatibility between his, genuinely limited, European clearing system and the policy of multilateral global trade espoused by the ordo-liberals and Dr Erhard. For Kreyssig's strategy was clearly oriented to the relationship between western and eastern Europe, which in substance corresponded with his industrial and agricultural sectors. It meant the integration of Europe as a whole, not western integration.[59]

Kreyssig's model of a 'balanced' two-sector economy, largely protected from the vicissitudes of the world market, reappeared in Richard Lowenthal's essay, 'Die Westeuropäische Wirtschahtseinheit'.[60] By the time the article appeared, though, in the early 1950s, the division of Europe had been consolidated. The gulf separating the world in which Kreyssig wrote from that in which Lowenthal, himself an advocate of the Third Way in 1947, now wrote is striking. Lowenthal's work is interesting for three other reasons. Firstly, it criticizes European integration, in accordance with prevailing SPD policy, and in doing so adopts arguments similar to those employed by the British Labour Party. Secondly, and for similar reasons, it exhibits some conformity with the ideas of the ordo-liberals, themselves no supporters of European integration. Thirdly, it is dismissive of the emphasis upon productivity. Lowenthal agreed with Kreyssig that Europe had to find a new pattern of trade. Its old position of dominance, based upon early industrialization, had been lost. There was a new dominant power, the United States, whose leadership rested, however, upon different factors: namely, its raw-material reserves and the fact that foreign trade was no more than 3 per cent of national income. The United States then, as a balanced domestic economy, was to that extent a model. Even more so were Sweden and Switzerland, both with relatively balanced domestic economies but also relying upon highly specialized exports. Whereas Kreyssig looked to a balance within Europe as a whole, Lowenthal now sought it within each European state. His attitude to intra-European economic relations took something from the British and something from the ordo-liberals. Analogously to the British he looked to policy convergence between planned economies. This had the advantage that:

the merger of planned economies of this sort – not the administrative command economies of the eastern type, in which state directives to every individual factory replace the market, but rather the western full-employment countries, which are steered by credit policy and guided investment – does not require an awesome superstate.[61]

Lowenthal's agreement with the ordo-liberals paradoxically formed a compliment to this idea of policy convergence between states committed to full employment and exchange controls: all of whom, he noted, were less enthusiastic about European unity than states with more liberal domestic policies. For he said, the fragmentation of Europe into different sovereign states had not been problematic in Europe's heyday. Hence he agreed with the recently expressed view that: 'all efforts towards European "Integration" should intend as their first step to restore that degree of economic unity which existed between the thoroughly sovereign nation-states up until 1931'. This was the argument of the ordo-liberal Wilhelm Röpke, for whom 'integration' meant the restoration of lost unity, the reintegration of the economies that had been isolated from each other during the era of autarky.[62]

Lowenthal also came close to Röpke in his rejection of the prevailing arguments about productivity. Their agreement consisted in a common opposition to the idea that American economic strength was derived from the large internal market that facilitated specialized mass-production by large-scale plants, resulting in higher productivity, and opposition to the idea that Europe's salvation lay in imitation of the American model. The way they criticized this assumption indicates the severe limits to their agreement. Röpke accepted that there were cases where the model seemed justified but denied that they were typical, There were, he said, highly profitable small and medium enterprises in the United States itself. Moreover, the Swiss export industry was primarily based upon medium-sized concerns. The way forward, consequently, was to allow the laws of the international division of labour to determine the distribution of production. What size of production unit would emerge under these conditions could not be decided in advance.[63]

Lowenthal proceeded on a broader front. He pointed out that the enthusiasm for the combination of productivity and unity was inspired by the predominance of the United States; he suggested there were other reasons than a large internal market and high productivity for that status. He promptly added that Europe's problem was not competition from the United States anyway. It was the newly industrializing countries that were driving Europe's exports from the market. Productivity alone, were it to be miraculously increased overnight, would be of no avail. The United States would retreat behind the walls of protective tariffs and no increase could overcome the advantages of location enjoyed by the new challengers. To drive his point home he claimed that industrial productivity had risen faster in parts of postwar divided Europe than in the United States. The successes here were due to increased investment facilitated by commitments to full-employment, not the absent benefits of a large market.[64]

In both Britain and Germany then the Marshall Plan ideology was interpreted in terms of national and domestic conceptions, which is not to say that it was interpreted in a purely pragmatic sense. The British Labour movement, German Socialists and ordo-liberals had their own ideologies, which in varying and discriminating degrees allowed them to accept, modify or reject the American model. Despite the radically different circumstances in which they found themselves, not to mention the different traditions and recent experience upon which they drew, there were numerous similarities in the responses of British and German Socialists to the Marshall Plan and to America in general. There were fears that interdependence between Europe and the United States would expose Europe to economic collapse, as in the past. From this viewpoint the American economy appeared as the archetype of unrestructured Capitalism. Those who saw the United States in these terms cast doubts upon the motives of the Americans in launching the Marshall Plan. As the land of rampant capitalism America was prone to aggressive competition and imperialist expansion. Yet this attitude was not a plausible basis for national policy, especially not when the ethereal hopes for a Third Way had dissipated. The more pro-American stance could, moreover, rely on recognition and exaggeration of changes in American society. The United States might still be capitalist but it was, it appeared, a restructured Capitalism that exhibited traits little different from the aspirations of many European Socialists. The motives bolstering suppositions of this kind are easy to list. In the western zones of Germany dependence on the goodwill of the most powerful occupier mingled with admiration for the American democratic and republican tradition, and increasingly for American anti-Communism, and the bonds established between the AFL–CIO and the new German unions. In Britain, faith in the 'special relationship' was buttressed by feelings of superiority and suspicion towards other Europeans.

These general predilections did not necessitate wholehearted acceptance of American strategies or prevent the reinterpretation of American plans in terms of national traditions and goals. This is clearest in the case of the British response to the productivity campaign within the Marshall Plan. In Germany, increased production was no less desired but it had different connotations, bound up as it was with overcoming simple hunger and removing Allied restrictions on the levels of production. There is also evidence in both cases of a clear rejection of the American argument for the association between increased production and

European unity. For the British, increased productivity and increased production was a road towards Socialism in one country and the heritage of Empire still beckoned as an alternative to Europe. In Germany the equivalent of the Empire was tainted and, even in its more benign formulations, soon exposed as implausible in the prevailing geopolitical climate. Restoration of international trade on the other hand was attractive, for the immediate reasons of reconstruction: it provided a way back to the comity of nations and marked a rejection of the autarky of the 1930s and the War years. But neither the Socialist Lowenthal nor the ordo-liberal Röpke accepted the notion that *Europe* should be remade in the image of America; both met the argument from productivity head on.

The point of these observations is, in the first place, to reaffirm the autonomy and coherence of European Socialism without mitigating its weaknesses. If European Socialists, as even their leaders were wont to complain, suffered from a lack of socialist vision or, often with the approval of their leaders, succumbed to parochial obsessions with Socialism in one country, this had less to do with Americanization than with deep-rooted problems about the nature and implementation of Socialism and, equally importantly, with the resolute refusal of their domestic opponents to compromise. This does not mean that European Socialists were immune to the image of America. Indeed, they were often more impressed by the vision of America than they were by the vision of Europe. That meant, in turn, that they were confronted by the apparent ambiguities of America – a capitalist land with, for some, the reputation of being among the most socially progressive, a democratic model whose representatives behaved imperiously, a foredoomed economy that continued to prosper and an imperialist power that aided the recovery of its competitors. By comparison Europe was a less-potent image, save perhaps in the disreputable form given to it by the National Socialists. There were exceptions whose visions of Europe were clear and passionately held; but they were often overtaken by events and could not, at least in Britain and Germany, displace older beliefs rooted both in Socialist and national experience.

5 Americanism and Anti-Americanism in Italy

P. P. D'Attorre

Before the First World War, Italians were acquainted with two myths about America. The first positive myth was reflected in diverse sources. Among the travellers and historians, Filippo Mazzei, Carlo Botta and G. Compagnoni, a founder of the 'democratic' Constitutional Law school in Italy, were prominent. Leaders of the Risorgimento looked to the American War of Independence as a model. A positive image of 'Merica' also emerged in the letters of Italian immigrants to America from the last decade of the nineteenth century.[1] Alongside this enthusiasm for America ran a more negative stream which can be found in the young *maîtres à penser* of 1900–14. Ojetti and Prezzolini, the latter playing a leading role in the exchange of perceptions between Italy and America for over a century, criticized the triumphant materialism of American society and culture, which was so distant from the 'spiritualism' of the 'new man' they were defining in reviews such as *La Voce* and *Il Leonardo*. Even if America reveals our future to us, argued Ojetti, we cannot accept it but must oppose this modernism. A negative image also prevailed in Catholic public opinion – though the entrepreneur Alessando Rossi was one of the most intelligent translators of 'Americanism' in the business community. Socialists were at best predominantly indifferent if not disillusioned.

Before the First World War indifference was understandable.[2] There were few students of the American political and social system, or of American literature. Indeed, not until 1897 was a distinction drawn, by Nencioni, between American and English literature. The limited number of commentators, to say nothing of the emigrant correspondents, had a limited audience. For most Italians, like their contemporaries in France, Germany and England, albeit for different reasons, America was a distant and not particularly interesting land. It was simply too far removed from Italian political and cultural concerns to be anything more.

Italians learned more about America during the First World War, partly as a result of American propaganda.[3] Propaganda, however, should not be over-estimated: just as in 1948, postcards, ribbons and buttons were less important than the content of policies. A key role here was played by 'Wilsonism'. Initially this enjoyed great support but disillusion soon set in. Indicative of the transition was the poet D'Annunzio. In 1918 he wrote an ode, *All 'America in armi*. One year later he was the most violent critic of Wilson's policy towards Italy. The end of mass-emigration to the United States, following legislation in 1923, also increased the latent anti-Americanism of the Italian middle classes. These general trends swept over the more discerning analyses of individual observers, like, for example, Papini, who saw the philosophy of pragmatism, advanced by Henry James, as an interesting development, or Antonio Gramsci's comments on Americanism and Fordism. But these commentators were read by a small number of Italians at best. A more influential impact arose from Fascist propaganda.[4] Initially, in the 1920s, when the loans from the American finance house of Morgan were still important to Mussolini, criticism was muted. In the 1930s the restraints were removed. Cultural institutions, magazines and columnists propagated the image of a society diseased with crass materialism. Attempts to disguise its imperialism were futile, it was claimed, in a society where gangsters and plutocrats were popular heroes. The Right-wing philosopher, Julius Evola, and the mediocre authors of books such as *Babilonia stellata: gioventù americana di oggi* (*Starry Babylon: American Youth of Today*) or *Razza in agonia* (*Agony of a Race*) bolstered Fascist leaders like G. Pini or Biscaretti di Ruffia, who compared Mussolini's brilliant civilization to the supposed disaster of Roosevelt's New Deal. These opinions were, however, scarcely unique to Italians nor even to Italian Fascists. The clichés of Fascist writers on America differed little from prewar Italian anti-Americanism, or from the anti-Americanism of other European countries. In, for example, *America 1934* by N. Quilici, who had direct experience of America, or in the Strapaese movement, which had none, there are the same clichés as in Aron and Dandieu (*Le cancer américain*), and the same fears as in Romier's *Qui sera le Maître?*

Research on the loans of small-town Italian libraries in the period shows that the journalist, A. Fraccaroli, was particularly appreciated, especially his *New York ciclone delle genti* (*New York, Melting Pot of People*), *Donne d'America* (*American Women*) and *Hollywood paese dell'avventura* (*Hollywood, Land of Adventure*). The title of the latter points to an important element in the image of America and an important channel of influence. Hollywood was a key element of the image of America and its products an important, if disputed, influence. According to Renzo de Felice, the American dream, as disseminated by the movies, was the most active antidote against the fascist culture of the 'new man' and the 'new order'.[5] This probably goes too far. There were many Fascists who exalted the Empire and Roman heritage in the daytime, then spent their evenings '*al cinematografo*' – Mussolini amongst them. There are also more obvious antidotes to Fascist propaganda, especially Catholic and Communist ideologies. Yet there are two different images here: that of Fascist propaganda and that of the Hollywood movies. Quite what the long-term impact of these images was is a question that still remains unanswered.

More attention has been devoted to the pro-American authors of the interwar decades, including Mario Soldati's *America prima amore*, more than Emilio Cecchi's *America amara* and the works of Carlo Linati and Mario Praz, or Cesare Pavese and Elio Vittorini. It is necessary, however, to take care in grouping these authors together. Cecchi and Soldati both failed to escape the bonds of Fascist propaganda. They insisted upon the pettiness and sordidness of American life, from its slums to its lynchings, without any attempt to come to a real understanding of America as a civilization. The myth created by Pavese and Vittorini on the other hand was diametrically opposed to Fascist propaganda. They presented a society that was vigorous and vital, not decadent. In their myth America was, to be sure, untamed and tinged with brutality but it was always human and often humane. Yet it remained a myth, based, as it was, upon the novels of Steinbeck and Faulkner, rather than upon direct experience. In this form the myth of America played some role in anti-Fascist ideology, though how much is uncertain.

But the most important question is this: did Fascist anti-Americanism and anti-Fascist Americanism have a more extensive impact upon Italian society than the pre-First World War debates? How many people read *America prima amore* or A. Guidi's *Cose vuole Roosevelt*? In both cases the answer is: not many. Until 1943 the United States remained a largely unknown country. For élite groups it could conjure up a dreaded future or a dream of freedom, but for the masses America meant something else. The use of slang reveals a predominantly negative connotation. Before the terms 'Americanism' and 'Americanization' became widespread the phrase *all 'americana* meant a confidence trick, while *americanata* meant boorish or cheating behaviour, or bluff. Such indications are, however, rare. There is, for example, little evidence of the diffusion of the phrase, *vivere all 'americana* (living in the American style), before 1950. This is important for understanding just how remote America was from the Italy of the 1940s. It is difficult, or rather impossible, to find evidence of 'Americanization' in Italy before the Second World War. The main reason for this is the simple lack of any sustained and extensive direct contact. Italy was acquainted with America only through the movies. It is true that attitudes and fashions indicated that something was changing, but only for the élite. Even jazz remained a peripheral underground passion up until the 1950s, a sort of cultural status symbol for Left-wing élites. Advertising remained rooted in national attitudes and concerns. There was, after all, little need for American-style advertising in a country where even *mille lire al mese* (a thousand lire a month: that is to say, a safe salary) remained for most people an impossible dream.

The most dramatic change in the history of the Italian perception of America was undoubtedly a product of the Second World War. After the landing of Allied troops in Sicily a new phase began, not only in political relationships but also in mutual perceptions.[6] The traditional approach to this change emphasizes the pro-Americanism of conservative and moderate public opinion, in contrast with the anti-Americanism of the Resistance which developed during the difficult winter of 1944 and the disappointing months of Allied control of local and national government. But the most important fact is that, for the first time in Italian history, Americans were not a dream but a part of everyday life. Differences in perception were closely linked to different experiences of daily reality and to the uneven progress of the Allied advance up the Italian peninsula. In the north, which remained under German occupation much longer, a deadly civil war developed; in the south, Allied liberation and occupation had already left its mark. In the south the development of the popular mood was particularly

striking. Initially, in 1942–3, naive hope predominated. The Americans were seen
as liberators from war and Fascism. By 1944–5 this optimism had given way to
disappointment; the Americans were widely blamed for inflation and the black
market.

The change is evident in the writings of Curzio Malaparte, who also exhibits an
interesting continuity with the prewar anti-Americanism of the *Strapaese* movement. It is also evident in the letters censored by the *Ispettorato Censura Militare*
up until 1946.[7] Typical was the infantryman who wrote that, 'In Italy Americans
always behaved like friends, without the arrogance and hate we found in the
English.' His sentiments are confirmed by early opinion polls. America meant
power, food, medicines, bulldozers and jeeps. 'Goods are coming in all the time,'
wrote another soldier in April 1945. The direct impact of this flow of men – well-
dressed, well-equipped and shaved – and goods was certainly substantial and
equally certainly overstated by American propaganda. The Americans even
produced eulogies to the jeep in *ABC italoamericano*. Many Italians saw the short
film *Autobiografia di una jeep* produced by the omnipresent OWI. Films like
Sergeant York and *Joe Smith, American* were shown in Naples in the spring of 1944
and greeted in the *Corriere* with 'Welcome, American Films'. The message of these
films was consistent: the United States was a democratic and prosperous country
– prosperous because democratic and democratic because prosperous. The
enthusiasm that greeted this message was short-lived as inflation came to cast a
shadow over the American dream. A typical letter accused the Americans of
starving liberated Italy: 'I thought they meant to free people from starvation, as
they claimed in their leaflets before they came; instead we're hungrier than ever.'
Another added: 'With the excuse of war operations, the Allies think of
themselves and themselves only.'

The conclusion that emerged from this disillusion was summarized in the
question of a third correspondent: 'How can we deliver ourselves from our
deliverers?' The impact on daily life was reflected in the play *Napoli milionaria* by
Eduardo De Filippo, first performed in 1945, in which one character observed:
'Today, when you go out, you will find yourself in a foreign country. . .' The
sense of cultural shock was extensive: no one was safe, no value respected.
'Americans with their gold changed all values,' wrote a man from Palermo. This
sense of shock hit the middle classes particularly hard, compounded as it was by a
broader crisis affecting their moral values, financial standing and social status.
Yet there were distinct limits to Italian anti-Americanism, even among the middle
classes. Giannini's Right-wing *Uomo qualunque* movement soon turned from
criticism of the Americans and sought a scapegoat in Italian political parties and
the labour movement. The underlying basis of this shift was bluntly expressed by
a southern writer of a letter mailed from Catania to Cleveland on 16 June 1945:
'Let's hope the Americans will sort things out'. The United States was regarded as
Italy's mainstay against chaos, ironically the more so as its actual presence was
diminishing.

But what had happened in the north? Here the evolution of perceptions was
similar, though experiences were different and more affected by indigenous social
and political structures, especially that of the Church. As recent regional studies,
for example of the strongly Catholic Veneto region, have shown, the Church was
suspicious of all ideas and patterns of behaviour coming from a materialistic and

Protestant country.[8] The Church was resistant to any involvement with the Allies. There was a strong line of continuity connecting the reviews of American films published by the *Centro Cattolico Cinematografico* before and after the War, between the prewar Vatican policy on education and the postwar opposition to the project of the subcommission of the Allied Control Commission for reform of teaching. Despite all this the Church was led by its anti-Communism to a sort of 'historic compromise' with American politics and even with American ideology. The mediators of this compromise came from the new Christian Democrat party, including Emilio Taviani, founder member of the Christian Democrats and champion of Atlanticism, and Giulio Pastore, who opened Catholic trade unions to the influence of American labour in the 1940s.

At the other end of the political spectrum, the Left was much more suspicious of the politics and ideology of the United States, even before 1947 and the announcement of the Marshall Plan. This suspicion did not entail opposition to all things American. The myth of America as the 'land of Socialism' was persistent and deep-rooted. This general sympathy was continued in postwar works such as E. Vittorini's *Americana* or C. Pavese's *La letteratura americana*. But these works purveyed the myth of *un' altra America*, an America different from the country of Truman and Eisenhower, a myth that survived in the success of Howard Fast in Communist newspapers a decade later. Confronted with the real America, and the fear of cultural colonization by Hollywood, the reaction was harsh, extending well beyond the confines of the Communist Party to embrace part of moderate public opinion.

The distinctions that had to be drawn were not easy ones and the initial anti-Americanism of the Italian Communists reflected the contradictions and ambiguities of the situation. One interesting example of this emerged in a debate as to whether the cultural medium or the content of cultural transmissions was the main problem. At one level this was discussed by Gianni Rodari, the most famous Italian writer of childrens' stories, and N. Jotti. Rodari argued that the content, in this case Mickey Mouse, might be rejected, but the cultural form of cartoons could not, for cartoons were the children's literature of the future. The point of the argument was not lost on the Communists. *Il pioniere*, the Communist children's magazine, consequently published the cartoon strips of Cipollino and, among foreign cartoon strips, those of the French dog, Pif.

Resistance to Americanization was broadly based, even in the years of the Cold War. The Left naturally produced a great number of images of 'the other side of America', from the Rosenbergs to Wilma Rudolph. There was also considerable sarcasm in *L'Unita*'s discussion of *Cindarella* or Coca Cola. But the case of Coca Cola demonstrates the existence of a wider consensus on the need to resist cultural colonization. The underlying motives were diverse and mutual perceptions often inconsistent. At the end of the 1940s the Italian government quietly introduced a tax on soft drinks 'in order to defend Italian wine producers'. The Americans perceived the measure as yet another example of protectionism, like the quota system restricting the importation of American films or the maintenance of Fascist laws in certain strategic areas such as mining or oil exploitation. In this case, too, the Italian attitude appears to be the same as that of the French: an inexplicit, undifferentiated anti-Americanism. In a different area another strange alliance arose between conservative and progressive resistance to American

ideology. The Productivity Drive associated with the Marshall Plan was unacceptable to the main labour union, the CGIL, because the union rightly perceived it as
an instrument of exploitation. But it was also unacceptable to the entrepreneurs
led by A. Costa, who resented the perceived external interference in the
management of their businesses.

American cultural mobilization during the Marshall-Plan years was unique in
the long history of Italo-American relations.[9] Its novelty should not, however, be
confused with its efficacy; there were substantial impediments to the latter.
Inherent contradictions in the American programme, like that between reform
and stabilization, were often solved by the United States in favour of the
conservative option. In the second place, American ideology did not fit Italian
circumstances. Throughout the 1950s, Italian society underwent a process of
large-scale forced accumulation, rather than a boom based on increases in
productivity, revenues and mass-consumption. In 1957, the average monthly
wage of a worker was still below the sum of 70,000 lire which public officials held
to be the minimum necessary to maintain a family. There was, to be sure, an
unfulfilled craving for goods, with 65 per cent of workers aspiring to own a car
but only 1 per cent actually achieving their desire. The American dream remained
a dream. Thirdly, the impact of the American ideology of growth was limited by
the strength of traditional subcultures. These subcultures were able to organize
the modernization of society within their own frameworks, to canalize the fears
and hopes of common people, producing an uneasy mixture of ambivalence and
inconsistency. Italian nationalism and Catholic mistrust of Americanism
coincided with Atlanticism. Entrepreneurs received American aid, while rejecting
the philosophy that underlay it. Socialists and Communists, roused by the world
of *The Grapes of Wrath*, adopted an alternative myth: the Soviet one. The myth of
the United States as a free, peaceful, democratic country was counterbalanced, on
the Left, by other myths of emancipation and social justice, and, on the Right, by
a traditional conservatism that was able to adjust itself to new circumstances. For
some Italians the champion of peace in the world was the Soviet Union; for others
the Pope; for very few, the United States.[10] The contradictory internal cultural
dynamics were acutely perceived by the novelist, Giovanni Guareschi, whose
successful series *Don Camillo and Peppone* testifies to the weakness of Italian
Americanism. In fact, in comparison with France, anti-Americanism in Italy was
much less explicit, though the actual policies developed by these two countries to
defend their national interests were the same.

'American myth', 'Americanism' and 'Americanization' are certainly not
synonymous with each other. They belong, however, to the same semantic
family: a very rich one. Even in the 1950s no other nation induced such a wide
range of ideologically laden images, not even the Soviet Union. The natural desire
vigorously to separate out the overlapping and adjacent meanings associated with
the projection of American power is misguided. It is the coexistence of different
meanings, filtered through different ideological channels, which lies at the heart
of the image of America. The myth of the United States, with its positive and
negative poles, runs through the whole of the twentieth century, dying and
coming back to life within different, sedimented national cultures. There is, in the
culture of the Socialist movement at the beginning of the century, a 'mythical'
image that reappears in some Communist literature of the post-1945 period. There

is also, in nationalist ideologies, the ever-recurring cliché of the contrast between the materialism of America and the humanistic values of Latin (or even European) culture.

Such a long duration of continuity points both to a complex interplay of mutual perceptions and opinions – for instance, between Protestant America and Catholic Italy – and to a broader background of hope for, and fear of, novelty and modernity. Acknowledgement of the entwinement of images need not entail a refusal to draw any distinctions. 'Americanism' is something different from the myth of the United States as our promised or threatened future, but no more stable in meaning. Even Gramsci had used the term 'Americanism' equivocally: a tendency even more marked in his interpreters. From the sale semantic starting point of 'Fordism', meaning innovation in the organization of work, in class composition and in production – with the words 'Americanism', 'Fordism' and 'rationalization' used as synonyms – there has been a transition, which began in the 1920s, to an emphasis on the change in the functions of the market and consumption. The idea of 'Americanism', increasingly removed from the context of Gramsci's *Quaderni*, has been linked to allusions of Gramsci's about the role of intellectuals and then to broader reflection about our consumer society and contemporary patterns of social consensus. At the end of the day, this post-1945, 'consumer modernization' is a different type of Americanism to Gramsci's. This result reflects the changing intensity of America's impingement on European life. In Umberto Eco's words: 'America, as a model, as a display and system of goods, as a political influence, as an image transmitted by the mass media, invaded Italy. Before, it used to be merely something one read about in books or saw in the movies. Afterwards, it became something that affected the life of the average Italian citizen, involving everything from chewing gum and records to the spread of cars and television.'[11]

The context of this cultural transformation forms the subject of recent historiography of the post-1918 and post-1945 periods. Emphasis has been placed upon the emergence of the political and economic supremacy of the United States, and upon the cultural consequences of that supremacy. From the 1920s onwards, it is argued, a close, and as yet inadequately understood, connection emerged between material supremacy and ideological consensus, between the public and the private sphere. This is the locus of the concept of 'Americanization'. Yet the concept is all too frequently associated with an all-encompassing, pervasive and clear-cut process that has never truly occurred, not even in those countries where there has been the most conspicuously passive acceptance of, or adoption of, Americanization as a system of values, of behaviour, and as a social and political strategy. The assumption that certain countries were especially receptive to Americanization is understandable. During the post-1945 period the ideological consequences of the crisis of the national state were becoming evident. Especially in the defeated countries, the main generator of cohesive myths and ideologies, the national state had lost much of its authority. Nationalism undoubtedly survived; in the Italian case it remained an element in all the basic political subcultures. But it was no longer a state ideology and it could no longer act as the unifying axis for collective beliefs and behaviour. This entailed an unprecedented receptiveness to external sources of ideology and symbols, which, in turn, was reinforced by the bipolar confrontation of the two superpowers.

Applied to Italy this argument lead to the following conclusion, voiced by Silvio Lanaro: 'The absence of a "centre", that is to say of a central secular code of behaviour, spread osmotically or radiated from authoritative beacons, is intolerable in the historical stage of the expansion of consumption, the stage which creates the demographic preconditions for a mass society. Nowadays the absence of a centre is compensated by the apparatus of symbols and objects represented by the United States.' [12] Steven Gundle puts forward an even more explicit conclusion : 'Thanks to the peculiar characteristics of Italian society and of its stage of development during the 1950s, Italy was the European country most receptive to American cultural inputs.' [13] These conclusions reinforce each other. Italy is seen as the most receptive country, because here, more than anywhere else, Americanization and consumerism – symbols and objects – are inextricably interlaced. This involvement made it possible to achieve the ideological unification that the dictatorial nationalization of the masses had not been able to bring about during the Fascist period.

This interpretation reaches far beyond the vision of the 'Cold War consensus' developed by American historians to describe the United States in the 1950s. The trend of unification does not lie in allegiance to one side of the Cold War, or in the identification of the 'enemy' – crucial for the national identity of the United States during the same period – because in Italy, Atlanticism, the expression of ideological allegiance, resulted in contrasting domestic political identities and divisions. Instead, it is claimed, the path of unification consisted in the pursuit of the American 'dream' in its latest form, that of consumerist modernization. Hence, a sequence – Americanization to modernization to legitimation – is often suggested, which underrates the negative reactions, the national interpretations and the new combinations that took place in Italy, and elsewhere, in the 1950s. [14]

If we reflect upon this model, several worrying assumptions emerge. In the first place, this view of Americanization seems not too far removed from the response of anti-American authors who complained that Americanization was no longer a mere possibility, as in the 1930s, but a reality and a malignant one. Furthermore, there is a surprising persistence in the dubious argument that the very backwardness of Italy rendered it more susceptible to Americanization: an Americanization that always seems to be a coherent and systematic strategy. Yet it was the multiplicity of American initiatives that was the significant reality. There was a plurality of organizations and departments pursuing a plurality of goals. The State Department, the embassies, individual agents in Rome and Washington, civil and military organizations often came into conflict and not just because of temporary disputes about their respective authority. Non-governmental bodies also had their own short-term and long-term goals, including the trade unions, Italo-American groups and industrial interests. Corresponding to the divergency of goals and agents there was an equal diversity of channels through which they sought to impart their message. Alongside the more traditional means for disseminating propaganda new forms sprang up. Attempts were made to transform Italian intellectuals into independent mediators of Americanization by a policy of cultural exchanges, by supporting publications like *Il Mulino, Tempo presente, Epoca*, or *Selezione, del Reader's Digest*, by setting up American libraries and by the projects on 'productivity'.

But perhaps unity can be extracted from this diversity. There is, after all, no doubt that policies of 'productivity', ideas of mass-consumption, economic interdependence and also military security, coexisted. Indeed these four dimensions – productivity, consumption, interdependence and security – do form the basis of the leadership of the United States in the 1950s and 1960s. It is, therefore, easy to agree with Leonardo Paggi's *Americanismo e riformismo* that American supremacy in Europe is based neither on the strengthening of the nation-state nor on simple power politics, but rather on its capacity to orient the process of modernization by expanding the market and creating new collective, 'consumerist', identities. Paggi errs only when he writes that: 'this is the revolutionary, subversive side of the American challenge to the old European society, which can hardly be placed alongside the categories of stability and containment'.[15] The problem is that he overestimates the subversive impact of Americanization. The Italian experience is a case of Americanization without reformism – and not because of the prevalence of Einaudi's *laissez-faire* doctrines, whose influence in Italian political history Paggi overrates. There was a substantial convergence of goals – political and social stabilization at the domestic level, the acceptance of a subordinate position in Italian foreign policy – that united the Christian Democratic leadership with American administrations. But Italian élites were discriminating in their response to Americanization. Paggi comes closer to the truth when he writes:

The Italian experience shows how, from the second postwar period on, the theme of ideological and political conservatism, of prudence and hostility toward any measures for the redistribution of wealth and for social justice, begins to merge (imitating the American conservative model aptly described by Hofstadter) with the management of an economic process which is deeply innovative and tends to unsettle the previous social balance.[16]

This conclusion is more convincing but still does not go far enough. The failure of reformism in Italy was vital, for it cut off the potentialities for the Americanization of Italian society. American efforts to transform Italy, which reached their highest point in the 1950s, were unparalleled in any other time or country. Yet their impact was limited. Americanization became part of local conflicts: it deepened not only the divisions of the Cold War, but also other, older, cleavages that cut across Italian society. The American model did help traditional cultures (Catholic, Socialist, Communist, Nationalist) to become less provincial but it did not dominate the more complex process of social modernization. The 'via italiana' to a consumer society prevailed. The American way of life turns out to be a propaganda cliché belied by everyday life during the years of 'forced accumulation'. For subsequent decades conclusions might be different.[17] But by then the limits of American supremacy had been revealed, in some cases (on the Left) giving rise to new myths of an alternative America.

During the 1950s even advocates of active adaptation, such as a considerable part of Catholic or Liberal-Democratic culture, could hardly be considered an American party. Nor is the picture clear-cut on the other side: opponents, for instance Italian-Communist culture, could be 'contaminated'. The limits of Americanization can be measured not only in the great gap between expectation and reality that characterized the trend towards mass-consumption up to the 1960s, but also, indeed even more, in the persistence of other myths, of the Soviet

Union as synonymous with peace and social justice, of the Catholic message, which was Carolingian rather than Atlanticist, and above all in the disillusioned, sarcastic portrayal of the 'Americanized man' by the actor Alberto Sordi (*Un americano a Roma*) and the singer Renato Carosone (*Tu vo fa' l'americano*). The political hegemony of the United States in postwar Italy is beyond question. Cultural colonization, on the other hand, is more difficult to demonstrate.

6 Postwar Misery in Eastern Europe: Glosses on an Hungarian Perspective*

R. N. Berki

István Bibó, whose historical perspective provides the conceptual basis as well as the original inspiration for this paper, is now widely regarded by informed Hungarian opinion as its most eminent political thinker in the present century. His work though, alas, is not as yet sufficiently well-known in the West. Bibó (1911–79) was a professional academic jurist and political scientist who, however, also held high positions in public service and, for a brief but dramatic period in November 1956, political office as Minister of State in the last Imre Nagy government, toppled by Soviet armed intervention. Bibó suffered many years of imprisonment directly as a result of his participation in events connected with this popular uprising. From the voluminous Bibó-*oeuvre* we have selected just two noteworthy pieces for summary exposition and glossing in this paper; neither of these has to date been made publicly available in the English language. They were both published in 1946: a longish historical excursus, 'The Misery of the Small States of Eastern Europe', as an independent pamphlet, and a shorter, topical tract, 'The Peace Treaty and Hungarian Democracy', in *Válasz (Response)*, a periodical associated with the National Peasant Party and a group of radical populist writers around it.[1] Bibó's intellectual home was with this group: a Left-of-centre radical democrat, he was a genuine advocate of coalition politics and government and an enthusiastic supporter of the new democratic republican régime in Hungary, arisen out of the ashes of defeat in the Second World War. Note should be taken, therefore, of the fact that although Bibó's perspective is unmistakably Hungarian – in terms of its intellectual background, political interest, style, emphasis and topical concentration – it is by no means a narrowly nationalist or parochial one on that account. It is in fact quite the contrary. Bibó,

* The author wishes to thank the Nuffield Foundation for a research grant which, *inter alia*, assisted in the preparation of this paper. He also acknowledges with gratitude the constructive criticism and advice received from G. Borbándi, I. Z. Dénes and I. Vida on the first version.

as we shall see, is indeed a stern critic of historic states and frontiers (while he upholds the principle of nationality), and besides, his clearly articulated historical principles and analysis are, as they are certainly meant to be, of *general* application, being relevant to a proper understanding of democratization and international cooperation in modern and indeed contemporary conditions.

The literary activity of 'glossing' in this paper refers in fact to an attempt on our part to utilize Bibó's perspective in dealing with a contemporary problem – or rather a problem which, present at the time of the publication of these two texts, is now assuming even greater prominence in the all-European political theatre. The problem, though somewhat simplified, could perhaps be defined like this: why has the endeavour to achieve transnational regional integration in eastern Europe been such a telling failure, in sharp contrast to the success attained in recent decades by west European countries in this regard? The answer it might seem permissible to flesh out of Bibó's historical analysis can serve, among other things, as a welcome corrective to the well-meaning but somewhat idealistic and utopian advocacy of immediate 'federation' in the east European region, while it also appears to throw into sharp relief those often encountered, but rather simplistic, ideologically-oriented and unhistorical explanations charging the Soviet Union with sole or overwhelming responsibility for the chronic disunity of eastern Europe in the post-1945 period. The roots of regional disunity and conflict, and more profoundly the rather poor showing of democratic social and political structures in eastern Europe in the past, are in terms of Bibó's perspective to be located much deeper than postwar Soviet occupation and imposed Stalinist one-party régimes. These, Bibós line seems implicitly to suggest, might be looked upon much more usefully as at least in part effects, rather than causes, of a deeper-lying malformation or 'misery' in the region. On the present interpretation Bibós perspective certainly does not appear overly flattering to east European *amour propre*; yet this is not to say that his remarks are onesidedly condemnatory, defeatist or pessimistic. The fundamental presupposition behind his analysis is one he shares, to a considerable extent, with most democratically-minded proponents of eventual east European *rapprochement* and with most fair-minded critics of Soviet policy in the region after the Second World War. This is that transnational integrative processes which are non-imperialistic and non-hegemonic (like those underlying the present European Community) must have operative political democracy – understood in the current mainstream 'Western' sense – as their necessary historical precondition. It should be stressed that we are talking here about an historically 'necessary' precondition, to be clearly separated from others, and especially from anything that might be construed as a 'sufficient' condition of integration. It is obvious that in the postwar west-European situation a number of other factors, conducive to integration, have played an important part; these have also been absent in the east (e.g. comparable economic development).

Bibó's essay depicting the 'misery' of east European countries takes us back to the beginnings of the modern age, to the historical period that witnessed the emergence of modern nations in Europe. This ran parallel, in the western part of the continent at any rate, with the gradual – though at certain points traumatic and revolutionary – triumph of the principle of democracy. It is crucial for Bibó's analysis and argument, to be sure, that the 'nation' should be clearly recognized as a basic, enduring unit of society, by no means invented wilfully or accidentally in the modern age, and not to be expected (or wished) to wither away in the future either. The number of genuine nations in Europe, concrete cultural communities to which individuals feel they belong, he argues, has hardly changed in the last thousand years. Therefore, there is nothing arbitrary or objectionable in patriotism or 'national' sentiment as such; ruling classes (like the landowning aristocracy in eastern Europe) could exploit this sentiment for their own purposes only because it has objectively existed in the popular psyche. 'National sentiment, even though narrow and petty, is still a serious mass emotion, germane to democratism.' And: 'Serious mass sentiment can only spring from *passion* and passion can only result from *real experience.*'[2] In the West dynastic state-formations had, over the centuries preceding the onset of the modern age, themselves performed the task of 'nation-building': the frontiers of kingdoms like France, England and Spain, came to be the settled, accepted boundaries defining the territory of linguistic-cultural communities. National sentiment in these conditions could therefore become, without any serious friction, the most important active carrier of popular movements working towards the attainment of political democracy. In these conditions the 'people' and the 'nation' thus became synonymous terms and entities; democracy came to signify the politicization, the emancipation *of the nation*, the successful endeavour of the common people to lay their hands on the sate, to take over the reins of government themselves.

Not so, as Bibo observes, in eastern and parts of central Europe, including Germany and Italy. Here the main stumbling block was the long and baneful persistence of large transnational dynastic states, like the Holy Roman Empire, the Ottoman Empire, and last but not least – as he puts it – that 'fatal state formation', the Habsburg Empire, which to begin with had been anything but a genuine 'Danubian state'.[3] Thus it came about that the spirit of modernity, of popular political movements, affected the awakening nations of this region in a way markedly different from the West. While in the West the concept of the 'people' signified a dynamic force of social emancipation, in the East it came to be seen as the 'decisive carrier of distinct national characteristics',[4] alone appointed to guard the true components of national identity, like language and traditional folk customs. It was only the common people who could assume this role, owing to the simple but decisive fact that the dynasties, the courts and the ruling aristocracy constituted in each case a heterogeneous and, so to speak, cos-mopolitan mix. Bibó observes that while the two terms 'populaire' and 'völkisch' (both translated as 'népi' in Hungarian) have the identical logical meaning, their emotional connotation differs a great deal. Populist movements in this region of the continent therefore – those that in more fortunate conditions would have been straightforwardly metamorphosed into democratic movements – became instead linguistic-cultural 'nationalisms', with a horizontal, rather than vertical, political focus, more concerned with identity than with social emancipation. This preoccupation in turn necessarily led to the fluidity and destabilization of state frontiers. The main problem was not that existing frontiers were topsy-turvy or failing to conform to 'natural' geographical boundaries or economic entities

but that the historical sentiments of these nations – and the majority of them did possess historical memories – were attached to other, and as a rule larger, territories than those on which the population speaking the appropriate language lived.[5]

Hence practically all reborn nations in the east European region soon came to be locked in relentless hostility against their neighbours over the frontiers of the national territory. 'This is the main source', Bibó writes, 'of the political hysteria of Central and East European nations.' [6]

A substantial section of Bibó's essay is devoted to a detailed and incisive analysis of the persistent – indeed, cumulative – misery of the three 'historic' states of the region: Poland, Hungary and Bohemia. His comments do not spare the sensibilities of his own nation but not, to be sure, of those of the other two nations either. His specific comments on Poland are not of direct relevance to the argument of this paper, so they will be omitted here. As a matter of fact, Bibó considers the three historic states to have been afflicted essentially by the same malady: the growing contradiction between their 'historical memories' and their existing linguistic-cultural realities. Hungary had possessed its ancient 'thousand-year-old' kingdom, a politically viable state in the past which, however, was revealed to contain a multinational population in the modern age: at that time nationality really began to count. In 1848–9, in the course of Hungary's popular democratic revolution and war of national independence from the Habsburgs, nations within the kingdom other than the 'state-forming' dominant Magyars, (Croatians, Serbs and Rumanians) took the side of the dynastic, conservative Empire. In Hungarian political consciousness, so Bibó, two unfortunate lessons came to be embedded as a result of this experience: that Europe (the liberal, progressive West) would always leave Hungary in the lurch in the latter's struggle to achieve freedom, and that other ethnic groups belonging to the Hungarian state would use their democratic freedom to secede from historic Hungary. The dominant (until 1945) ideology in Hungary was therefore unable to draw a distinction between the perfectly justified secession of territories populated by other nations, which in the modern age became 'ripe' for such a step, and the unjustified loss of linguistically pure Hungarian (Magyar) territories, equally hostile to and condemning both. This ruling ideology could not free itself 'from the illusory picture of historic Greater Hungary and hence sunk even deeper into the mentality that Europe was guilty of a serious injustice against Hungary'.[7] Hence the ruling class considered itself exonerated from any European commitments in 1938 and, chasing after the illusion, it brought on itself the catastrophe of 1944 – which meant the final collapse of the illusion, adds Bibó, without registering any regret or sympathy.

Bohemia, land of the Czechs, entered the modern age also as a multinational community. In 1918 the modern, democratic Czechoslovak republic came into being, professedly multinational but nevertheless asserting an ethnic character as its chosen name demonstrated. No wonder therefore that the sizeable German minority in the West, and the less-substantial but hardly less nationally conscious Hungarian minority in the South, came from the start to be alienated from this new state formation, the 'democratic' character of which in other respects Bibó is happy to acknowledge. All the three states in question clung to their inherited or acquired territories with steadfast determination and emotion but could not help the fact that their 'national' lands were *not* held together by any real sentiment of national cohesion; they remained multinational states, increasingly subject to centrifugal pressures. It was a vain hope to imagine that democratic institutions and freedoms would succeed in a short time in welding the various ethnic groups into one national community, on the French model:

Behind the French model, however, there stood 2000 years of cultural development, a political framework of 1500 years, 1000 years of centralized government, national consciousness going back 500 years, and the prestige of the great *French* revolution.[8]

The catastrophe of these three historic states lay in the fact that even when, in given periods, they were in the forefront of European progress, simultaneously they were acting out a reactionary, undemocratic role in the domestic scene. While fighting against European reaction, they were suppressing their own minorities. Thus they perished: Poland in the eighteenth century, Hungary in 1848–9, Czechoslovakia in 1938–9. Since their downfall in each case occurred as a direct result of brutal and unjust foreign intervention, they were not in a mental position to acknowledge the presence of 'historical logic' in these traumatic events.

Bibó's descriptive penetration of the phenomenon of 'political hysteria' enveloping east European consciousness is deserving of special emphasis and attention. (Another one of his celebrated seminal texts from the period deals intensively with the causes and nature of the 'German hysteria'[9], akin to the east European affliction and of even greater global significance.) Occasioned by the peculiarly painful and confused process of modern nation-building in the region, in the absence of politically viable, modernizing state structures and ethnically endorsed frontiers, hysteria came to manifest itself essentially in the predominance of the emotion of *fear*. No ordinary fear just experienced by individuals *qua* individuals, but the more distorting, more disturbing sentiment of collective fear: what Bibó calls 'existential anxiety for the community'. In dramatic contrast to the experience of west European peoples, and as reflected in their political consciousness, east Europeans have lived in constant fear for the life and survival of their national communities. In the West, as Bibó points out, it is mere rhetoric to talk about the 'death of the nation' but not so in the East:

Here one need not actually go to the length of extirpating or expelling a nation, here for the perception of danger it is sufficient to hear strongly and violently expressed doubts that a given nation exists at all.[10]

Enduring existential anxiety, in this way, came to overshadow, and indeed derail, the processes of modern social development and in particular the movement towards democracy. It is one of Bibó's most striking, frequently stated axioms that democracy and fear are incompatible: to live in a democracy means first and foremost not to be afraid. Freedom from fear, in turn, presupposes the taming and dispersion of power, whereas existential anxiety has demanded its concentration and augmenting; east European peoples have always been in a double bind, a cruel historical catch-22. And Bibó does not regard this characteristic east European 'existential anxiety for the community' as being anything imaginary, artificially induced or purely subjective: it is the direct effect of 'real experience' and must therefore have a real solution. We shall later see the solution Bibó advocated.

The consequence of collective fear, historically speaking, was therefore an arrest in the democratization process, a halt and even a reversal in the movement that intended the 'liberation of individuals', and its replacement with struggles for 'the conquest of the national community'; national sentiment came to be completely distorted in a dominant 'territoriocentric perspective'.[11] The fatal divergence between these two dimensions of modernity – smoothly dovetailing, even congealing, in the West – led in due course to the re-emergence of traditional European reaction and autocracy, reinforced and in a modern guise. A new, distinct type of politician appeared on the scene, one whom Bibó calls the 'false realist', whose function – as a rule successfully performed – was to consolidate the hegemony of the old ruling classes and hereditary castes, precisely by keeping the embers of existential anxiety aglow, making minor and meaningless social gestures when unavoidable and engaging in aggressive, imperialistic ventures. For Bibó, prime examples of false realism are Bismarck, Pashich, Bratianu, Venizelos and the prewar Hungarian political leaders Tisza and Bethlen. While in the West the logical, natural, desirable, morally prescribed progression of democracy has meant for the individual citizen more and more exclusive reliance on the *law* – impersonal and impartial – for protection, eastern Europe has witnessed the reappearance of the paternal 'head of state', the ruler of predemocratic times, now still figuring as the fountain of wisdom, authority and grace in the state.

Politically speaking, that is, with direct application to the period that saw the publication of both pieces by Bibó summarized here, the past and protracted 'misery' of the small states of eastern Europe came to the fore after the end of the Second World War with particular acuteness and, again, with the 'real experience' of pain, agony, trauma and existential anxiety on all sides. Perhaps most of all this occurred in Hungary, which had the dubious distinction – not altogether undeserved – among countries of the region of being considered the only unqualifiedly 'defeated' nation: the last Nazi satellite. Defeat in this case meant not just, and in subjective terms perhaps less importantly, complete exposure to the power of the victorious Soviet army, replacing German hegemony and (in the last six months of the war) occupation. It meant the reappearance of the long-festering conflict between Hungary and its immediate neighbours. The dispute in particular between Czechoslovakia and Hungary came to occupy a position of special salience, both in Bibó's eyes and those of most of his compatriots. Bibó's specific comments on Czechoslovak claims with regard to Hungary in the immediate postwar situation are perhaps not exactly demonstrative of 'academic detachment' but they are essentially fair, objective and, most importantly, logically consistent with Bibó's general principles concerning democracy; whether agreeing with him or not, one has to acknowledge the writer's acumen in causing high moral consideration and down-to-earth political observation fruitfully to cross-fertilize.

In the essay on east European 'misery', while taking the traditional ideology of Hungary severely to task for its hopeless anachronism, Bibó is no less-incisive in criticizing Czechoslovak 'modern' national ideology for – what it amounts to – its short-term political unrealism and not-so-hidden inconsistency with professed democratic principles. One of Bibó's main concerns, was reflecting the attention of Hungarian public opinion on the eve of the impending peace treaty, with the categorical Czech insistence, joined by Rumania and Yugoslavia, with the Soviet Union lending unqualified support, on the restoration of the 1938 frontiers between Hungary and its neighbours. These frontiers had been determined by the Treaty of Trianon in 1920. They were revised in favour of Hungary by the two Vienna Awards in 1938 and 1940, directly resulting from German ascendancy in the region. In no sense whatsoever does Bibó wish for even a consideration to be given to this short-term, ill-fated and unlamented settlement. But in his view the (perfectly justified) revocation of these awards does not *eo ipso* justify the restoration of Trianon; the latter, apart from its flagrant violation of the principle of national self-determination, was according to him also a major cause of the instability of the region, permitting the eruption of the Second World War. Hence he considers it proper to rebuke the line taken by Czechoslovakia after the War, in the first place on account of its historical shortsightedness. The Czech position, as he says, is unrealistic 'because it endeavours to restore precisely those elements of the 1918 peace settlement which once already caused it to crumble'.[12] Going beyond this, however, he is apprehensive that Czechoslovak aims and actions are more than likely to do long-term damage to the cause of democracy in the region, especially in his native country where it has but tender roots.

At this point it may be thought advisable for us to digress briefly and outline the situation of postwar misery in eastern Europe as it appeared in these early years from the Hungarian angle. There were a number of events and developments that caused widespread resentment, shared to some extent even by the 'Muscovite' and 'Stalinist' leadership of the Hungarian Communist Party. The country had suffered utter unqualified defeat in the War. Its immediate neighbours, on the other hand, including Rumania (which had successfully managed to 'change sides' only a short time before Horthy's abortive attempt), were classed among the 'victorious' nations by the Allied Powers. The former were not tardy in asserting their claims on defeated Hungary, backed by immediate 'action' on the ground. Mainstream democratic public opinion in Hungary readily accepted that the *states*, as such, of Yugoslavia and Czechoslovakia had suffered aggression during the War, had in fact been destroyed as states, and hence were properly counted among the victors, among members of the United Nations. Hungarians remembered, however, that the attitude of the wartime German puppet-states of independent Slovakia (under Tiso) and independent Croatia (under Pavelich) were just as reprehensible, if not more so, as Hungary's under Horthy. While Hungary had a hidebound, conservative, even if you like 'quasi-fascist' régime, these two were Nazi states, pure and simple. They, too, stood by Hitler up to the last ditch. (Antonescu's Ironguardist régime in Rumania had little to learn from the Germans or Hungarians either.)

All this was conveniently forgotten in the immediate postwar period when the native Hungarian population of these neighbouring countries was branded 'fascist' *in toto* and held collectively responsible for aggression and atrocities during the War. The neighbouring 'Allies' were now paying back in kind, with added interest. The returning Rumanian administration and freebooters of the Maniu Guard were wreaking havoc in Northern Transylvania. According to an Hungarian Communist historian, these gangs 'perpetrated bloodbaths which often exceeded even the atrocities of fascist régimes'.[13] The Soviet Deputy Foreign Minister Vyshinsky, too, considered that the volunteers were terrorizing the Hungarian population; the situation was so desperate that the Allied Control

Commission (dominated by the Soviet) decided on 14 September 1945 to remove the Rumanian administration from this territory and place it under direct Red Army control.[14] In Slovakia, too, Hungarians lived 'under a reign of terror', suffering 'inhumane persecution and despoilation', as the United States representative in Hungary, A. Schoenfeld, reported to Washington on 31 August.[15]

Interestingly, in the light of subsequent developments, the conflict between Hungary and Czechoslovakia assumed greater salience at this time than the Hungarian-Rumanian wrangle which subsided. With Yugoslavia there was no conflict, properly speaking, in spite of the heavy Serbian retaliation for the wartime massacre in Novi Sad – but then, under total Communist rule from 1945, Yugoslavia became a genuinely multinational state, as Hungarians noted with approval and relief. Czechoslovakia, it appears, proclaimed a new 'principle', elaborated by its émigré leadership during the War and this was acted upon with speed and determination thereafter. Eduard Beneŝ, Zdenek Fierlinger and other Czech leaders made no secret of the fact that their intention was to turn the interwar 'nationalities state' of Czechoslovakia into a pure 'nation-state' of Czechs and Slovaks after the war. Beneŝ made it abundantly clear in an authoritative article in *Foreign Affairs* in 1946 that in his view Czechoslovakia had an absolute moral right to its prewar frontiers, because of the manner in which these had been changed in 1938:

In my opinion it is inadmissable, under present conditions, to allow the question of revisionism to be opened. The pre-Munich frontiers of Czechoslovakia with Hungary, Austria, Germany and Poland are intact. No political, military or economic considerations can change this reality. After what happened to her in 1938, Czechoslovakia has a right to complete moral satisfaction.

And his assertion of the new principle for the postwar Czechoslovak state is equally straightforward and unambiguous:

The choice is between the concept of a national state and the formerly recognized Wilsonian concept of a state of nationalities, with all that that involves. In a national state there is no room for minority problems . . . Even the Great Powers have recognized that in the interest of peace in Europe there remains no other solution but the removal of the Germans and Hungarians from Czechoslovakia.[16]

Accordingly the Sudeten Germans and Hungarians in Southern Slovakia, the largest nationalities in the state and which lived in homogeneous territorial blocs, were accused of 'disloyalty' to Czechoslovakia, were maltreated and intimidated on the spot, and immediate measures were taken to effect their forcible removal *en masse*. The postwar Czechoslovak government demanded an immediate large-scale 'exchange of populations' with Hungary, which was to involve approximately half a million Hungarians on the Czech side (the Slovakian population in Hungary was much smaller). The Allies, it should be noted, did not entertain the Czechoslovak demands *in toto*. The Paris Peace Treaty reduced the original figure of Hungarian expellees, and later, after a great deal of wrangle, a 'compromise' solution was reached. But the interesting and relevant point to note in our context is that the proclaimed Czechoslovak 'nation-state' principle – which, it might be thought, is just about compatible, *ceteris paribus*, with modern democratic principles such as those upheld by Bibó – was combined with an absolutely adamant, rock-like refusal to consider even minor revisions of the frontier with Hungary in the latter's favour, and in regard to territories that were adjacent to Hungary and where the population was overwhelmingly if not purely Hungarian. Thus while Czechoslovakia wished to keep all the territories it had been granted in 1920 on the assumption of it being a 'nationalities state', it now proceeded to 'denationalize' the same stretches of land to fit it into the new homogeneous 'nation-state'. And not only that. Czechoslovakia demanded *further* Hungarian territory, on purely strategic and economic grounds, on the south side of the River Danube, to extend the Bratislava 'bridgehead'. In the event, of the five villages (purely Hungarian) demanded, three were awarded to the new 'nation-state'.

Such occurrences and denouements – nothing if not 'miserable' from the Hungarian point of view – go some way towards illuminating the proper context in which to approach Bibó's article, 'The Peace Treaty and Hungarian Democracy', which in a way supplements and renders vitally concrete the general principles and historical observations set out in 'The Misery of the Small States of Eastern Europe'. Bibó in this shorter text begins with the valid recognition that the Peace Treaty, restoring the Trianon frontiers, will be received in Hungary with 'resigned bitterness'; for that reason he enjoins his countrymen to bear this new adversity calmly and not to abandon the perspective of democratic progress achieved hitherto, since the liberation in 1945. To Bibó it is clear that democracy faces perhaps the most difficult passage in Hungary (and Poland) among all small states in the east European region. Those to the West (Czechoslovakia) have a stronger, larger middle class and are more advanced industrially. Those to the east and south (Rumania and the Balkans) have a smaller, weaker aristocratic ruling class and also possess an intelligentsia directly related to the common people. However, Bibó argues, this is merely a sociological fact the employment of which in futuristic political debate amounts to 'cheating' and would present a serious obstacle to further democratic development. He points out that lack of democracy in Hungary was in no way responsible for the adverse Trianon peace settlement following the First World War; on the contrary, it was the harsh, unjust terms of that treaty that caused the downfall of Károlyi's democratic republic at the time. Today, he observes, the situation is similar: every advantage squeezed out of Hungary on the grounds of the 'democratic merits' and moral superiority of the neighbouring victorious states is a 'wicked obstacle put across the painful path which leads to Hungary's democratization'.[17] He likens the victors' conduct to the condemnation of an unmarried mother for killing her infant by the person who has abused her in the first place.[18]

With reference to the forcible expulsion of populations Bibó asserts that 'democracy issues in only one directive in territorial questions and this is called the right of self-determination'.[19] Hence he considers it farcical to appeal to democracy when people are forced to live in a state where they do not feel they belong or to be booted out of their native land. Let us admit, he says, that in east European history (as contrasted to the conduct of Denmark in 1919) there has never been found a single nation (Hungary included) which would have stood fast by democratic principles for their own sake and in opposition to its own territorial interests. Instead of appealing to merits, he goes on, we should admit that we have all been stumbling downwards on the same slope of political immorality, regressing to baseness. The oppression of minorities in historic Hungary earlier is now exchanged for semi-fascist methods employed by the democracies. We should certainly not equate the intentions of Hitler and Beneŝ:

But however firmly the value distinction between democracy and nazism is sustained, there is no difference at all between the grief of a mother whose child was killed in a German death-camp and the mother whose child, having died in a Czechoslovakian internment camp or on the highway, is buried wrapped in a newspaper. And if these mothers were further to proliferate in Central Europe, there will be nobody left to whom to explain the value distinction between democracy and nazism.[20]

But notwithstanding outbursts like this, the general tone of Bibó's article is, though displaying 'bitter resignation', serene, conciliatory and filled with realistic optimism. He accepts – *very* realistically, as it turned out – that the impending Paris Peace Treaty, with the restoration of the 1938 Hungarian frontier, will introduce long-term territorial stability into the region. Hungary has no choice but to live with it and to work quietly for the consolidation of its own new democratic system. The duty remains nevertheless, he emphasizes, to see that Hungarian populations living in the neighbouring states are accorded proper minority rights – a duty in the performance of which subsequent Hungarian governments were sadly remiss until recent times. It is also in this article that Bibó makes the remarkable – and seen from the traditional nationalistic viewpoint undoubtedly 'revisionist' – statement that Hungary should try to forget and overcome its largely self-imposed posture of 'tragic solitude' in the east European region. Though linguistically isolated, Hungary has had a great deal in common with its Slavonic neighbours. 'In past and present we have had so much in common with the Slavs, that it is up to us to get involved with the Slavonic cultural and political community. For a long time there has been a vacant place left for us . . . The principal obstacle has been our own anachronistic clinging to the "Turkish cavalier" heritage or the "German-Hungarian community of destiny" directed against the Slavs. It is true that the opposite "fatal perspective", according to which the historical significance of Hungary had been as a "wedge" between Northern and Southern Slavs, was invented and propagated by the Czech historian Palacky, but why has it been necessary for us to take this seriously and interpret it as our historical vocation?'[21]

At this juncture we shall again take up the thread of argument in Bibó's historical essay on the misery of eastern Europe. The principle advanced by Bibó aiming to defuse political hysteria in the region is unsentimental and straightforward; perhaps it might appear a bit simplistic at first glance but *qua* principle it is surely unexceptionable. Starting out from his basic conviction that nations are objective, historically enduring entities, properly functioning linguistic-cultural units that in the true order of things serve as indispensable vehicles of democratic transformation, Bibó affirms the right of national self-determination. This means above everything else a mutually agreed and satisfactory settlement of national frontiers. But in eastern Europe no such thing can be done on the basis of 'historic states', be they of medieval foundation or the products of modern power-political settlements, like Trianon in 1920 and (in anticipation) Paris after the Second World War. It is precisely this retrospective, neurotic, 'hysterical' nostalgia over historical frontiers that has caused all the trouble in the region. History, if employed in this manner, equals hysteria which in turn equals misery, shared all round. It must, therefore, be overruled, resolutely cast out of the armoury of interstate negotiations. The frontiers of east European states must instead be fixed along *existing* linguistic-cultural lines by a settlement which, by using tested mechanisms like local plebiscites, will declare these frontiers to be henceforward permanent and unalterable; irredentist agitation as well as the forcible assimilation of minorities will then have to be prevented or punished by the collective might of the peacemakers.

Bibó does realize, obviously, that not all interstate disputes could be solved in the region by the direct application of this general principle. There are ethnic conclaves, 'islands' within homogeneous national blocs, which will require special consideration, e.g. the Danzig Corridor (as it appeared in the interwar period), the areas north of the Aegean Sea and, from the Hungarian point of view looming as most important, Transylvania. But these special considerations must still logically follow from the general principle: otherwise they have no proper moral foundation and are thus unlikely to lead to stable results. We might add here, however – and this is implied in Bibó's perspective rather than explicitly stated – that the general principle enunciated by him *would have* had direct relevance and application in the case of southern Slovakia and large stretches of land alongside the Rumanian and Yugoslavian frontiers with Hungary (and other parts of the region such as Kossovo, Macedonia and Bukovina). But the principle was never applied and thus east European misery, now latent, now erupting, has continued to the present day.

In the context of this chapter, however, what assumes particular significance is Bibó's severe verdict on what he regards as a proffered alternative strategy for the solution of east European misery. It will be recalled that at the start we have posed the question – to which the Bibó perspective on modern European history can provide, *ex hypothesi*, at least part of an adequate answer – why east European 'integration' has been lagging so far behind the western achievement. Bibó's stand on this question is clear and forceful: successful integration presupposes properly functioning democracy. The latter's indispensable prerequisite are nations with a settled (cultural as well as territorial) identity who can go about their business unhysterically; this desired state of affairs in turn presupposes settled national frontiers. Integration is the final, highest achievement, not a panacea to be administered immediately. Hence Bibó is scathing in his dismissal of the 'dangerous superstition' according to which frontier adjustments are useless exercises, since the solution of the problem is the 'creation of some kind of supra-national federation'. There *was* once such a supra-national construct in the region, he points out, namely the Habsburg Empire,

and this was exploded and in consequence drowned the whole area under the waves of despairing uncertainty precisely because it could not bring about satisfactory boundary solutions among the nations under its rule. Federation is like marriage: you must not enter into it with unsolved problems, for its essence is the setting of a new perspective and with it lots of new problems, and it does not enable us to save the bother of dealing with unclarified questions. Any kind of future federation will operate only if it is preceded by the creation of minimal stability in respect of boundaries, this being the psychological precondition of federal union.[22]

In Bibó's view – and this might sound rather quaint in the retrospect of forty years, though it was by no means an absurd consideration at the time – east European countries ought not to look to the Soviet Union as an example for emulation. The coherence of the Soviet Union as a multi-ethnic nation rests on the long tradition of the Russian Empire, reinforced by the experience of the Socialist Revolution of 1917 and the Great Patriotic War its peoples have just victoriously concluded against the Germans. Hence the Soviet Union, like the British Commonwealth, can safely permit a large degree of regional autonomy to all the ethnic and national entities within its borders, even the right of secession, knowing full well there is no real danger of sundering the federation. Even if, continues Bibó, there is to be a 'unifying experience' for the peoples of the east European region in the near future, this is likely to be confronted with 'much stronger historical realities' [23] of a centrifugal character than those which the old Tsarist dependencies had to face following the Russian Revolution.

Bibó's perspective, as formulated in the immediate postwar period, does obviously look a little bit skewed, and in certain respects somewhat starry-eyed, if judged with historical hindsight. As a genuine, committed democrat he certainly seems to have been, in these years, more concerned with the potential danger of a traditionalist restoration in Hungary than with the threat posed by Stalinist Communism. Though self-consciously occupying a centrist position on the spectrum of coalition forces, being an intellectual advocate of the Third Way, his wary eyes are now fixed more on the Right than on the Left. Hence the particular force and fervent character of some of his strictures against traditional nationalism and 'historic' state formations, coupled with – or rather logically resting on – his touching faith in the effectiveness of popular democracy and its unproblematic fusion with patriotic sentiment. He was soon to learn from bitter personal experience among other things, and his later writings, though never losing his judicious sense of balance, display a perfect awareness of the tragic way in which Soviet postwar policy in general, and the conduct of the Hungarian Communist Party in particular, came to exacerbate the misery of eastern Europe. But in order to explain Bibó's emphasis, one ought to venture the remark in this context that his postwar analysis does assume a considerable amount of credibility when applied to the domestic Hungarian scene in isolation. It would be reasonable to suggest that the Communist-engineered distortion of the democratizing process in Hungary after 1948 was in the main foreign-led, rather than indigenously prepared and produced, a direct effect of the Cold War (whoever is being arraigned as the 'guilty party' for the eruption of that blemish in postwar history) and not reflective of east European, and a fortiori Hungarian, domestic social and political developments. In 1945–7, at any rate, the Right in Hungary did not appear any weaker than the Left; if anything, it appeared stronger, more deeply rooted in popular culture. The implication thus seems to be – and hopefully our interpretation does not stretch Bibó's perspective too far – that in the absence of Cold War divisions and Communist takeovers the historical 'misery' of the east European region could just have continued festering in the old accustomed way.

But whichever way we may want to judge on this rather controversial matter, the deeper thrust of Bibó's postwar analysis is certainly not affected in an adverse way by developments in the region in the past forty years. On the contrary: its basic validity appears to be proven in many ways. The crucial point is surely this: since democratic progress, for whatever ostensible and immediate reason, could not take place in the east European region paralleling or even remotely following the west European path, it was to be expected that transnational integrative processes would also be lagging behind. Integration, as Bibó sees it, can be a consequence (though not an inevitable consequence) only of 'consummated' democratic development; and consummated democracy *equals* consummated nationality, i.e. 'unhysterical' patriotism. The sad, but – following Bibó – not altogether surprising fact to be recorded in the most recent history of the region is that decades of Soviet power-hegemony and enforced political uniformity there were not capable of generating the 'common experience' that would have been conducive to harmonization, let alone integration. Indeed, if anything Bibó seems to have erred on the side of circumspection by referring darkly to 'historical realities' that could stand in the way of progress in this respect. These are certainly still there, blocking the way. The gradual mollification and relative recession of Soviet power in the area led directly to the gradual but unmistakable resurfacing of conflict along ethnic, linguistic, national lines all over the place, involving the rights of minorities. It follows therefore that territorial disputes cannot be lagging too far behind – and it is useless to say that these constitute the legacy of the Stalin-era, since they were there to begin with, sorely festering under, as it has turned out, a thin, fragile veneer. A spectacular dimension of this current turbulence is the dynamic presence of ethnic centrifugality within the Soviet Union itself, endangering the coherence of that complex 'nation' from the Baltic to the Caucasus and central Asia. On this point, Bibó was perhaps somewhat too easily led into accepting the Soviet Union as a proper 'national' community but he was certainly not alone among non-Marxist writers to make that assumption, plausible in the period in question. We may also make the point here that the Leninist-Stalinist theory of nationality – in contrast to the practice – could, and did, have a favourable resonance among east European thinkers and politicians seeking a way out of the imbroglio of inter-ethnic conflict.

But more relevantly to the present discussion, we are now witnessing yet another phase in the long-drawn-out misery of the small states of eastern Europe, with some novel features but basically faithful to the hallowed pattern. Conflicts that have so far hit the headlines loudest are those involving the Hungarian minority in Rumania and the Albanian minority in Yugoslavia but there are plenty of others rapidly brewing up. Poignancy is added to these issues by the differing character of the political systems of the countries involved but it would take a large amount of ideological naivety to believe that relative 'democracy' and relative 'totalitarianism' have an essential bearing on the matter, beyond supplying the appropriate rhetoric and (as the case may be) the power-political wherewithal to put desired state policies into effect. Had Hungary been stead-fastly Stalinist and Rumania pluralistic, or Albania decentralized and Yugoslavia monolithic, the conflicts developing in the last few years would probably have looked much the same. The truth is that – as of old, in the last 150 years as so masterfully described by Bibó in his essay – immature and near-hysterial nationalism is always the first, easiest, readiest-to-hand weapon to be employed by the powers that be in critical situations. National sentiment, based, as Bibó says, on real experience, is objectively there, to be used or abused, to serve reactionary

or progressive democratic purposes. In eastern Europe, as a sad repetition of
events of a not-so-remote past, the same national sentiment and assertive national
self-identity as have assisted the small states in their endeavour to achieve
relative independence of the Soviet Union have also been instrumental in keeping
their minorities, if any, in a subordinate position, thereby continuing to prevent
rapprochement among neighbours. Misery is further enhanced and the chances of
reconciliation and accommodation pushed even further into a mist-enveloped
future, when intolerant nationalism fuses with intolerant neo-Stalinism, thus
preventing even the first prerequisite of regional harmonization, namely
democracy in the domestic field.

Currently as everyone knows and views with wonderment, eastern Europe is
undergoing a tremendous process of political transformation at an incredibly
rapid pace. With Poland and Hungary showing the way, and Soviet perestroika
supplying the one indispensable external permissive factor,[24] by now practically
all countries in the region (with the possible, and no doubt temporary, exception
of Albania) are firmly set on the road towards democratization. It is, however,
still an open question how far – and how fast – internal changes in the several
countries are capable of bringing about decisive improvements in their relationship to one another. It seems that, although the period of postwar oppression
failed to generate any 'unifying' experience among the nations of eastern Europe,
most of them have by now progressed to a remarkably mature state of *domestic*
reconciliation and unification, severally and as yet perhaps in an inward-looking
way, which certainly augurs well for the prospects of democratization. Like
charity, democracy must begin at home. And here we can appreciate the validity
and relevance of Bibó's dictum to the effect that the relative paucity, or even
absence, of long-standing democratic 'traditions', in the institutional and sociological sense, has precious little to do with a nation's present and future capacity
in achieving democracy. What is needed (in addition to the permissive factor of a
favourable international constellation) is the maturation of *common experience* on
the domestic front, of tragedy and tribulation as the case may be, the saving
experience which – in historical terms – is to be likened to the great cataclysmic
revolutions inaugurating democracy in the West at the time. Poland and Hungary
in 1945 looked (to Bibó and many others) to be the most problematic cases from
the viewpoint of democratization. Forty years on Poland and Hungary are in the
forefront. This relative, and probably temporary, advance confers no more
privileges, of a moral or political nature, on Hungary and Poland than its interwar
democratic 'merits' should have conferred on postwar Czechoslovakia. Still, these
cautious national advances currently provide the most hopeful signs that eastern
Europe as a region might after all, and given sufficient time, transcend and escape
its past history of misery. Bibó is consistently emphatic that all nations have the
capacity to attain to democracy, given the historical opportunity; deformation is
contingent, not innate.[25]

Our last observaton concerns an intriguing point, inextricably connected to
Bibó's historical perspective, as interpreted in the foregoing, but on which the
conclusion of this chapter might to some extent diverge from Bibó's own scenario
and predilections – although it is logically consistent with the line taken in the
two texts commented on here, inspired by Bibo's dedication to the cause of
democracy, and in addition mindful (as Bibó could not have been) of lessons

suggested by most recent developments. Yet it will not be denied that our conclusion is deliberately speculative and may be unintentionally controversial. The question is: in what sense are we entitled to conceptualize, in a political discussion, eastern Europe as a 'region'? Bibó's analysis, it seems, identifies eastern Europe as a region only in the *historical* sense, as an entity 'in itself', a unity to be characterized in terms of negatives and contradictions. The identity of eastern Europe is first and foremost a 'miserable' identity: its *differentia* are constituted by a set of absences, arrests, dead-ends, halfway-houses, distortions of national character, of societies and political cultures caught in the web of reaction and false realism, of nations suffering from the affliction of political hysteria, of infantile, defective western-type institutions existing amid eastern-type conditions.[26] From this it certainly follows that east European nations must accomplish the 'common' – or rather 'parallel' – task of internal democratization, which is the same thing as becoming proper, mature, modern nations. There is no alternative: this is the only way out of their condition of misery. But from the same set of historical premises what does *not* seem to follow is that there is any likely purchase in endeavouring to accomplish this task in the context of some kind of 'regional unity'. Since the ultimate objective is democratization equalling nationalization equalling 'Europeanization' in the only valid sense, striving towards the achievement of an intermediate east European identity might well appear to be an unnecessary, indeed pointless and self-defeating, detour. In other words, from Bibó's historical perspective alone it does not appear logical or politically desirable to construe eastern Europe or central Europe as a region 'for itself', to be cast in the role of a positive factor assisting in the movement towards democracy, freedom, pacified conditions in Europe and leading ultimately to European unification. And it is at this point that we have to note, explicitly and with emphasis, the relevance of the current phenomenon of 'uneven development' in the east European region: those countries enjoying the lucky historical break of being in an 'advanced' position have little choice but 'to go it alone', to push forward on a single-country basis, to accomplish Europeanization one by one. This is, indeed, what is precisely going on at the present time. We should feel reassured that this process is not just dictated by short-term expediency but represents the playing out of deep-seated historical forces active in the social development of our continent.[27]

7 The Hungarian Draft Treaty for the Protection of Minorities

Mihály Fülöp

The Peace Treaty Division of the Hungarian Ministry of Foreign Affairs presented its proposals about the fate of Hungarians living outside the national frontiers in the summer of 1945. The head of the division, István Kertész, in accordance with the armistice, started with the principle that, 'At present, Hungary holds state supremacy both *de facto* and *de jure* exclusively over the territories defined in the Treaty of Trianon. Thus our policy and behaviour at the postwar conferences can be realistic only if we start from, and base our arguments on, the territorial decisions of Trianon.' Accordingly, it would be consistent with:

international justice, human development, the ideals of democracy and socialism, and the provisions of the agreements between the Allies, if the borders of Central Europe were drawn on the basis of the principle of self-determination propagated by President Wilson and the principle of national minorities so often stressed in Lenin's works . . . If, however, the Trianon borders, or similar ones, remain, then we are forced to request the abolition of the new economic, transport, waterway and cultural anomalies by international conventions. The fulfilment of these requests is not merely in the interests of Hungary, but in the common interests of all the peoples living in this area. It should be stressed that during their re-establishment the borders should lose their significance and not provoke despair in the peoples, but rather contribute to their pacification. This request also accords with paragraphs four and five of the Atlantic Charter.[1]

In its note to the representatives of the great powers in Budapest on 14 August 1945, the Hungarian government proposed that:

since national minorities most probably will still be found outside the mother country, no matter how the borders will be drawn, it is absolutely necessary to provide for their protection by means of some international arrangement by the United Nations.

The protection afforded to minorities by the League of Nations undoubtedly justified certain adverse criticism, but at least there was some protection. In many cases the very fact that this machinery existed was sufficient to restrain governments which were planning oppressive measures against minorities. It will be a regressive act if even this protection is not granted in the future to national minorities.[2]

At the London session of the Council of Foreign Ministers (11 September 1945 to 2 October 1945), the great powers presented their drafts for the Peace Treaty. The Soviet proposals were based on the armistice agreements and the resolutions of the Berlin (Potsdam) Conference. They were intended to reinforce the decision of the Allies to compel ex-enemy countries, that is Italy, Rumania, Bulgaria, Hungary and Finland, to readmit their nationals who had fled from their countries and to be fully responsible for them. The draft of the United States, seeking to uphold the human rights and fundamental freedoms of the Charter of the United Nations, included guarantees of freedom of speech, religion, choice of language, political conviction and right of assembly. On 20 September 1945, during the sole debate on the Hungarian issue at the London Conference, the French Foreign Minister, Bidault, proposed using the ethnic line as the border between Rumania and Hungary, adding that: 'due to the regional distribution of the Hungarian population in the centre of Rumanian populated areas, the problem can only be partially solved, *thus the situation provides an opportunity for strengthening and developing the rights of minorites*'.[3] Yet no decisions were taken at the London Conference and substantial talks were postponed to the spring of 1946.

This was the position at the turn of the year, as Hungary faced some of the gravest problems of the postwar period: the resettlement of Hungarian nationals from Czechoslovakia and of the German ethnic minority in Hungary. In his summary of 1 January 1946, Pál Sebestyén, Secretary General of the Ministry of Foreign Affairs, explained that the Government was obliged to accept responsibility for the fate of Hungarians living beyond its territorial remit and to act as a 'trustee' for them. Sebestyén warned that the Government must resist the temptation to 'try to obtain, or even accept, concessions to, and advantages for, the Hungarian state and its inhabitants at the expense of those Hungarians who are separated from us. This temptation is extremely strong in relation to neighbouring states.' He added that the postwar migrations and transfers:

occur in the spirit of political and ethnic regrouping and restratification, the aim of which is to exploit the fluid situation arising from the destruction of the German Reich in order to create new positions of power. The new situation will be set for a long time through the peace settlement, and the fate of nations and peoples will depend upon what state and position they can secure for themselves in the settlement.

He considered that 'the assurance of political freedom, economic welfare and a free cultural life for all Hungarians to be a fundamental and justifiable aim. The optimal condition would be for all Hungarians to live within the bosom of a single state.' However, if this could not be achieved, 'we have to ensure those basic conditions for the Hungarians compelled to live outside our borders, which enable them to live a life without fear, free of political persecution and oppression, and to have their human rights respected, so that they may prosper economically and continue a free cultural life.'

At the turn of 1945–6 the threat of deportations – of Hungarians from Czechoslovakia and Germans from Hungary – cast a darkening shadow. Sebestyén came to doubt the possibility of returning to the so-called minorities' treaties concluded at Paris:

Our neighbours, who at the time allowed these minorities' treaties to be forced upon them by the victorious powers only after the utmost resistance and in exchange for the implementation of their maximum territorial aspirations, would, today, when – with more or less justification – they look upon their territorial positions as an acquired or even historic right, be even more reluctant to submit to such an arrangement. Since their territorial aspirations have been satisfied, the powers cannot offer them sufficient compensation . . . At a time when relocations and deportations are taking place to an unprecedented extent the necessary disposition and tact for dealing with the question of minorities through such sophisticated legal machinery is entirely absent, both from world public opinion and from our neighbours. The extent to which the current atmosphere, probably created as a subconscious remnant of fascist methods, affects international public opinion is shown by the fact that the very same great powers who raised their voices with such moral loftiness for the respect for human rights and human dignity, seem to consider forceful resettlement an appropriate solution to the problem of Germans living outside the German state; a method hardly compatible with human dignity. To varying extents, the same atmosphere is evident in our neighbours, who have abandoned the minority protection arrangements of the past and wish to treat, and solve, the problem of Hungarians within their borders as their internal affair, each in his own way. This disposition does not allow us to entertain any hope of solving the problem of Hungarians living within their borders by means of bilateral treaties.

Sebestyén saw little point in trying to revive the old minorities' treaties since they would be quite inadequate for the new state of affairs. The old solution was regarded by the Secretary General as a last resort if all else failed or as a bargaining counter. The only solution he could see was to consolidate all Hungarians into an ethnically homogenous and economically viable state. He wanted the great powers to delimit the borders of the new Hungarian state. Our neighbours, he explained, 'could establish good relations, without internal or external friction, without fear of ulterior motives, with a democratic Hungary, which has given up her historic ambitions for ever and, reconciled to her position, is starting a new life.' [4] These hopes were rudely shattered by the decision of the great powers, in the spring of 1946, to return to the frontiers of Trianon. Hungary was forced to return to the idea of the codification of the rights of minorities.[5]

In a draft Preparatory Peace Note of 27 March 1946 the Ministry of Foreign Affairs had appealed for the elimination of those factors that had caused political and social discord between the states of south-east Europe.[6] It started from the articles of the Charter of the United Nations which proclaimed that one people should not exercise hegemony over another nor oppress national, racial or religious minorities. It then called for special measures to be adopted in the region. The Peace Treaty itself should bind parties not to enact laws whose avowed or hidden intent was to oppress any nationality. Minority groups left after the revision of the frontiers should, it argued, be recognized as autonomous bodies according to the model adopted by the Soviet Union. Furthermore, these autonomous bodies were to be placed under the protection of permanent local delegates of the United Nations, who would also guarantee the rights of individual members of the minorities. The Hungarian Government, it said, would accept such supervision for any minorities remaining within Hungarian territory, on a reciprocal basis, and agree to be bound by the decisions of the supervisory agencies. It added that there should be explicit provision that every inhabitant of any territory should be guaranteed citizenship, recalling that in the interwar period hundreds of thousands had been arbitrarily deprived of their citizenship and observing that this lamentable practice was still in operation. To prevent the persistence of resentment, those who had been expelled from their homes or forced to flee from them should have the right to return and be offered compensation for the losses sustained. It acknowledged that an international loan would be required to facilitate this. It also called for measures to counteract the general growth of mutual suspicion and mistrust in the Danubian region, which was making the frontiers practically impenetrable.

This note was handed to the representatives of the great powers after the 7 May 1946 decision to restore the Trianon borders between Hungary and Rumania.[7] From then on the Hungarian Government recognized that a more favourable settlement of the borders was unlikely and it concentrated on obtaining guarantees of protection for minorities. Indeed, on 7 May a meeting was held in the Prime Minister's office to formulate a draft Treaty to Protect Minorities. This was presented to the Council of Foreign Ministers on 11 June 1946 by the Hungarian envoy in Paris; copies were given to representatives of the great powers in Budapest on 2 July. The Hungarian Government proposed that provisions protecting minorities should either be included in the Peace Treaty or that the permanent members of the United Nations Security Council should conclude separate agreements with each of the countries of south-east Europe for this purpose. It also proposed joint commissions and courts to settle disputes arising from the implementation and interpretation of the provisions.[8] The leaders of the Hungarian representatives in Paris, István Kertész and Zoltán Baranyai, gained the impression that the great powers would give serious consideration to the proposal.[9]

Indeed, at the beginning of June 1946, the British Foreign Office mentioned the possibility of including a minorities protection article in the Peace Treaty with Rumania. Some impetus was given by the planned visit of Prime Minister Ferenc Nagy to Washington and London and the desire to strengthen the position of the Smallholders' Party. The British Foreign Minister, Ernest Bevin, sought to gain the support of the American State Department. Bevin acknowledged that nothing could now be done about the frontiers, but added:

We have however been impressed by the case which the Hungarian Government have put forward that something should be done to protect the Hungarian minorities in Rumania and Czechoslovakia. The disabilities under which the Hungarian minority in Rumania at present lives are described in the Hungarian Government's memorandum summarised in Budapest telegram No. 568 (May 24).[10] Although the Hungarian statement may be exaggerated in certain respects I have no reason to doubt the general accuracy of the Hungarian allegations. It has not hitherto been our intention to insert minority clauses into the peace treaties and it had been our hope that such matters would be satisfactorily covered by the human rights Article . . . We now think however that we should try to do something more to protect the Hungarian minority in Transylvania. One of the principal disabilities under which they seem likely to have to suffer is the denial of Rumanian nationality and full civic rights.
We are therefore inclined to propose for inclusion in the peace treaty a clause on the following lines: 'The Rumanian Government undertake, as the case may be, either to confirm in the possession of Rumanian nationality and full civic rights following therefrom, or to confer such nationality and full civic rights upon, all inhabitants of the territories subject to the Vienna Award, who remain therein after the date of the coming into force of the present Treaty.[11]

The reply of the State Department came quickly. Despite doubts about whether Bevin's proposal would actually provide any greater protection for the Hungarian minority, the State Department agreed that the inclusion of such a clause would aid the Smallholders' Party and that it was, for this reason, desirable. Lord Inverchapel, reporting on the American reply concluded that:

Provided therefore that the discussion regarding the Rumanian Treaty at Paris develops favourably and there appears to be a reasonably good prospect of securing Soviet agreement to it, Byrnes would be prepared to support you in proposing the inclusion of a nationality clause on the lines which you suggest. The State Department considers however that it would be unwise to raise hopes which in the event may not be realised and they have therefore thought it best to refrain from discussing this possibility with the Hungarian Prime Minister during his visit here.[12]

Accordingly, Deputy Secretary of State, Dean Acheson, explained to Nagy that the problem of Hungarian minorities would be considered by the three great powers, adding by way of reassurance that the United States was fully aware of the situation and that it had always supported the possibility of Hungary undertaking direct negotiations with its neighbours on the problem.[13]

The British Foreign Office, in a memorandum of 19 June 1946 concerning preparations for the forthcoming visit of the Hungarian delegation, reaffirmed Bevin's view that the Hungarian minorities were suffering from mistreatment. A restoration of the Versailles machinery for the protection of minorities was excluded, on the grounds that it had proved to be inadequate. Nevertheless, the memo suggested Nagy be told that the way forward lay in the United Nations Charter and the insertion of human rights clauses into the treaty. It did concede there was a need for additional protection of the Hungarian minority in Rumania and advised that Rumania be obliged to accord full citizenship to all inhabitants of its territory. It was admitted that no similar protection could be provided for the minority in Czechoslovakia.

The complexity of the problem became apparent when the two sides met in London. The British Minister of State, Noel-Baker, felt obliged to refute rumours that Britain had supported Rumanian claims to Transylvania because of British interests in Rumanian oil. He argued that the Soviet Union was quite intransigent on the issue of the border and that it would be futile to raise the matter again. Noel-Baker held out the hope that under the Charter of the United Nations all minorities would receive better treatment than in the past and noted that both Hungary and Rumania would soon be members of the United Nations. This did little to reassure the Hungarians, who expressed concern about the fate of the 650,000 Hungarians in Czechoslovakia. Czechoslovak claims that 200,000 could be exchanged for Slovaks in Hungary were disputed. The Hungarians doubted whether the figure would exceed 50,000 or 60,000 and pointed to the fact that only 68,000 Slovaks in Hungarian territory had volunteered for the exchange. In reality, they claimed the Czechoslovak Government was intending to 'slovakize' 200,000 and to expel most of the rest, that is 300,000–400,000. The Hungarians protested vigorously against both policies. The expulsions, they argued, would impose an intolerable burden on the Hungarian economy, which was already the most densely populated of the agrarian states. Furthermore, Czechoslovak policy would leave Hungary no choice but to pursue a policy of revision. Noel-Baker showed some impatience with protests against Czechoslovak attempts to consolidate a nation-state, pointing out that, in the wake of Munich, the British Government could hardly criticize Czech attempts to create a nation-state. Ferenc

Nagy refused to be swayed and reaffirmed to Attlee the Hungarian hopes of regaining territory from Rumania as well as securing minority rights for Hungarians in other countries. Attlee's response was to remind the Hungarians that democracy entailed tolerance of other opinions and that tolerance had been notably lacking in south-eastern Europe. He placed more emphasis upon creating a spirit of cooperation and cordial relations than upon any juridicial guarantees, whether these were enshrined in separate treaties or fell under the auspices of the United Nations. He agreed that Hungary faced severe problems and that ethnic divisions did not correspond to economic realities. Nevertheless, he reaffirmed that the boundaries had been set by the four powers and that he did not know if the Russians would agree to any changes. The solution, he suggested, lay in direct discussions with Czechoslovakia and Rumania.

The Hungarians encountered much the same response when they met Bevin in Paris on 25 June 1946. Nagy reiterated the difficulties caused by the Trianon boundaries and asked for Bevin's help in reopening the question of Transylvania. Bevin refused to be drawn. The impasse was reflected in the ensuing discussion. According to the British record Bevin declared:

that as regards Transylvania he had originally supported the US proposal that some adjustment should be made. At the present conference, however, it had been decided that there was no point in going on with it. He hoped, however, that it could be arranged, after the peace treaty was signed and the Rumanian elections had been held, that the Rumanians and Hungarians could meet and arrive at a common settlement. It should be possible for neighbouring countries to come to such amicable settlements, particularly in the economic field. The problem of minorities was of course always present. It was impossible to move all these peoples from one country to another. But if the question were raised at Paris or at a subsequent conference, he would be sympathetic to making adjustments in order to minimise the difficulties which had arisen. The Hungarians should, however, understand that it was not really possible to give complete satisfaction in these matters. He had always been in favour of the Eastern European countries getting together in the economic field in order to achieve, if not necessarily customs unions, at least the freest possible exchange of goods.
At this point Mr Auer interjected the remark that it was difficult to achieve a customs union unless a good atmosphere were first created in the area.
The Secretary of State said that he realised this but the good atmosphere depended on the efforts of the small powers as well as on the Big Four. Racial feeling was one of the major problems which the Council had to face. We would try, however, not to make these things too rigid and to ensure that there would be provision for these matters to be reviewed.
As regards the minority in Czechoslovakia he felt that wholesale evacuation of minorities would place an excessive strain both on Czechoslovakia and Hungary. He recalled that provision had been made in the treaty for the exercise of human rights. It was the duty of the United Nations to see that effect was given to this clause which, he hoped, would prove to be more effective than the minority clauses in the Treaty of Versailles. He hoped in fact that a moral code would be built up in regard to the treatment of minorities and he was determined to urge full use of the human rights clause in the Charter in order to establish proper protection for everyone. This, he felt, was a better method than bilateral arrangements between the two countries alone.[14]

Thus, Bevin declined to take up the Transylvanian issue, referring to Secretary of State Byrnes's opposition to having the problem discussed again.[15] In the days that followed, the British and American diplomats, now increasingly engaged by the tensions between the superpowers, backed away from the idea of including a new article on citizenship in the Rumanian Peace Treaty. Bevin returned to his earlier standpoint: 'I still feel that minority clauses were no good in the treaties and that the questions could be settled without the intervention of the Big Four.' [16]

The Soviet Union's view was clarified in comments by the Deputy Foreign Minister Dekanozov, explaining the outcome of Soviet-Czech talks to the Hungarian envoy to Moscow, Gyula Szekfü. Dekanozov expressed strong support for Czechoslovakia's policies, including the expulsion of some 200,000 Hungarians. He was a little more sympathetic in the other major area of concern: Transylvania was to go to Rumania, though he added that the rights of the Hungarian minority would be protected, in accordance with the guarantees in the draft treaties. [17]

Hungary's last chance to obtain more favourable conditions was the forthcoming third session of the Council of Foreign Ministers (4 November to 12 December 1946). This was to consider the draft treaties that had emerged from a series of meetings earlier in the year. The second session of the Council of Foreign Ministers (15 June to 12 July 1946) formulated texts that were sent to the affected countries on 19 July and made public on 29 July. Significantly, the Rumanian and Hungarian draft treaties provided for guarantees of human rights and fundamental freedoms, but not specific measures for the protection of minorities.

Hungarian efforts focused on the Paris Conference (29 July to 15 October 1946) which was to consider the draft treaties before submitting them to the Council of Foreign Ministers. The Hungarian Council of Ministers met on 6 August to discuss their approach to the Paris Conference. Foreign Minister János Gyöngyösi raised the possibility of making territorial claims against Rumania, claims he knew the great powers would not support, as a tactical measure. The idea was that the Allies might then be persuaded to establish some form of institutionalized protection for the Hungarian minority as compensation for the rejection of these claims. This, however, was regarded as absurd by Hungary's own experts. Turning to the Czechoslovak question, Gyöngyösi stated that Hungary's main aim had to be to try to thwart the Czechoslovak plan to expel Hungarians and to assure some form of effective guarantees for them. The problem was that the 'Czechoslovak state does not want to take upon itself any kind of minority protection, because it does not want any minorities within its borders unless there is a general article adopted by the United Nations Organisation, which is of binding force for every member of the United Nations.' [18]

The experts on the minorities question, Béla Demeter, István Révay and Sándor Vájlok, put forward a series of concrete demands they thought Gyöngyösi should make to the Paris Conference. They wanted, in the first place, the appointment of a Peace Conference Committee to investigate the ethnographical, economic and political problems in Transylvania and Slovakia, to hold hearings of the representatives of Hungarian minorities in the disputed areas and to arrange a plebiscite. Rumania and Czechoslovakia were to remove discriminatory legislation, with retroactive effect, prior to the signing of the treaties. Furthermore, the minorities should be guaranteed participation in the legislative, judicial and executive functions of the host states. Provision should also be made for measures of self-government and international supervision. The existing proposals of the Allies, they complained:

fail to provide effective guarantees of a life without fear and the enjoyment of all the benefits of human rights for the more than three million people of Hungarian nationality remaining outside the national borders. The leading powers might have proceeded from the idea that they had signed the United Nations Charter, thereby undertaking that their foreign and domestic policies would uphold the basic principles and spirit of the United Nations. However, the attitude of Czechoslovakia profoundly contradicts these principles.[19]

At the Paris Conference itself, on 14 August, Gyöngyösi argued forcefully for more precise measures:

If the borders cannot be changed, then their significance has to be modified, and all those fundamental freedoms ought to be provided for the Hungarians living in other countries ... that is, the right to a life free of distress and fear, as well as the right to protect their nationality. Unfortunately, I have to state, that in our case, belonging to some national minority does not only mean a different citizenship, but the deprivation of practising one's human rights and partly of one's human dignity.
The settlement which followed the First World War had clauses concerning territories peopled by minorities. These clauses have not always guaranteed the full respect of human rights, but with their application being controlled by the League of Nations, it was at least possible to have a right of appeal.
We are also aware that Hitlerite Germany has known, for its own imperialist political needs, how to make full use of the guarantees assured to national minorities by the treaties. But the fact that she misused them does not justify the abandonment of a necessary guarantee. This is confirmed by the claims advanced by the international representatives of Jewish organisations, the most authoritative in the matter, as a result of the cruel persecutions they have endured.
It is known to the Hungarian Government that the United Nations Organisation intends to prepare a charter on human rights. This will take time. On the other hand, the United Nations Charter and the declarations of principle contained in the drafts of the peace treaties only mention certain liberties, leaving out the right of choosing one's domicile, the right of choosing one's language of instruction, the right to work and the right of enterprise. In a world torn by passions and national intolerance resulting from the war, it is precisely these liberties that it is essential to assure. It would then seem necessary, until the entry into force of the code to be issued by the United Nations Organisation, to come to an agreement whereby the states of Central and Eastern Europe should pledge themselves to respect the exercise of these liberties.[20]

Gyöngyösi's impassioned plea was followed up by the suggestion, on 20 August, that Article 2 of the draft treaty for Hungary, which offered purely formal guarantees, be amended to make specific mention of the rights Gyöngyösi had enumerated.[21] The Hungarians continued to explore every avenue and argument to secure better protection for minorities. On 29 August Gyöngyösi sought discussions on Article 3 of the draft treaty for Rumania, which was similar to Article 2 of the proposed treaty for Hungary. On the same day Béla Demeter suggested that detailed proposals be submitted to the Conference.[22] On 30 August the Hungarians presented a Draft Treaty on the Protection of National Minorities to the French Secretary General of the Conference.[23] This text returned to the idea of agreement between the permanent members of the Security Council on the one hand, and Hungary, Rumania, Czechoslovakia and Yugoslavia on the other. It also sought to establish international supervision and jurisdiction with a direct right of appeal by political, economic, cultural and ecclesiastic minority organizations to the Security Council. Pál Auer, in a 31 August speech on the problem of the Hungarian-Rumanian border, requested that the Hungarian and Rumanian delegations be called upon to begin direct talks on special guarantees that would protect the rights of the Hungarian minority and provide extensive self-government for the homogenous bloc of Hungarians living in the eastern part of Transylvania. In the event that no agreement was reached within a specified time, he suggested that the Council of Foreign Ministers should implement an equitable solution themselves.[24] Gyöngyösi continued, in a letter of 4 September 1946 to the chairman of the Rumanian Political and Territorial Commission, to seek permission to expound his views in person. This request, like all the other Hungarian efforts, was ignored. None of the great powers supported the numerous and varied appeals for a full and extensive settlement of the minorities problem. In the end, on 13 September, the Hungarian Political and Territorial Commission accepted, by a vote of eight to three (the Soviet Union, Bielorussia and Ukraine), with two abstentions (Czechoslovakia and Yugoslavia), a British proposal that studiously avoided the specific guarantees sought by the Hungarians.[25]

All that was left now was the hope that one of the great powers might put its weight behind direct Hungarian-Rumanian negotiations on minority protection, citizenship and cross-border traffic. The Soviet representative in Budapest, Pushkin, favoured this idea.[26] However, when Gyöngyösi briefed the Soviet Foreign Minister, Molotov, the response was less helpful. Molotov agreed that talks should begin but he would not commit the Soviet Union to support the Hungarian position.[27] Despite this rebuff the Hungarian Foreign Minister tried again in a letter of 12 October addressed to Molotov in his capacity as Chairman of the Paris Conference. He argued that if the Conference did not wish to deal with the matters that concerned the Hungarians, it should at least press the Hungarians and Rumanians to reach an agreement between themselves. Yet even this request was turned down. Molotov's reply of 22 October coldly declared that:

the settlement of issues between Rumania and Hungary does not fall within the scope of the Paris Peace Conference, all the more so, since the problems mentioned in your letter should be dealt with as an item on the agenda of a Hungarian-Rumanian bilateral agreement. In connection with your statement, that the Paris Conference did not consider it necessary to guarantee the democratic rights and the protection of cultural and economic interests of the Hungarians living in Rumania, I am obliged to draw your attention to Article III of the Rumanian Peace Treaty draft, which prescribes such obligations for the Rumanian Government, which will guarantee the rights and interests of the Hungarian population to the necessary extent.[28]

The protests and arguments of the Hungarians did as little to change the final text of the Peace Treaty as the final note sent by Istvan Kertész on 10 February 1947, the day the Treaty was signed.[29] Yet the Hungarian Draft Treaty for the Protection of Minorities is still significant, for it remains the most comprehensive effort to codify the rights of minorities and to resolve ethnic conflict in accordance with the United Nations Charter.

8 British Policy Towards Western Europe 1945-51

Stuart Croft

During the tenure of office of the first postwar Labour governments, British policy towards western Europe was largley conditioned by two factors. First, the German problem: what should be the status of postwar Germany in both political and economic terms? Second, how should the great powers interact with one another over the major problems of the day? These two factors were interrelated. One of the major problems of the day was the future of western Europe. The future of that part of the continent was deemed to be largely dependent on decisions taken by the great powers about the future of Germany. There were many concerns. Were the great powers not to fashion some stability for Germany, then political instability was likely to dominate the rest of western Europe, notably in France and Italy. Should the great powers, and notably the Americans, not be committed to some framework to control Germany, then many feared that Germany might once again pose a threat to European and indeed global security. Finally, there was a concern that the great powers should not allow the Germans too much economic recovery, for fear of Germany once again dominating Europe; but too little economic recovery would have prevented a regeneration of economic activity in the rest of western Europe.

Britain's policy towards western Europe during the first postwar Labour governments was therefore closely linked to British policy towards Germany on the one hand, and towards the United States and the Soviet Union on the other. Consequently, as the nature of Britain's relations with the Americans and Soviets changed throughout the late 1940s, British policy towards Germany and western Europe went through a series of transformations. In the early postwar period, Europe was seen as the area over which the great powers could concert their efforts in a new system designed to manage the problems of the world collectively. By 1946, it had become apparent that such a concert system would not work; instead Britain sought to integrate western Europe into a third force between the Americans and the Soviets. This too proved not to be a viable policy as the cold war deepened and the Americans became more interested in the future of Europe. But the economic collapse suffered by the British in early 1947 led to a period of retrenchment in British foreign policy. By late 1947, however, Britain came to view western Europe as an appendage in a Western alliance dominated by the British and Americans, a view that led to frequent Anglo-European and Anglo-American tensions. By 1951 it was clear that this view of British policy towards western Europe was also not tenable. There were thus a series of policy changes, each of which were entirely logical given underlying assumptions. This chapter will examine these transformations in British policy towards western Europe in order to amplify these themes. It will also seek to identify British policy-makers' underlying assumptions towards Europe during the first postwar Labour governments.

Developing a concert-style approach to the problems of the world had been a favourite choice of British policy-makers since at least the Congress of Vienna: it had been a policy option chosen several times during the nineteenth century and an option explored after the Great War. By a concert system, what was meant was an agreement between the great powers to meet to discuss and resolve the major problems of dispute without recourse to major war between the great powers. It did not imply that nations involved in the concert system would be allies: far from it. Britain had not been an ally of either Metternich or Bismarck but had worked with both in a concert system during the previous century. Supporters of the concert approach did not therefore see any qualitative difference between Stalin's Russia, Metternich's Austria and Bismarck's Prussia in terms of being able to deal with an adversary over the major issues of the day. The concert approach was seen as a mechanism that would institutionalize conflict-management and resolution. It was therefore perhaps natural that in the aftermath of the 1939–45 War British policy-makers should again explore this option.

The British origins of this approach to the postwar world can be traced back to at least 1942. At that time, an important document was drawn up in the Foreign Office entitled 'The Four Power Plan' which argued that the major powers should work collectively to prevent any nation from achieving hegemony.[1] Looking back on the immediate postwar period, Gladwyn Jebb wrote in 1947 that 'all our own papers were then based on the assumption that there should in no circumstances be any Anglo-US line-up against the USSR or against Communism'.[2] Once the Labour government came to power in the summer of 1945, the incentive to pursue a concert approach was enhanced. Many in the Labour party, especially on the parliamentary backbenches, felt that Britain should work actively with the Soviet Union. The most determined proponent of the view that Britain should work with both the Soviet Union and the United States was the Prime Minister, Clement Attlee. 'What he [Attlee] wanted was nothing less than a drastic revision of the principles governing British foreign and defence policy; and he believed that the implications of the newly formed United Nations Organisation . . . [were] an overwhelming justification for such a revision'.[3]

The four-power or concert approach therefore entailed the British working with both the Soviets and the Americans over the major issues of the day. Europe's role in this concert approach of the British was twofold. On the one hand, Europe was seen as a major problem area, solutions to which could only be found through the concert approach. On the other, part of Europe, that is to say, France, was in the British view an integral part of that concert approach.

In the summer of 1945 there were many problems that such a concert approach would have to address. However, quite clearly one of the most significant related to the future of Europe and above all Germany. Germany lay defeated in the hands of the wartime Allies. Should it be dismembered, pastoralized or reintegrated into the international political system? The German problem was one over which the British hoped the concert system would work; yet by early 1946, it had not proved possible to reach agreement with either the Soviets or the French on the nature of German recovery, while the Americans had yet to agree to maintain some presence in Europe during the recovery period. The future of France posed different problems for the British than did the future of Germany. Germany was a defeated enemy that had to be reorganized by the major powers to prevent it from threatening to disrupt the peace once more. France, on the other hand, was seen as an important ally once it had recovered from the physical and psychological effects of war and occupation. The desire to include France as one of the major powers at Potsdam and in the occupation of Germany may initially have appeared to be something of a whim on Churchill's part. Yet once the Labour government came to office, it was clear that Anglo-French collaboration would be a major platform in British policy. On return from Potsdam, Foreign Secretary Ernest Bevin argued for 'extensive political, economic and military cooperation throughout Western Europe, with an Anglo-French alliance as the cornerstone'.[4] Such an approach had been an integral part of Deputy Under Secretary of State Sir Orme Sargent's important 'stocktaking after VE Day Memorandum' of 11 July 1945.[5]

Yet France was unable to play a major role in world affairs and unwilling to play the docile junior partner to Britain. The French had their own policies, notably over the future of Germany, which did not always reflect British desires. The concert approach to world affairs broke down by early 1946. There had been many in the Foreign Office and particularly among the Chiefs of Staff who had believed this was always likely.[6] The end of the concert approach was probably marked in February 1946 by the promotion of two people in the Foreign Office who were hostile towards the concert approach. Christopher Warner was appointed Superintending Under Secretary for both the Southern and Northern Departments, while most significantly, Sir Orme Sargent, described by one contemporary as one who 'laughs at the United Nations as he did at the League' became Permanent Under Secretary.[7]

Although there were voices raised in the Cabinet in favour of the concert approach during the same month, from this point British policy moved towards a different conception of great power relations.[8] Although the problems in Germany did not break the concert approach to great power relations, success over the German problem would surely have ensured that the concert approach would have proved more enduring. As it was, British officials began to show interest in notions of a third force. British policy-makers believed in early 1946 that the concert approach was failing for two reasons: the hostility of Moscow and the unpredictability of Washington. British policy-makers began to agree that there was a qualitative difference about the Soviet Union: in effect that it was not possible to deal with Stalin's Russia as previous generations had dealt with

Metternich's Austria or Bismarck's Prussia. Throughout 1946 the Soviet Union put pressure on Iran and Turkey, refused to withdraw its forces from Rumania and Hungary and encouraged its Yugoslav, Bulgarian and Albanian allies to put pressure on Greece. In Poland, the Peasant Party was put under increasing pressure despite apparent popular support.

British attitudes towards the Soviet Union darkened from February 1946 with a Joint Intelligence Committee report on Soviet strategic interests, while in April, the Russia Committee was set up in the Foreign Office to analyse Soviet global strategy.[9] In the Foreign Office's update of Sir Orme Sargent's VE Day memorandum, written in January 1947, it was concluded that 'the only real danger to peace is now the Soviet Union. If the Soviet Union disappeared, or Russia were under a different ideology, the world could soon settle down to peace'.[10]

The problem for Britain, however, was not only the attitude of the Soviet Union. The United States was also deemed to be a problem. In mid-1946, the United States suggested that its zone of occupation in Germany should be merged with the other zones. Only Britain reacted positively, but only after agonizing that it was dangerous to deal 'with the Americans lest they should suddenly change their minds and leave him [Bevin] in the lurch.'[11] With regard to Europe, it was felt that 'the American public are very ignorant of the state of affairs in Germany, and at the moment it is more than ever true that public opinion goads the administration'.[12] In the January 1947 memorandum, the Foreign Office dismissed the Americans as 'a mercurial people unduly swayed by sentiment and prejudice'.[13]

Facing problems with both the Soviet Union and the United States, Britain sought an alternative means of managing global problems, that of developing a third force. This was very much a second-best option to the concert approach but was nevertheless all that Britain seemed to be left with by early 1946. The third force was to incorporate the Empire and the states and empires of western Europe. Naturally, this gave a pre-eminent position to France. As already seen, France had an important role to play in the concert system. Bevin had rejected in November 1945 'the view that all my policy and the policy of H.M. Government must be based entirely on the "Big Three" . . . In the case of France there is a great history and I am convinced that there is a great future.'[14] For Britain, the importance of France to the third force approach was even greater.

The development of the third force offered Britain the possibilities of minimizing the serious dollar difficulties that the United Kingdom faced in 1946 and 1947 through the exploitation of raw materials found in Africa for export. This idea had been supported by the Chancellor of the Exchequer, Sir Stafford Cripps, as well as Bevin.[15] Ideally, this had to be achieved in collaboration with other European nations with imperial possessions in Africa, as part of the development of the third force. Bevin initially sought cooperation between the British, French and Belgian empires in Africa; he hoped later to include the Portuguese and Italians.[16]

As clever as these ideas were in theory, they could never come about in practice. The dollar problem was serious but the central problem for Britain was the instability in Europe and the requirement for its economic reconstruction. For the third force conception to be viable, it would have to address that issue.

Unfortunately for the British, it did not prove possible to coordinate policy with the French. The key problems were in Germany. France sought to annex the Saar and to separate the Ruhr politically from the rest of Germany. Britain, however, feared that the latter would damage European economic recovery, and having rejected ideas about dismembering Germany in January 1945 was unable to support the French position.[17] Thus the ideas about forming a third force based on Anglo-French cooperation could not be realized in terms of practical policy.

The issue that finally ended British interest in the third-force approach was not Anglo-French differences, however, but related instead to changes in American policy. Early in 1946, the British had been convinced that the United States was too unpredictable to rely on. Events throughout 1946 began to question that assumption, however. At the Paris Council of Foreign Ministers in the spring and summer of 1946, the United States made two commitments to the future of Europe. First, Secretary of State Byrnes proposed a draft Treaty on the Disarmament and Demobilization of Germany. The Foreign Office argued that 'we should certainly welcome the proposal as coming from the United States. Although no doubt intended as a cover for a comparatively early United States withdrawal from Germany, it would bind the United States Government nonetheless to the principle and practice of inspection in Germany for 25 years after and the use of force against violations'.[18] Second, the United States proposed that the occupying powers should join their zones of occupation together in economic terms. Britain accepted on 25 July 1946, having agonized over the decision for a month.[19]

The decision was taken for economic reasons, but had two important political effects. In the autumn of 1946, the Foreign Office noted that Bevin 'wished to have the Americans so heavily committed with us in the administration of the British and United States zones that they would find it difficult to leave. He is most anxious not to be backward in all these matters since they would become discouraged.'[20] Further, after the quadripartite control machinery collapsed, the French refusal to join the joint zones meant that British officials in Germany had virtually no contact with the French until the establishment of the High Commission in 1949. Thus the Bizone, as it was called, strengthened Anglo-American ties and weakened Anglo-French ties over the future of Germany and hence Europe. The third important step in the evolution of American policy in Europe came in September 1946 with a speech made by Secretary of State Byrnes in Stuttgart. Byrnes said: 'I want no misunderstanding. We will not shirk our duty. We are not withdrawing. We are staying here. As long as there is an occupation army in Germany, the American armed forces will be part of that occupation army.'[21]

American foreign policy underwent a major change in 1946, but it was a change the British only dimly perceived.[22] As already noted, the third-force conception only arose out of the failure of the United Kingdom to be able to work closely with both the United States and the Soviet Union. By the end of 1946, British policy-makers began to realize that, after all, it might be possible to work closely with the Americans. Yet by early 1947, it was becoming clear to American policy-makers (though not to British) that any such collaboration, due in large part to Britain's economic difficulties, would not be one of equals. With the passing of the third-force approach and the onset of massive economic and financial problems, Britain entered a period of readjustment.

The first half of 1947 was disastrous for the United Kingdom; Hugh Dalton, in his memoirs, called it 'annus horrendus'.[23] By the end of 1946, Britain was seeking a renegotiation of the Fusion Agreement that was to join the British and American zones of occupation, even though the agreement would not come into effect until January 1947. In mid-1946, the Fusion Agreement had appeared to be beneficial to the British since they had to accept half of the financial burden, whereas their zone accounted for two-thirds of the Bizone's deficit.[24] Even the reduced deficit seemed to be too much for Britain six months later. 'The economic situation in the British zone is extremely bad and it is clear that very heavy capital investment will be needed . . . It is clear that this capital investment cannot be found on anything like a fifty-fifty basis . . . The Americans will therefore have to help.'[25]

The British therefore had reason to feel that they had lost control of their policy towards Europe by the end of 1946. Early in 1947 the situation worsened. There was a serious shortage of coal, a problem exacerbated by the exceptionally cold weather, both of which combined effectively to close British industry for three weeks. British foreign policy also seemed to be in full retreat. The Palestine problem was to be referred to the United Nations; an announcement was made that aid to Greece and Turkey could not be renewed, and that British troops would be withdrawn from Greece; while Attlee announced that Britain would withdraw from India within fifteen months.

At this moment, American Secretary of State, George Marshall, announced his initiative to aid the reconstruction of western Europe. It was an initiative that the British warmly welcomed. However, discussions about its implementation were to present the British with problems. The Americans sought to aid Europe as a whole; Britain sought a position apart from the rest of the continent. The arguments came to a head with the visit of American Under Secretary, Will Clayton, to London. Clayton came to London on 24 July 1947 and left two days later. The purpose of his mission was to discuss American financial aid to Britain and Europe. The British felt they deserved a special position in the programme, apart from the rest of Europe. Clayton strongly disagreed, arguing instead for an integrationist strategy for Europe in which the United Kingdom should be treated in the same way as the rest of Europe.[26] British policy-makers were outraged. For Bevin, this American policy was designed to reduce the Anglo-American relationship to the level of that 'between the USSR and Yugoslavia'.[27] Marshall aid was thus interpreted by the British as 'the prelude to an American strategic withdrawal from Europe, not to a vastly stepped-up defence commitment'.[28] The American desire for the British to become involved in European affairs as a European state and not as a great power standing aloof was to be an important theme in British foreign policy for the rest of the decade. However, by that time the British had been able to develop counter-arguments and counter-strategies. In 1947, British policy-makers had been rather caught out by the American approach.

British policy at this time towards Europe could perhaps be characterized by drift and defensiveness. The British sought to maintain their interests as best they could vis-à-vis the United States, while seeking further American involvement in Europe. From the end of 1947 and into 1948, however, the British regained some measure of influence and direction. Ironically, this came in part from the exploitation of the position of weakness into which they had fallen.

Britain had become noticeably weaker in terms of its economic position and political influence by the summer of 1947. Yet it had become more influential with the United States. By October, negotiations had begun once again over the Fusion Agreement. Unlike the previous year, this time an agreement was reached that was widely welcomed in Britain. The new agreement, reached in December, limited Britain's dollar liability in Germany for 1948 to just £28 million, with every likelihood that the actual figure would be only £10 million.[29] Britain's success in these negotiations was due to two factors. First, Britain's economic collapse of the first few months of 1947, which had made it quite clear that the United Kingdom would need major American help in order to remain in Europe. Second, the deepening of the cold war, particularly after the ending of the Moscow Council of Foreign Ministers in the spring of 1947 without agreement. A greater perception of Soviet hostility made more apparent to the United States the costs it would have to bear if the British were forced out of Germany and Europe in the way they had said they had been forced out of supporting Greece and Turkey. In the aftermath of the British withdrawal from the eastern Mediterranean and the promulgation of the Truman Doctrine, the American Military Governor in Germany, General Clay, had sought an assurance that Britain would not withdraw from Germany within twelve months. That gave the British a perfect bargaining opportunity. Attlee gave Bevin permission to give 'the US Government an assurance that, on the understanding that a satisfactory new Fusion Agreement is negotiated, our forces will not be withdrawn before 30 June 1948'.[30] Britain was not looking for an opportunity to withdraw, since 'the presence of British troops in Germany is not merely a guarantee of order in the British zone, but is one of the bases of our whole German policy'.[31] Whereas Byrnes had been unwilling to concede ground to the British, the significance of the deepening of the cold war and Britain's economic collapse were not lost on the new American Secretary of State, who, according to Hugh Dalton, 'would have been horrified at the prospect of our pulling out'.[32]

By the end of 1947, the British felt they had learnt several important lessons. First, that it was no longer possible to work with the Soviet Union. This had been the conclusion confirmed for many who had long suspected this outcome after the Moscow Council of Foreign Ministers in early 1947; British policy-makers, with one or two exceptions, expected the London Council in the winter of 1947 to collapse. It was therefore important to work without Moscow. The second lesson was that the United States was concerned with the future of Europe and amenable to British influence, as had occurred over the new Fusion Agreement. This was a new state of affairs in the postwar world. But there were limits. Britain's economic decline clearly meant that the United States did not regard the United Kingdom as anything like an equal, as Will Clayton's visit to London in the summer of 1947 had demonstrated. Further, the United States had made no long-term commitment to Europe. Thus Britain sought to place the emphasis on political rather than economic policy and to encourage the Americans to commit themselves to Europe's future. The third lesson was that immediate action was needed. Soviet actions seemed more aggressive, while the situation in Europe was serious. It had been apparent from the spring of 1947 that 'the Allied occupation was heading for a disaster of such proportions that it threatened to destroy not only the Germans, but the other nations of western Europe as well; for if Germany became depopulated its neighbours would inevitably be dragged down to a pastoral existence'.[33]

The British were particularly concerned about France in this context. The failure of the European economies to recover after the War had been one factor in the growing strength of the French Communist Party. On 5 May 1947 the coalition government, which had included members of the Communist Party, was dissolved and the Communist Party moved into opposition. Britain was concerned for two reasons. First, it was not clear that Ramadier's Socialist-MRP government would be able to survive without the support of the Communists, who had attracted some five million votes. If it could not, then the Communists might well be strengthened and return to dominate the government. Second, if Ramadier was successful, the British had no faith in the Communists staying within the constitution.[34] The economic crisis, centred on Germany, thus threatened the future of France.

Faced by these three lessons and challenges, British policy-makers devised a bold new line of policy outlined in a paper presented to the Cabinet on 8 January 1948. In the paper, Bevin argued that 'we shall be hard put to it to stem the further encroachment of the Soviet tide . . . This in my view can only be done by creating some form of union in Western Europe'. In response, the Cabinet agreed to 'consolidate the forces of the Western European countries and their Colonial possessions'.[35] This allowed Bevin to make his famous 'Western European Union' speech in the House of Commons on 22 January. In that speech, Bevin argued that 'I hope that treaties will thus be signed with our near neighbours, the Benelux countries, making with our treaty with France an important nucleus in Western Europe. We have then to go beyond the circle of our immediate neighbours . . . We are now thinking of Western Europe as a unit.'[36]

It is a matter of legitimate historical dispute as to the motivations of the United Kingdom in seeking western European union. It has been argued that union was 'a sprat to catch a whale – a device to lure the Americans into giving Western Europe backing in the face of the Soviet threat'.[37] Further, 'Bevin never had any doubt that the key lay in America's willingness to give political as well as economic support to Europe.'[38] Thus, union was used to obtain the protection of the United States. The records can be read in a different way, however. Gladwyn Jebb talked about union as an alternative to the current policy which would lead Britain to 'eventually have to make the dismal choice between becoming a Soviet satellite state or the poor dependent of an American pluto-democracy'.[39] In addition, Bevin's Cabinet paper of 8 January talked about the creation of an Anglo-European 'bloc which, both in population and productive capacity, could stand on an equality with the western hemisphere and Soviet blocs'.[40]

It is statements similar to these that lead some to argue that Britain was seeking the creation of a third force that would act independently of the Soviet Union and the United States. There is, however, another interpretation. During the 1960s debate over French membership of the integrated military structure of NATO, there was much discussion over the distinctions between Europe as a third force and Europe as a second pillar. As a third force, Europe would seek to be independent from both superpowers. As a second pillar, Europe would seek a relationship of equals with the United States, although still be closely associated with Washington. It is this latter form of relationship that the British were probably striving for in early 1948. After all, why should the British suddenly decide not to work with the Americans when that had been their aim throughout the 1940s? Why should Britain, with its large empire and still a great power seek to be dominated by the United States? The notion of second pillar, or the dumb-bell approach, does much to explain British motivations at the time. American strength would help to 'stem the further encroachment of the Soviet tide'. In his speech to the Commons, Bevin had argued that for Western union to be viable, 'The power and resources of the United States . . . will be needed if we are to create a solid, stable and healthy world.' [41] The strength of the west European states working together, however, would prevent Britain from becoming the 'poor dependent of an American pluto-democracy'. [42]

Yet the British desire was to lead to major British arguments with the Europeans and the Americans during 1948 and 1949. On the face of it, this appears rather strange. After all, like the west Europeans and Americans, Britain sought to solve Europe's balance-of-payments' deficit with the western hemisphere through increased production, liberalized trade measures and improved payments measures. Britain also sought a single west-European economy that would have led to major British compromises on economic sovereignty and links with the Commonwealth. The differences between the British on the one hand, and the Americans and Europeans on the other were, however, profound. The Labour government was the only major socialist government in western Europe at the time, unconstrained by coalition. There was therefore an inevitable dispute over the role accorded to free-market forces in the new European economy. Britain preferred 'an extension to western Europe of the principles of economic planning which the Government had adopted for the United Kingdom'. [43] Such a solution was unlikely to be acceptable to Britain's non-Socialist allies.

A further problem arose over the role of sterling. The United States felt that the sterling area prevented the United Kingdom from behaving as a European power, and hence acted as a block to economic union. For the British, however, the sterling area provided the foundation of a multilateral trading area, the loss of which would lead to 'the end of the United Kingdom as a World Power'. [44] This was an issue over which there was no difference between the Labour and Conservative parties. The third major problem arose over the question of supranational authority. Many became interested in the federalization of Europe, notably Averell Harriman, special representative in Europe of the American Economic Cooperation Administration (ECA), David Bruce, the ECA mission chief in Paris, and Henri Spaak, Belgian Prime Minister. Britain, on the other hand, was determined that ultimate decisions should stay under the control of national delegations, and that any interstate organization should be intergovern-mental, not supranational, and should only act as a planning agency. There were therefore three issues that separated Britain from its allies in western Europe and North America: Socialist politics; national ambitions; and British political culture, which would not allow for the loss of so much sovereignty.

There were at work two basic conceptions that varied greatly. The British conception of union was intergovernmental in nature; it looked to the United States to aid Europe economically and politically in order to produce a balance of power that would prevent Soviet domination of Europe. That is, the British

interest in west European union was deeply rooted by 1948 in the politics of the
cold war. Continental European opinion was somewhat different. For France in
particular, the overriding concern was to control any resurgence in German state
power. Perhaps more accurately this notion might be termed unity, an attempt to
pool west European resources in order to control continually the scope of German
decision-making. For the United States, the cold-war problem was central but
European unity would allow the German problem to be greatly diminished,
allowing the attention of the continental Europeans to turn to constraining any
threat of Soviet expansion. Thus, for the Americans, unity would bring the
rewards the British hoped to achieve through union.

These differing conceptions came to the fore in procedural disputes throughout
1948 in the Organisation for European Economic Cooperation (OEEC). The
OEEC was formed in April 1948, after which the Americans sought appointments
from the Europeans of ministerial rank. This was designed to give the OEEC an
independent status and an institutional importance within Europe. That was
something the British wanted to avoid and, as a consequence, appointed Sir
Edmund Hall-Patch who, although extremely able, was only an Under Secretary
in the Foreign Office. As a consequence, by July Harriman was arguing the need
for the appointment of a director who could speak for all the Europeans as he
spoke for the Americans. Since the Belgian Prime Minister, Paul-Henri Spaak,
was the only Cabinet-rank representative, he seemed the natural choice. The
French and Italians also seemed to support his candidacy. British opposition led
Harriman to accuse Britain of not entering wholeheartedly into the work of the
OEEC, while British officials talked about the 'Harriman problem'.[45] The
Americans, however, felt they could not push the British too far. In March, the
American Ambassador in Paris, Jefferson Caffrey, had argued that 'in the absence
of British participation and leadership, it is unlikely that enough European
countries can be brought together to create a unit of sufficient economic
dimensions'.[46] Britain's weakness was relative; France was still weakened by
internal political strife, Italy an ex-enemy power and Germany had not yet
achieved statehood. British influence with Washington came through its position
as a major European power; however in 1945 the United Kingdom had been seen
as a major world power.

The western union approach also had important implications for Britain's
policy towards Germany. There were important moves towards German statehood
but this was to be a divided Germany, associated with the western union. The
British calculated that 'a centralised Reich with 65 million inhabitants would tend
to swamp . . . the present Western system, and there is every reason to believe
that the French Government and indeed the Benelux Governments would decline
to admit such a Germany into Western Union. From this point of view the
division of Germany is essential to our plans.'[47]

The project of western union was undoubtedly hastened by the implementation
of the Berlin blockade. The British had not been confident of being able to resist
Soviet pressure on Berlin. In February the concern was that 'If it seems certain
that whatever our efforts we shall have to withdraw within a fairly short period
we should take the initiative and find some excuse for leaving Berlin voluntar-
ily.'[48] Yet the airlift was a success. Britain lifted some 31 per cent of the total
between 28 June and 8 November, yet it was British rather than American

airpower that was stretched to the limit.[49] Britain was determined not to be defeated; as the Cabinet noted, 'if the Western Allies were forced out of Berlin, the project of Western Union would be fatally weakened'.[50]

The western union approach was widely deemed to have been a success with the signing of the North Atlantic Treaty in April 1949. With that formalization of the European-American relationship, Britain sought to ensure that within the Western alliance it was seen as the leader of western Europe, and consequently the equal of the United States.

After the successful signing of the North Atlantic Treaty, the British sought to use western Europe as a multiplier of diplomatic strength, to assert leadership in Europe and equality with Washington. This, however, was never really to come about. The issue that made this most obvious was the Korean War, which began on 25 June 1950 when the Communist North invaded the South. On many occasions the British sought to restrain what they considered to be American excesses. In July 1950, the British sought to encourage the United States to enter into negotiations with China over the conflict, at a time before the Chinese had entered the war. In reply, Secretary of State Acheson argued that this was not possible due to the twin issues of Formosa and accession to the United Nations. However, Acheson also added that 'the implications of your message and its possible consequences on the relationship between your country and mine might be very serious indeed'.[51] In November, Britain sought to dissuade the Americans from launching an offensive to the Yalu River; within a month, MacArthur's forces were being driven southwards by Chinese forces.[52] Attlee's visit to Washington in December to restrain American thoughts about using atomic weapons and to gain a British veto over their use (certainly from British airfields) was similarly rebuffed. The British had sought a role that Attlee described as 'unequal no doubt in power but equal in counsel' with the Americans; but the Americans had not allowed them this position.[53] Permanent Under Secretary of State, Sir William Strang, recognized this in January 1951. 'We have in fact no alternative but to work with them [the Americans]. For us to join the Soviet bloc would be unthinkable. The establishment of a neutral or independent European block manoeuvring between the Soviet Union and United States, has repeatedly been examined and as often rejected . . . Our problem is to deflect the Americans from unwise or dangerous courses without making a breach in the united front.'[54] More bluntly, Pierson Dixon, formerly Bevin's Principal Private Secretary and Ambassador to Prague, argued that 'we should accept the disagreeable conclusion, in the end, that we must allow the United States to take the lead and follow or at least not break with them. It is difficult for us, after centuries of leading others, to resign ourselves to the position of allowing another and a greater power to lead us.'[55]

If the United Kingdom failed to achieve a position 'equal in counsel' with the Americans, what about the other aspect of policy, leadership of western Europe? In July 1950 the British Ambassador in Washington, Oliver Franks, had written to Attlee to argue that Truman's recent agreement to Attlee's proposal to hold talks over a variety of political and military affairs represented 'acceptance by the US of our partnership in world affairs. This would have been impossible three or four years ago when we were one of the queue of European countries. Now . . . we are effectively out of the queue, one of the two world powers outside

Russia.'[56] Certainly in early 1948 it could have been argued that Britain was exercising a position of leadership in western Europe, but in the intervening two years much had changed. The British had gained a reputation for undermining the movement towards European unity and indeed refused to have any involvement with more radical notions of integration.[57]

British attitudes to European unity also emerged out of British economic weakness. Britain's position had been weakened by the growing dollar deficit, which rose from £82 million in the first quarter of 1949 to £157 million in the second. This led to a devaluation of sterling from $4.03 to the pound to $2.80 in September 1949.[58] The Americans were informed during a meeting between Cripps and Acheson in Washington; the French were not. The French Prime Minister, Henri Queuille, complained of the lack of loyalty of the British; the Americans regarded the handling of the situation as 'a severe setback to the cause of European cooperation'.[59]

The French were able to gain some measure of revenge for what they considered to be the British betrayal in May 1950 with the announcement of the Schuman Plan. Monnet had worked with Bruce in Paris and also Harriman on the Plan while consulting with the German Chancellor, Adenauer. Britain, however, was not informed. Further, once the Plan was announced, Britain was not to be included unless it would endorse the idea of a federal Europe, which it felt unable to do. Unlike early 1948, by 1950 western Europe was unwilling to be led by the British. In the intervening years, France had developed a coherent foreign policy and the Federal Republic had been formed. Britain's central role was therefore lessened. Indeed, the announcement of the Schuman Plan at the London Conference of Foreign Ministers did much to upset British plans. The Conference had been organized according to British views of how the West should be organized: on a strictly hierarchical basis. First, the British and Americans met for two days. Then the French were admitted, as partners in the occupation of Germany. Finally, a full NATO Council was held. The Schuman Plan did much to upset this hierarchy. The ability of the British to act as leader of western Europe was also lessened for political reasons. The Americans had become relaxed about any possible German threat, focusing solely on the Soviet Union. The British, too, had become more relaxed, although to a far lesser extent.[60] In contrast, in October 1950 'it seems that the French are still more obsessed with the dangers that a revival of German militarism may lead than they are with the Soviet menace'.[61] In contrast, the focus of concern for Britain was the Soviet Union, and the consequent need for American support. As Bevin said in May 1950, 'with the support of the Commonwealth, Western Europe was not strong enough to contend with the military danger confronting it from the East'.[62]

These differences led to dispute over the European Army, an idea put forward by French Prime Minister, Rene Pleven, in October 1950, one month after Acheson had put the issue of German rearmament on to the political agenda at the New York Foreign Ministers Meeting. Acheson had offered to send more troops and an American commander to Europe should Germany be rearmed; were rearmament not to be agreed, there was a danger of total American withdrawal. After consideration, Bevin informed the British Ambassador in Paris that 'It is the interest of His Majesty's Government, as a North Atlantic power, to ensure that the defence of Europe is established on a broad North Atlantic, and not a narrow European, basis . . . The first objective of His Majesty's Government is to secure the agreement of the German Federal Government and the German Parliament to a German contribution to the defence of the West. The creation of a European Army and the incorporation in it of German military units is secondary.'[63] The British felt in general terms that 'to keep Germany from the arms of Russia, is bound to invoke some cost to the countries of Western Europe and not least to the United Kingdom'.[64] This perception was not one likely to be articulated in the same way in Paris.

British policy in the period was therefore not greatly successful either in terms of achieving an equality in counsel with Washington, or the leadership of Europe on which that equality was to be based. But, as in the entire postwar period, Britain's policy towards Europe was conditioned by the attitudes and policies of the Soviet Union and the United States.

It is clear from this analysis of British foreign policy aims in the 1945–51 period that the United Kingdom set its policy towards western Europe very much into the context of its relationships with the Soviet Union and particularly the United States. To put it at its most blunt, Britain's policy towards Europe was dependent on its relationship with the United States. Throughout this period, Britain saw Europe both as something separate from the United Kingdom, and as an entity that should be dependent upon London. Therefore in 1945 western Europe was an area in which the great powers were supposed to work in concert. Once this approach had failed, Britain sought to lead a third-force Europe. After the readjustment of early 1947, the United Kingdom sought to organize western Europe into an entity that London could lead in order to gain a position 'equal in counsel' with Washington. Discussions about British integration with western Europe during 1948, 1949 and 1950 were therefore never realistic; as this chapter has tried to demonstrate, Britain saw Europe as an object, not a subject, in international politics and this clearly coloured British attitudes towards the OEEC and the integration of Europe.

The key nations for Britain in western Europe at this time were Germany and France. British policy towards the two was obviously different; one was a defeated enemy, the other a wartime ally. Yet the context for British policy towards both nations was the same. The problems facing both were seen by London in terms of the overall policy-framework of the day. Britain for much of the period sought to obtain loyalty from both and to lead both. In a sense, for British policy-makers, both were within the British sphere of influence. This was a privilege the French refused to recognize and one the Germans also rejected once they formed a government in 1949.

This chapter has sought to examine British aims as well as achievements and failures. In that light it is clear that for the United Kingdom, western Europe had a second-rate status in the global scheme. As Bevin said in February 1951, Britain saw itself as a 'North Atlantic power'.[65] This reference to the special relationship with Washington (which was non-existent for some of the time and rarely worked as the British hoped) was in effect a euphemism for the maintenance of Britain's great-power status. This was a delusion that was to dominate British policy well beyond the first postwar Labour governments.

9 British Perceptions of the European Defence Community

David Weigall

The Pleven Plan, proposed on 24 October 1950, provided for German participation in the collective defence of western Europe without creating a German national army. It was the French reply to the call by Dean Acheson, US Secretary of State, the previous month for German rearmament in the shape of ten divisions within NATO. Like the Schuman Plan, the proposal of a European Defence Community was an attempt to deal with the problem of a reviving Germany. It was a hybrid in which the idea of further European integration was combined with reluctant French acceptance of a West German military contribution.

The French government's tactic was clear. The idea of rearming Germany was understandably highly unpopular, particularly in France. Arguably, though, it could be made acceptable to public opinion if such rearmament was accompanied by firm guarantees and assimilated to the seemingly acceptable process of European integration. This proposal which, with modifications, became the EDC Treaty, would involve both a high degree of supranationalism and a further consolidation of the Cold War in Europe. On the one hand, the European army would contain the Soviet Union and her allies; on the other, it would implicitly contain the revived German military capability by Europeanizing it.

On 27 May 1952 the EDC Treaty was signed by the Six. It was bolstered by further undertakings: a treaty of mutual assistance between the Six and the United Kingdom against external aggression; a protocol extending the NATO guarantees to the Federal Republic; and a declaration by the United States and the United Kingdom to station in Europe 'such forces as they deem necessary and appropriate to contribute to a joint defence of the North Atlantic area'. As a necessary preliminary to the signing of the EDC Treaty, the three occupying powers and the Federal Republic had signed a convention the previous day that terminated the Allied Occupation and returned to the government in Bonn the essential sovereignty of Germany that had been thrown into commission as a result of unconditional surrender. It was intended that the Bonn Convention should become effective after the EDC had been ratified by the parliaments of the signatory states. In March 1953, following Article 38 of the Treaty, the Common Assembly of the European Coal and Steel Community was instructed to work out a draft treaty for a European Political Community embodying the supranational-ist intent.

After much delay, in August 1954 the French National Assembly refused to ratify the Treaty. This promptly led to the very eventuality that the Pleven Plan had been contrived to avert – the rearmament of the Federal Republic as a sovereign state within NATO. Acheson's demand and Pleven's counter-proposal had been advanced against the background of rising international tension and fears for western Europe that followed the outbreak of the Korean War. The United States pressure for German rearmament was emphatic. The British Chiefs of Staff reported that if Britain was subjected to immediate attack she could last only a month at the most before her defences were overrun.[1] As Alfred Grosser put it, 'Could the American General Staff afford to do without the human potential of a country whose population voted 95% anti-Communist and rely on France, whose voters gave the Communist Party 25% of their vote and whose professional army was in Indochina?'[2]

At the time of the signature of the North Atlantic Treaty, serious expectation of a Soviet armed attack on western Europe was not high. While it increased in 1950, western Europeans and Washington were arguably less conscious of any immediate Soviet military threat than of western Europe's relative weakness, disunity and the inability to cope with such a threat if it developed.[3] The United States presence in Europe had been required by western European governments not simply as a deterrent but as a reassurance. For a variety of reasons, which emerged in the long controversy surrounding it, the EDC seemed to many people anything but reassuring, in spite of its double objective of containing Soviet pressure and frustrating any revival of militaristic German nationalism.

During the debate within France over the EDC, which Raymond Aron compared with the Dreyfus Affair for its capacity to divide public opinion, the sheer unpopularity of the prospect of rearming Germans diminished the popular-ity of the idea of European integration. French advocates of the Treaty and Europeanists became identified as slavishly pro-American, as accepting that German rearmament was 'the price France had to pay for the maintenance of the Atlantic Alliance, and not as a free choice corresponding to her own view of her own interests'.[4] Nationalist, neutralist and Communist opinions combined to reject the Treaty, but this outcome illustrated the extent to which the debate in France had been based on certain illusions about the significance of French power within the Atlantic Alliance. As Lerner and Aron commented: 'A substantial number of deputies in the National Assembly voted on the EDC as if the choice available to them was: German rearmament or no German rearmament. As was subsequently demonstrated by events, this was an error of overdefining French freedom of choice . . . Only after the EDC was rejected did it become clear to many deputies that the alternative of no German rearmament had already been foreclosed by the joint Anglo-American decision that, one way or the other, Germany would be rearmed. The only choice left open to French policy was – which way, EDC or NATO? In closing the EDC way that National Assembly made the NATO way inevitable.'[5]

The Labour and Conservative governments in Britain between 1949 and 1955 found themselves faced with the double issue of German rearmament as such and the form that it should take. Both the United Kingdom and the United States originally favoured the NATO option and concurrent negotiations on both options began in 1950. The Pleven Plan and the subsequent EDC Treaty raised the further issue of the extent to which Britain would be willing to involve herself in the process of western European integration and accept supranational institutions. The fact that should be remembered is that, though France acceded to the treaty, both Britain and France rejected participation in the EDC. The sequel of Eden's military offer of 1954 which paved the way for the rearmament of Germany within NATO has raised the question as to whether such a British guarantee in the EDC would have tipped the balance in favour of French ratification.

From the closing years of the Second World War, Churchill, the Foreign Office and the Chiefs of Staff had perceived that the Soviet Union could pose a major threat to western Europe. In such circumstances the United Kingdom would not be able to abandon her wartime commitment to the continent. The establishment of a British zone in north-west Germany, the Dunkirk (1947) and Brussels (1948) Treaties and membership of NATO (1949) indicated a long-term military attachment in peacetime such as no earlier government had contemplated. Britain was, inescapably, committed to Europe. At the same time, such a commitment was only convincing if the United States was persuaded to involve herself on a long-term basis in Europe. The European and transatlantic aspects of British foreign and defence policy were, therefore, intimately connected, as were the British defence commitments east of Suez and the trading ties of the Commonwealth.

The British governments in this period thought not simply of a European balance of power but of a world balance of power, which involved collaboration between western Europe, the United Kingdom and her Commonwealth and the United States. Indeed, throughout the 1950s Britain's foreign preoccupations were primarily extra-European. Through her participation in these alliances, she had though become part of the European balance. She could no longer play the role of the insular arbiter, intervening from time to time. In the words of Chester Wilmot, the military correspondent, 'The ringmaster has become part of the act and the whip is in other hands.' [6] Even if she did not participate in such a union as was envisaged in the EDC Britain would have to continue to maintain substantial military forces on the Continent in peacetime, not only to protect the Atlantic seaboard but also to provide a reassurance of her determination to uphold the freedom of her European neighbours upon whom she was now more militarily dependent than ever in the past.

The response of the British Chiefs of Staff to the issue of West German rearmament was to submit a memorandum on 18 August 1950 which Ernest Bevin, the British Foreign Secretary, enclosed for discussion among the Foreign Ministers of the occupying powers at their forthcoming meeting. Entitled 'German Association with the Defence of the West', this proposed a German contribution far greater than anything discussed to date: twenty active and ten reserve divisions, a tactical air force with 1,100 aircraft for army support and an air defence with 1,000 fighters. It also called for local naval forces. There was also at this time a particular British apprehension about the northern flank, especially the gap between Iceland and southern Norway. To cover this Britain needed to have the use of radar stations and fighter airfields in Norway and Denmark, which, so far, had been refused to Britain or any other member of NATO. This problem was directly connected with the defence of Germany. One of the main reasons given by the Danes for their refusal was that they could not afford to provoke Soviet hostility. The overland route to Denmark through Schleswig-Holstein could not be protected until the Allied armies in West Germany were reinforced by German divisions. If West Germany were not rearmed there was little prospect of the United Kingdom obtaining the facilities she needed to cover the gap in her own air and naval defences.

While Bevin pressed hard and successfully for government acceptance of the need for German rearmament, his initial response to the Pleven Plan was very critical. It was, in the main, he considered, 'a manoeuvre in French domestic politics . . . (with) the subsidiary purpose of securing that the Deputy Com-mander-in-Chief of the integrated forces would be a Frenchman'.[7] In a paper to the Cabinet Defence Committee he claimed that 'one of the ideas underlying the French plan is undoubtedly that of a continental bloc under French leadership which, while linked with the Atlantic Community, would constitute in world politics a force with some measure of independence'. Such a bloc, he said, was 'a sort of cancer in the Atlantic body . . . we must nip it in the bud . . . I thought it was a mistake,' he commented 'to lay too much emphasis on the word "Europe" and to speak in terms of a European Army. The United States and Canada, together with other members of the British Commonwealth, would all be involved and the issue at stake would be the defence of the whole free world.'[8] This reflected his own preference for a western union in which the United Kingdom would assume a pivotal role and be able, together with the Commonwealth, to develop her own power and influence to equal that of the United States and the Soviet Union. In any case, German armed forces, he argued, would be more acceptable and less dangerous if they were not part of a purely European defence force which they might well come to dominate. This was an argument strongly advanced within France by opponents of the EDC. On the other hand, any plan for the defence of western Europe only as far as the Rhine was plainly unacceptable. Among other things, it would mean the evacuation of the north-east provinces of The Netherlands in a crisis. The western powers, Bevin maintained, must be willing and able to fight as far east as possible in Europe.

In the United States General Marshall among others echoed Bevin's scepticism, regarding the Pleven Plan as 'hopeless'. He was concerned both by its seeming impracticability and the delay it would involve in a pressing matter. There were also some suspicions in the United States that this might be a scheme (at least to some extent) to exclude the United States from European affairs.

Bevin and Attlee's approach to western Europe was to favour piecemeal, functional collaboration. While they questioned whether western Europe would ever be strong enough to defend itself, they and their Conservative successors recoiled before the supranational, federalistic implications of the EDC. They were highly suspicious of the idea of European political union. At the OEEC Council meeting Sir Stafford Cripps, the Chancellor of the Exchequer, had stated that the United Kingdom could not integrate her economy into that of Europe in any way that would prejudice the discharge of her responsibilities towards the Commonwealth and the rest of the sterling area. (At this time only 25 per cent of British exports were going to Europe as against over 40 per cent to Commonwealth countries.) Though some Labour MPs were temporarily attracted by the neutralist potential of a united Europe, the Labour Party boycotted the Hague Conference organized by the European Movement. The National Executive Committee in its document 'European Unity' probably reflected general sentiment throughout the country when it commented: 'European peoples do not want a supranational authority to impose agreement. They need an international machinery to carry out agreements which are reached without compulsion.'[9]

During Herbert Morrison's tenure of the Foreign Secretaryship the Labour Government modified its attitude to the proposal for a European Army. There were two main reasons for this.[10] First the Truman Administration had come round to the view that the most practicable way of persuading western Europe, and particularly France, to accept German rearmament would be along the lines suggested by Pleven, though not without important modifications to the original proposals. Secondly, just as Pleven used the avoidance of an independent West German military contribution in the plan to placate widespread opposition to the idea of rearmament in France, so Attlee's government advanced the European army idea to pacify critics of German rearmament within the Labour Party.

The joint statement by Morrison, Schuman and Acheson in Washington on 14 September 1951 welcomed the Pleven Plan as 'a very important contribution to the effective defence of Europe'. Morrison also affirmed that the British government wished 'to establish the closest possible association with the European continental community at all stages of its development'.[11] The key word here was 'association'. The Cabinet were informed this was the 'first formal recognition by the US and France of the special position of the UK in relation to European unity, and of our inability to integrate fully with Europe'.[12] They were optimistically assured that this declaration would restore French trust in British policy. On the contrary. The view of successive French governments was to be that United Kingdom association with the EDC was inadequate. Nothing short of full British participation would suffice, to counterbalance the Federal Republic. French apprehensions at this time were both military and economic. The Federal Republic was experiencing soaring industrial production and investment, while the French economy was in the doldrums.

Before Pleven's announcement of his plan, Winston Churchill, Leader of the Opposition, had already called for a European army within which 'we would all bear a worthy and honourable part'.[13] He had even accepted an amendment by the Consultative Assembly of the Council of Europe calling for a European Minister of Defence. But, as he later explained to Anthony Nutting MP, 'I meant it for them, not for us'. He later explained in a message to Eisenhower, then President of the United States:

I disliked on military grounds the Pleven European Army Plan which began with mixing races in companies if not platoons. At the time when I saw you in Paris I was talking of it as a 'sludgy amalgam'. However when I came to power again I swallowed my prejudices because I was led to believe that it was the only way in which the French could be persuaded to accept the limited Germany army which was my desire. I do not blame the French for rejecting the EDC, only for inventing it. Also I accepted the American wish to show all possible patience and not to compromise the chances of EDC . . . All this time kept one aim above all others in view, namely a German contribution to the defence of an already uniting Europe.[14]

Eisenhower recalled of the earlier period that he used 'every resource . . . including argument, cajolery and sheer prayer to get Winston to say a single kind word about the EDC'.[15]

Anthony Eden had commented that he 'feared that the plan [for the EDC], imaginative as it was, might fail; for just that reason. It seemed to attempt too much. . .' He awaited the opportunity, he said, 'to work out a more modest scheme . . . without elaborate political superstructures'.[16] In practice he was to steer a narrow course between the need to support the EDC idea from the outside and the fear of being drawn into a European federation 'by the back door'. From the start he was ready to step forward with an alterntive, less ambitious, scheme if the EDC failed by itself. In his lecture 'Britain's Strategic Relationship to Europe' given in 1953, Chester Wilmot echoed the reasoning behind the Government's view when he said, 'Britain should not join the EDC because in the long run a European Army could only function effectively if it were responsible to a European political authority. Indeed, one of the main reasons why the United States has fostered the EDC is the hope that it will accelerate the development of a European Union, and Britain, because of her world-wide responsibilities to the Commonwealth and Empire, could not surrender her sovereignty to such a federal organization. If she were to do so, she would lose the position of leadership she now holds within the Commonwealth for her loyalties would be divided and she would not be so well placed as she is today to enlist the resources of the Commonwealth in Europe's support and defence.'[17]

The Truman administration originally hoped that the ratification of the EDC would take place before the end of 1952, an optimistic deduction based on the swift progress of the ECSC. In fact, though, the official United States attitude towards Britain's relations with the proposed army were ambivalent.[18] While there was general agreement in Washington that Britain's place, ultimately, was in a united Europe, the United States did not press immediate British participation. How do we explain this stance?

While, obviously, British opposition was a major consideration, there were others besides. Bearing in mind the global reach of the policy of containment, there could be no guarantee that the supranational EDC would be willing, suitable or able to divert any measure of its military resources to other parts of the world. Anyway, this was not its purpose. But Britain with her worldwide connections and interests could. There was, furthermore, the distinguishing fact that Britain had a nuclear capability. Some wondered whether this might not encourage third force and neutralist tendencies in western Europe – if Britain placed her deterrent at the disposal of a European defence force.

In attempting to resolve the question of German rearmament on terms acceptable to public opinion the EDC idea also crucially posed the issue of Britain's role in Western defence. If this had appeared to be resolved with the signature of the North Atlantic Treaty, it was now open to re-examination. Schuman had commented: 'Alliance defence and European defence . . . do not exclude each other and do not cut across each other. They occupy different

planes.' But where did this leave Britain? For the British, the United States and
the French perceptions were significantly different. According to Schuman 'the
Atlantic system may answer and satisfy urgent yet passing needs; the problem of
Europe persists'. To Anthony Eden, reflecting the official British view, the North
Atlantic Treaty was 'not merely some temporary expedient arising from the threat
of Soviet aggression . . . We regard it as a permanent association'.[20]

The initial United States response was to persuade the United Kingdom to
emphasize that she would undertake to support the EDC from the outside while
firmly anchoring the immediate security of the West on the Anglo-American
alliance. The integration of European defence would at the same time indirectly
assist the strategy of containment in other parts of the world: something that
could be undertaken by the United States and by Britain and her Commonwealth.

The Eisenhower presidency saw mounting United States impatience with the
slowness of progress towards ratification of the EDC combined with the Secretary
of State, John Foster Dulles's evident intolerance of British aloofness from the
scheme. (In the early stages of the debate Eisenhower had suggested that full
British participation might be 'a stumbling block rather than a help'.) Now
Congress clamoured for the immediate completion of the treaty and held out the
futher unification of Europe as a condition for future United States aid – the so-
called 'or–else policy'. This was explicit in the Richards Amendment of 1953
which provided that half of the military appropriations for Europe should be
made available only when the EDC was finally agreed. 'Asia first' and 'Fortress
America' were dominant themes in the United States debate over its global role,
the latter symbolized in the declaration of the strategic doctrine of 'massive
retaliation'. Within a week of becoming Secretary of State, Dulles had already
warned: 'If France, Germany and England go their separate ways, then certainly it
would be necessary to give a little rethinking to America's own foreign policy in
relation to Western Europe.'[21]

Time, though, was running out. While the Federal Republic ratified the EDC in
March 1953, followed by Belgium, Luxembourg and The Netherlands, France and
Italy had still not ratified it by August 1954; opposition to it was mounting in
both countries. In France two groups hostile to the EDC, the Gaullists and the
Communists, had strengthened their representation in the National Assembly.
Long-established doubts were encouraged by the relaxation in East-West relations
following the death of Stalin and the ending of the Korean War. Acheson had
detected a lessening of tension as early as September 1951: 'The bloom was off
NATO,' he commented. 'The fears of a year before had faded as music wafted
westward from the World Festival of Youth and Students for Peace in East
Berlin. All this led politicians and writers in Western Europe to question the
danger from the East and the need for rearmament upon which the Americans so
continually harped.'[22]

In Britain the Government did not question the need for German rearmament,
though the prospect of Four Power talks including the Soviet Union suggested it
would be diplomatically imprudent to appear impatient or strident about it.
Within the Labour Party, however, a major division had developed over German
rearmament: a division that was particularly acrimonious in 1953-4. Aneurin
Bevan criticized the United States for their insistence on arming West Germany
instead of seeking agreement with the Soviet Union for a united, neutral

Germany. Illustrative of this line of thought was the *Tribune* pamphlet 'It Need Not Happen'. This dismissed as worthless the safeguards under which German divisions were to be created in the EDC: 'The 12 divisions will be Nazi-led and Nazi-trained . . . The European Defence Community in fact is not an alternative to a German national army, but merely the first step towards its creation.'[23] The serious purpose behind such alarmism was the avoidance of a further consolidation of the Cold War in Europe before all possibilities had been explored in negotiation with the Soviet Union.

In France, Laniel's government fell on 12 June 1954 on the question of Indochina. Mendès–France, his successor, at once displayed his own doubts about the prospects of French ratification of the EDC Treaty by proposing yet further amendments. In the event, these were to satisfy neither the other members of the six nor the French National Assembly. While Mendès–France's motives in the ensuing crisis have been much discussed and remain far from clear, Britain's role was unmistakable. The United States expected her to ensure French compliance with Washington's wishes as promptly as possible. She was cast to be prime mover in French ratification. Dulles saw this as nothing less than an obligation on Britain, since he held her, at least in part, as responsible for the interminable delays. Unlike the ECSC, the Pleven Plan had been put forward with the firm hope that Britain would participate. Within twenty-four hours of signing the EDC Treaty the French Cabinet had let it be known that Britain must establish much closer ties with the army if there were to be any chance of its ratification. (It also insisted that Indochina be considered as part of the equation of Western defence.)

Churchill's position was unequivocal. In his statement to the House of Commons on 11 May 1953 he showed impatience with critics of British non-participation: 'We are not members of the EDC, nor do we intend to be merged into a Federal European system . . . We are 'with' them not 'of' them. We will exchange officers for command and training and cooperate in many other ways . . . We have stationed our largest military force on the Continent . . . We have the strongest armed force between the Rhine and the Elbe . . . have intimately associated our air forces . . . What more is there we could give, apart from completely merging ourselves with the European military organization? We have not got a single divisional formation in our own island. No nation has ever run such risks in times which I have read about or lived through, and no nation has ever received such little recognition for it.'[24]

During the four-year debate over the idea of a European army the French involvement in Indochina became a significant consideration in the arguments against signature and ratification. Just as British perceptions in this period were conditioned by the United Kingdom's extra-European role, so, too, French decisions in Europe and for Europe cannot be evaluated without an appreciation of France's commitment in the Far East. From the beginning the French military establishment had considered it essential for France to maintain the biggest force in any European army. But how could this be reconciled with the mounting demands on manpower and resources of the losing struggle in Indochina? In the absence of a British military counterweight in the EDC, the Federal Republic would come to dominate it – this was the French apprehension, shared by some on this side of the Channel as well. On the other hand, as Gladwyn Jebb warned, the whole saga of German rearmament would leave France an unwilling ally, resentful of Anglo-Saxon pressure.

There was a certain similarity in the British and French predicaments. Here were two old colonial powers respectively under pressure from the United States. In 1953–4 Britain's role was less that of a power enjoying a 'special relationship' with the transatlantic superpower than that of a junior functionary pressing American wishes on a reluctant France.[25] The question of prestige loomed large. France saw no reason why she should not have equality of status and recognition with Britain in international affairs. She consequently saw no reason why Britain should be allowed to stay outside the EDC. As it stood, the EDC condemned France to an inferior position *vis-à-vis* the Anglo-Saxon powers. Moreover, for those who wanted to see a more independent Europe emerge, it was by no means clear that the EDC would favour greater autonomy since Article 18 of the Treaty stipulated that the European defence forces would be assigned to SACEUR.

Both Britain and France, therefore, were constrained by overseas commitments. They also aspired to some role of independence in world affairs. In Britain's case this was both in her relationship with the United States and with Europe. The French apprehension is clearly summed up in the following comment by Bidault: 'While France wishes to build Europe, she does not wish to be engulfed by it and thereby lose her individual personality so that the continental character of France would no longer be considered except through the European Community of which France would be a part but not necessarily a spokesman. The position of France in the Standing Group could not be questioned. The creation of the European Defence Community could not separate France and the other territories and countries who were marching with her along the road to progress from the association of the Big Three.'[26] Churchill's habit of confining talks over a number of issues, like the Middle East and the Atoms for Peace proposal, to bilateral delegations with the United States did not help. Nor did the humiliation of Dien Bien Phu make the French less sensitive to considerations of national prestige. This has led one contemporary French scholar to conclude that by the time of the rejection of the EDC, 'the real issue was less the rearming of Germany than the reluctance of many French people to be the only ones to have a big army absorbed into this integrated force and to be deprived of a special position in NATO'.[27]

The threat by Dulles of an 'agonizing reappraisal' by the United States, which he explained, would have consequences for both Britain and the continent, impelled the British government to resolve the dilemma posed by French rejection of the EDC. The implication behind Dulles's warning was that the United States would fall back on 'peripheral defence', which meant the defence of their perimeter of bases stretching in a crescent from Iceland to Turkey. Eden explained to Churchill: 'I realize it would be an unprecedented commitment for the United Kingdom, but the hard fact is that it is impossible to organize an effective defence system in Western Europe without a major British contribution. The situation will persist for many years to come. By recognizing this fact and giving the new commitment we may succeed in bringing the Germans and French together and keep the Americans in Europe.'[28]

What emerged from Eden's brisk diplomatic initiatives was an intergovernmental rather than supranational grouping, the WEU, the Brussels Treaty

Organization reinforced by the membership of Germany and Italy. The agreement of 23 October 1954 was supported by the British undertaking to 'continue to maintain on the mainland of Europe, including Germany, the effective strength of the United Kingdom forces which are now assigned to SACEUR – four divisions and the tactical air force'. One can perhaps ask to what extent this commitment was additionally influenced by Britain's development of her own nuclear deterrent. The Defence White Paper of 1954 argued that this force 'should have an increasing effect upon the Cold War by making less likely such adventures on the part of the Communist World as their aggression in Korea. This should be of benefit to us by enabling us to reduce the great dispersal of effort which the existing international tension has hitherto imposed upon us'.[29] In fact the strategic nuclear capability proved irrelevant to the internal security problems normal in overseas areas. European and overseas security needs remained competitors for the same type of forces. Only three years after the Eden pledge, the 1957 Defence Review announced a 30 per cent cut in British forces in Germany.

The United States Secretary of State described the British commitment as 'a basic change in British foreign policy'. 'Now,' Dulles said, 'Britain, recognizing that modern developments have largely obliterated the Channel, was ready to identify itself irrevocably with continental Europe.' This observation was patently premature. In practice the second half of the 1950s did little or nothing to suggest any irrevocable reorientation. Until the Macmillan application in 1961 for Britain to join the Common Market, United States and British official thinking on west European integration were constantly at odds.[30] The Suez Crisis of 1956 dramatically illustrated the conflict between United States and Anglo-French perceptions. The attempt by Britain and France to play a major military role independently of both Europe and NATO and the extra-European preoccupations that lay behind this action further help to explain why both, in their different ways, had refused to participate in the EDC.

10 Italy and the European Defence Community: 1950-54

Antonio Varsori

The outbreak of hostilities in the Korean peninsula came as a shock for the Western world. Until June 1950 Soviet foreign policy had been perceived by Western leaders mainly as a political and propaganda threat, albeit supported by a powerful military structure. The dramatic events in the Far East seemed to confirm the most pessimistic views of Stalin's ambitions. The signature of the North Atlantic Treaty in April 1949 had not compensated for the apparent imbalance between Soviet military power and a weak Western defence system in the European continent. The Korean War, on the other hand, seemed destined to divert American troops from the European theatre to the Far East and to mean a slowing down in the flow of military aid to Europe.[1] In the opinion of the Western great powers, in particular the United States and Great Britain, German rearmament and West Germany's involvement in the Atlantic defence system became fundamental aims that the West had to achieve rapidly. In September 1950, American Secretary of State Dean Acheson put forward the proposal for the creation of German military units.[2] This project, warmly supported by most of the members of the Atlantic alliance, met with strong opposition from the French government. During the previous years the French authorities had been compelled, in particular by American and British pressures, to give up most of their ambitions about a settlement of the German question, which could have assured France a lasting guarantee against any German 'revanche'. So the French had agreed to the setting-up of a West German state and to the growing involvement of West Germany in the economic reconstruction of western Europe. The French government, however, still had deep suspicions about the role west Germany could play in the international context. The problem of the French attitude towards Germany's future was not confined to the almost traditional French fear of a new aggressive German 'Reich'. The French government aimed at recovering a leading role in the Western half of the continent: an early rehabilitation of Germany was regarded in Paris as a serious threat to such an aspiration. Moreover the hypothesis of a German rearmament was, in the opinion of French leaders, far more dangerous, as it would have given the Bonn government more room for manoeuvre in the international field. Some French authorities in particular feared that in such a case West Germany could be tempted to reach an agreement with Moscow on the reunification of the two Germanies in return for Germany's 'neutrality' in the cold war.[3]

From the summer of 1948 France had tried to face both the question of the relationship with her eastern neighbour and the problem of the leadership in western Europe by exploiting the ideals of European integration. Between 1948 and 1949 the French authorities had favoured the setting-up of the Council of Europe. After the minor role played by this organization became evident, French Foreign Minister Robert Schuman, with the advice of Jean Monnet, put forward the proposal for the creation of a European Coal and Steel Community in May 1950. Five European countries (Italy, West Germany, Belgium, Holland and Luxemburg) agreed to the Schuman Plan. Through this the French government could hope to maintain some form of control over two fundamental areas of the German – and European – economy. Moreover the French could please the Truman administration, which considered the recovery of western Europe and European integration as pillars in American policy towards the 'old continent'.[4]

In October 1950, after the difference of opinion with Washington and London on the issue of German rearmament had become evident, the French, who were conscious of their weak international position, believed it possible to resort to European integration as the best means to achieve both the strengthening of the Western defence system – which was also in France's interest – and a 'European' (i.e. French) control over West Germany's rearmament. In a speech to the *Assemblée Nationale*, Prime Minister René Pleven sketched out the plan for the formation of a European Defence Community along the lines of the ECSC project. The French plan was for small German units to be integrated into a European Army under a supranational authority. The Pleven Plan was the starting point of a complex political process on which the Western world was compelled to focus its attention during the first half of the 1950s.[5]

Italy's attitude towards the cold war and in particular to the military-strategic aspects of this conflict was ambivalent. Rome had been one of the founding members of the Atlantic Pact, but its accession to the Western military system had been perceived by many Italian moderate anti-Communist leaders and diplomats as an unpleasant necessity. The cabinet led by the Christian Democrat leader, Alcide De Gasperi, had come to the conclusion that it would be useful for Italy to become a member of the Atlantic alliance only in late 1948, when it was realized that Italy's involvement in the Pact was the prerequisite for the peninsula to be accepted by the major Western powers as a full member, not only of the Western defence system, but also of any future initiative aimed at developing political and economic cooperation.[6] Until then De Gasperi and Foreign Minister Count Carlo Sforza had carefully avoided any foreign-policy initiative that could be regarded as a symbol of Italy's involvement in the military aspects of the cold war. This cautious attitude had been mainly due to the lack of confidence large sectors of the Italian public opinion had, as a consequence of the bitter memories of the 1939 German-Italian alliance and of the ensuing defeat, in military commitments,[7] as well as to the existence of powerful pro-Soviet Communist and Socialist parties.[8] On the other hand Italy's involvement in the Atlantic Pact had mainly been the result of France's pressures on her 'Atlantic' partners, and, to a minor extent, of United States' goodwill. In early 1949 Paris and Washington had been able to overcome strong British objections to Italy becoming a full member of the Western alliance.[9] The sympathetic United States' view of Italy's request was evident, notably in the attitude of some State Department officials who hoped to strengthen De Gasperi's prestige through a 'diplomatic' achievement.[10] However, French policy had been based on more complex assumptions. The French had hoped to rely on a faithful Italian 'junior partner', and Italy's accession to the Atlantic Pact was part of a broader French policy aimed at diverting American strategic interests in the 'Atlantic' context from northern Europe to the southern flank of the alliance. France was thus to be seen as the vital link between the Atlantic Ocean and the Mediterranean Sea, as well as between the Anglo-Saxon powers and German.[11]

After April 1949 Italian foreign-policy makers could not forget the role the United States and France had played in supporting Italy's accession to the Atlantic alliance, but they often believed that it was now possible to rely on an unlimited sympathetic French and American attitude. On many occasions Italian diplomats and politicians overrated Western, in particular American, interest in the peninsula.[12] This misperception, on the other hand, was largely based on the sympathetic attitude the United States had apparently shown to Italy's needs from the Second World War onwards. During 1949 the Italian government tried to exploit its 'Atlantic' choice as an instrument in order to strengthen Italy's international position. In spite of Italy's early adhesion to Europeanist and Western ideals, the first aims of Palazzo Chigi – at that time the seat of the Italian Ministry for Foreign Affairs – were: (a) to overcome the political, economic and military clauses of the peace treaty; (b) to gain for Italy a major role in two traditional spheres of influence (western Europe and the Mediterranean); and (c) to recover a status in international affairs that would be similar to the one enjoyed by France and Great Britain.[13] Italy's ambitions, however, were often frustrated by its Atlantic partners. De Gasperi's 'Atlantic' choice, on the other hand, did not mean only the recognition, albeit a theoretical one, of Rome's role in the Western system: it also meant definite military and economic commitments. But the Italian government did not wish to devote its scanty financial resources to the strengthening of the Italian Armed Forces. The economic ministries in particular were obviously ready to accept any United States economic and military aid, but, in their opinion, any Italian financial effort in the field of defence could mean a severe blow to the hope of a quick economic recovery.[14] Moreover, a growing Italian commitment in the military aspects of Atlantic cooperation could be regarded by large sectors of the Italian public opinion as a symbol of De Gasperi's subservience to American strategy as well as a dangerous involvement of the peninsula in the cold war. De Gasperi and Sforza, on the other hand, had tried to convince Italian public opinion and political parties that Italy's accession to the Atlantic Pact had been a move aimed at preserving peace and a part of a broader 'Western' choice, whose ultimate aim was Euro-American economic and political cooperation.[15] As an obvious consequence of such a contradictory attitude, in early 1950 several Western diplomats were developing a critical view of De Gasperi's foreign policy and Italy was playing a minor role in the Western bloc.[16]

In the late spring of 1950 the Italian government gave a positive evaluation of the Schuman Plan and Italy became a partner in the negotiations aimed at setting up ECSC. Rome's choice had been mainly due to: (a) Italy's aspiration to an international status similar to the one enjoyed by Paris; (b) the need to maintain friendly relations with France; (c) the wish to please the American administration; and (d) last but not least, the hope of some economic advantages. Moreover it was possible to show to Italian public opinion that De Gasperi's and Sforza's 'Western choice' meant, above all, further progress in European economic cooperation, from which the Italians could get definite benefits.[17]

The outbreak of the Korean War was perceived by the Italian authorities as a serious threat to these goals. In the internal context the armed conflict in the Far East seemed destined to strengthen the 'peace campaign' developed after the signature of the Atlantic Pact by the Socialists and the Communists. In the international field, besides the obvious suspicions about any future Soviet move, De Gasperi and Sforza feared further American and Atlantic pressure in order to get a stronger Italian military commitment.[18] American proposals for German rearmament, however, were regarded favourably by Italian diplomatic and governmental circles. Germany's involvement in the Atlantic defence system could mean the move eastwards of a Western front from the Rhine to the Elbe and such a strategic development would represent a better guarantee for Italy's security.[19] The Italian government, on the other hand, was in favour of Germany's gradual rehabilitation. Germany had always been a traditional element in Italian foreign policy. In Bonn, as in Rome, there was a Catholic leadership.[20] The strong German economic system could add further resources to Western defence with less heavy commitments for other Atlantic partners. Last but not least, De Gasperi and Sforza hoped to convince a disappointed American administration of Italy's steady allegiance to Atlantic ideals and aims showing a firm Italian support for the plans worked out in Washington.

The appearance of a contrast between Washington and Paris on the issue of German rearmament led the Italian authorities to adopt a more cautious attitude. If the Rome government did not want to and perhaps could not oppose American plans, and wished to strengthen its relationship with Bonn, it was impossible to forget that France was an important partner. Paris had often been sympathetic towards most of Italy's international ambitions. Between September and October 1950, Sforza's instructions to Italian diplomatic representatives abroad largely reflected the uneasiness of the Italian position. Italy's embarrassment seemed destined to increase when, in October 1950, the French government launched the Pleven Plan. The project for a European army became the target of strong criticism on the part of the British and Americans, who regarded the French initiative as a mere device to delay the rearmament of West Germany. Italian diplomats and politicians partially shared such a view; they had more confidence in the feasibility of the American plan. But the Italian government was unable to refuse the French proposal for diplomatic talks, to be held in Paris, about the Pleven scheme.[21] Italy's rejection of the French offer would have meant a crisis in bilateral relations and could have caused doubts about Italy's allegiance to the ideals of European supranational integration. Italy, furthermore, was already involved in the ECSC negotiations. Last but not least, the Italian authorities feared that an early failure of the Pleven Plan could cause a major political crisis in Paris and, as there were similarities between the French internal situation and the Italian one, it seemed very likely that such a crisis could have serious consequences in the Italian peninsula.[22]

For a few weeks after Pleven's speech, the Italian government wavered between, on the one hand, stating its support of American plans and, on the other, agreeing to French proposals. This difficult situation led the Italian authorities to choose a 'wait and see' attitude: the French offer was not rejected but the Italian representatives in the Atlantic organization stressed the usefulness of Germany's involvement in Western defence.[23] In the meantime the French initiative made some progress and the Pleven government promoted a conference on the setting-up of a European army. A few days before the opening of the Paris negotiations, De Gasperi had important talks with Robert Schuman on the occasion of a bilateral French-Italian conference held in Santa Margherita Ligure. As for the Pleven Plan, the Italian statesman confirmed Italy's adhesion to the conversations to be held in the French capital, but he reminded his French colleague of the Italian government's doubts about the project worked out by the Quai d'Orsay. De Gasperi stressed in particular how any future European Defence Community had to develop close ties with the Atlantic alliance; the latter, moreover, in the opinion of the Italian government, had to maintain a leading role in the Western military system.[24] De Gasperi thought that the relationship between the United States and western Europe, embodied in the Atlantic Pact, was more relevant than any merely European defence scheme – and French projects could not disregard American opinions.

In February 1951 the conference on EDC opened in Paris. Italy, West Germany, Belgium and Luxemburg had agreed to the French proposal. The Dutch government sent observers and the Low Countries became full partners in the negotiations only in October 1951. The British, as in the case of the Schuman Plan, did not wish to be involved in a supranational scheme but could not neglect the progress of the Paris negotiations. As for the American authorities, they carefully followed the work of the EDC conference.[25] The Italian delegation was headed by an outstanding member of the Christian Democrat party, Paolo Emilio Taviani. Yet the role played by the Italian delegates during the early stages of the talks was a minor one. The EDC project was arousing growing suspicions among Italian diplomats, politicians and military leaders. The Italian authorities believed it was useless to take any active part in the negotiations, as in Italian governmental circles there was widespread conviction that the difficulties related to the technical aspects of the project and the contrast between French interest and American views and British scepticism would lead in a short time to a stalemate in the Paris negotiations. So it seemed possible for Italy to avoid any definite stand, while paying lip service to the ideals of European integration.[26]

During the first half of 1951 there was a sudden development in the American attitude towards the EDC plan. As a result of French pressures and promises, the influence of Eisenhower's views on European defence, and an internal debate in the United States about Washington's foreign-policy aims, the Truman administration began to regard the establishment of a European Army as a major element in American policy towards the 'old continent'. Also, as a consequence of the development in United States' foreign policy, in late July 1951 the Paris conference was able to formulate an important document, the 'rapport inter-imaire', which outlined the main features of the EDC. This document had to be carefully examined by the governments of the Six involved in the Paris talks but everybody regarded the 'rapport' as a significant step towards the setting-up of a European Defence Community. Since, in the summer of 1951 the Soviet Union was still regarded as a real military threat, France needed growing American support in the Indochina conflict and the Western world was developing forms of closer political, economic and military cooperation, from ECSC to NATO. The EDC seemed destined to become a military and political reality in a not too distant future.[27]

The apparent feasibility of the EDC plan was considered by the De Gasperi government as a serious threat to Italian interests. From the military and strategic point of view the Italians feared that EDC could replace the European structures of NATO. In the Atlantic context Italy had at least been accorded a definite role, in particular as a useful element in the southern flank of the alliance; Italian military authorities, moreover, were developing close ties with their American counterparts and hoped to benefit from American plans for European rearmament. These events, on the other hand, seemed to confirm Italy's aspiration to a 'special relationship' with Washington. In EDC, on the contrary, the Italians would have lost any opportunity for strengthening bilateral cooperation with the United States, while the French – or a French-German axis – would have become the real partners of the American administration in European defence issues. Furthermore the EDC would have confirmed the importance for NATO of the central European front to the detriment of Italy's security and Mediterranean interests.[28]

As for the economic aspects of the EDC plan, the hypothesis of a common defence budget under the control of a supranational body was regarded with deep suspicion by leading Italian politicians such as Giuseppe Pella and Giovanni Malagodi. They feared that the major partners in EDC (France and Germany) would work out the most relevant economic and financial decisions and Italy's peculiar interests would be forgotten. The Rome government would be compelled by its European partners to commit growing resources to defence needs, seriously threatening the process of economic reconstruction. Italy's European allies had already shown scant interest in the economic aspirations of the De Gasperi government. Finally, Italian economic authorities feared that the setting up of the EDC could mean 'European' wages for the members of the European army. That would have led to a sharp increase in the wages of Italian officers, NCOs and privates. Obviously, in a short time the other sectors of the Italian civil service would have requested better wages, fuelling a dangerous inflationary process.[29]

It was impossible for De Gasperi and the members of his government to forget the likely political consequences of the EDC. Most Italians thought the Pleven Plan was a consequence of the cold war, a further military alliance, whose main aim was to face the Soviet Union. The PCI and the PSI had already started a propaganda campaign, which singled out De Gasperi's 'subservience' to American 'imperialism', as well as the danger of German 'revanche'. The EDC issue had become a useful instrument, one which the parties of the Left were skilfully exploiting to provoke both opposition to De Gasperi's foreign policy in the country and open dissension among the political parties that formed the coalition government led by the Christian Democrat statesman.[30] De Gasperi could not forget the criticism of the Right-wing parties – monarchists and neo-Fascists – that openly stated it was the duty of the Italian authorities to exploit Italy's adherence to the EDC plan as the instrument of a nationalist policy. In their opinion, the Rome government had to make use of the EDC issue to compel the American administration and the British Cabinet to give Italy stronger support in the political and diplomatic conflict with Yugoslavia over the future of Trieste.[31]

As a result of these difficulties, De Gasperi and the Italian diplomatic service were compelled to work out more effective moves; once again, European integration appeared as the best solution to Italian international problems. Italian 'Federalists' had regarded the Pleven Plan as the easiest way to further the process of European political integration.[32] In the summer of 1951, Altiero Spinelli sent De Gasperi an interesting memorandum, in which the influential representative of the Federalist movement outlined a plan aimed at setting up a European supranational community through the EDC.[33] In De Gasperi's opinion the document drafted by Spinelli could be the basis on which the Italian government could develop an effective policy in the European context. The Italian government skilfully adapted the ideals of European integration to national interests and ambitions. In late 1951 De Gasperi publicly expounded Rome's objectives about the Pleven Plan. The Six had to regard the European Defence Community as a first step towards the creation of a European Political Community (EPC).[34]

This sudden development in Italy's attitude was confirmed by the appointment, as the new head of the Italian delegation at the Paris conference, of the Social-Democrat leader Ivan Matteo Lombardo, a staunch advocate of political integration. The Italian delegates in Paris made every effort to insert in the text of the EDC treaty clauses foreseeing the setting-up of a European Political Community.[35] Italy's plan received the immediate support of the European Movement and was regarded sympathetically by the Truman administration. As for Italy's European partners in the EDC negotiations, they seemed ready to comply with De Gasperi's wishes: they did no damage whatsoever to other – more relevant – aspects of the EDC scheme and the objective of political integration could be a useful smokescreen to conceal some more unpleasant implications of the treaty. So we must not overrate Italy's role during the final stage of the Paris negotiations.[36] Apart from the aspects concerning the EPC, the drafting of the EDC treaty was mainly the result of American influence, of French ambitions and fears, of German hopes and of an apparent strengthening in the relationship between the United States and western Europe.

At the end of May 1952, the representatives of the Six signed the complex treaty setting up the European Defence Community. In the final text, Article 38 dealt with the Italian proposal: it envisaged the creation of a European Political Community as the ultimate aim of the EDC treaty. In this context the consultative assembly of the European Defence Community was charged with the task of working out the structures of a political community.[37] Even if Article 38, as well as Italy's plan, stressed the issue of political integration, Rome's interest also focused on economic cooperation. Italy had already achieved some concessions in the context of ECSC but that was not enough compared with Italian ambitions. De Gasperi's objectives were: (a) to get access to raw materials for Italian industries; (b) to promote the mobility of Italian manpower (i.e. the emigration of Italian unskilled and semi-skilled workers to western European countries);[38] (c) to stimulate foreign investments in the peninsula; and (d) to open European markets to Italian industrial and agricultural products. But the Italian authorities understood that their European partners had only a scant interest in most of these economic aims, while the Benelux countries and West Germany were usually more interested in developing some form of customs' union, which would have favoured their stronger, more modern economic structures to the detriment of the Italian economy. If the Rome government wished to achieve its economic aims, it had to strengthen its international position. Such a condition was likely to be achieved through political integration. The Italian authorities hoped that in a European Political Community Italy would have been on an equal footing with its major European partners.[39] Obviously the Italian government also stressed the political integration aspects of the EDC treaty for internal reasons. De Gasperi hoped to convince Italian public opinion that the European Defence Community was a minor aspect of a broader 'peace policy' aimed at achieving economic and political benefits.[40]

Because of these objectives, during the second half of 1952 the Italian government focused its attention mainly on an early fulfilment of Article 38. De Gasperi was able to overcome French objections and the Six, mainly as a result of Italian initiatives, agreed to the setting-up of a body, the so-called 'ad hoc assembly', charged with the task of working out a definite scheme for a European Political Community.[41] In 1953 the 'ad hoc assembly' was able to draft a definite plan, which was also influenced by the opinions and ideals of the Italian members of the 'Assembly'. But the fulfilment of the EPC scheme was linked to the implementation of the EDC treaty and, in spite of the signature of the Paris agreements, it had become evident in a few months that the project for the creation of a European army was facing serious obstacles. The treaty had to be ratified by the Parliaments of the Six. In France, in particular, the ratification of the EDC almost immediately became a major political issue. The supranational aspects of the European Defence Community were regarded with deep suspicion by large sectors of public opinion and the political world. Paradoxically the European Defence Community was perceived by many Frenchmen as a major symbol of American interference in French internal affairs. Tough opposition to a European army was also developing in influential military circles, which believed the implementation of the treaty could threaten the tradition, the influence and the prestige of the *Armée*. Moreover, in late 1952, with the decline of the *Troisième Force* governments, France experienced a series of weak cabinets that were compelled to rely on the support of some sectors of the Gaullist movement, fiercely opposed to the EDC plan. French pro-EDC leaders quickly realized there was no clear-cut majority in favour of the treaty in the *Assemblée Nationale*.[42] In order to save both the EDC and a close relationship with the United States, Foreign Minister Georges Bidault, who had taken the place of Robert Schuman, thought it would be useful to obtain further concessions from the United States and from France's European partners. The French government's new proposals were labelled 'additional protocols' to the EDC treaty. In this context the French aimed at obtaining: (a) a British involvement in a European political and military 'status quo' based on a French leadership over the western half of the continent; (b) the recognition of a special role for the French armed forces in the

EDC structures; and (c) a settlement of the Saar question, which could preserve French interests.[43]

Obviously Italy could play only a minor role in the protracted and difficult diplomatic debate about the 'additional protocols', which involved, in particular, France, the United States, Great Britain and, albeit to a minor extent, West Germany. The Italian government publicly stated its critical views of the French proposals, especially as they seemed destined to postpone the fulfilment of EDC,[44] and De Gasperi put further pressure on Italy's European partners to develop the EPC project in the meantime.[45] In spite of Italy's public statements in favour of both the EDC and the EPC, the Christian Democrat leader felt himself unable to have the treaty ratified by the Italian Parliament. The general elections, to be held in June 1953, were approaching and De Gasperi's leadership was weaker than in the late 1940s. The Left parties' opposition was still very tough and the EDC issue skilfully exploited by both Socialist and Communist propaganda. The monarchists and the neo-Fascists harshly criticized De Gasperi's foreign policy. As in France, large sectors of public opinion resented American interference in Italian internal affairs as well as Anglo-American sympathy towards Tito's Yugoslavia. To strengthen his weakening position De Gasperi tried to enforce an electoral law, which would assure the Christian Democrats and their allies a steady majority in the Parliament. This law, quickly labelled *legge truffa* ('swindle law') by the opposition, became the main issue of the electoral campaign. In such a heated political atmosphere the ratification of the EDC treaty could have offered the opposition further opportunities for a more effective electoral proaganda.[46] During the first half of 1953 De Gasperi played down the European army issue, while stressing the EPC scheme.[47] The Christian Democrat leader thought that, strongly advocating the creation of the European Political Community, he could appease the American authorities who were increasingly disappointed by Italy's attitude towards the EDC ratification.

De Gasperi's task in the EDC context was not helped by the international events that took place between late 1952 and early 1953. The American Presidential elections seemed to mark a development in United States' policy towards western Europe. President Eisenhower and Secretary of State John Foster Dulles were deeply committed to the implementation of the EDC; the new Republican administration began to put further and stronger pressures on its European partners, in particular on France and Italy, to speed up the procedures for the ratification of the Paris treaty.[48] But Stalin's death, in March 1953, was rapidly perceived by several western European statesmen as presaging the end of the cold war. The achievement of West Germany's rearmament – and the setting-up of the European Defence Community – appeared less urgent than before. In Washington, on the contrary, there were fewer illusions about any real development in Soviet foreign policy; the Eisenhower administration regarded the EDC as the preliminary condition for negotiations with Moscow, as well as the instrument to achieve a different 'burden sharing' in the Western defence system.[49]

The 1953 general election marked the failure of De Gasperi's plans and the end of his political career. The Christian Democrat leader tried to form a new government but he was unable to obtain a parliamentary majority. He was compelled to resign from office and, already seriously ill, he retired to private life.[50] A few weeks later Giuseppe Pella was appointed President of the Council, heading an apparently weak Christian Democrat cabinet. But Pella had definite political ambitions and he began to search for broader support both in Parliament and from public opinion. The Christian Democrat Prime Minister singled out the solution of the Trieste question as the instrument through which he could strengthen his government and his own political role, while the EDC was regarded as a minor element in Rome's foreign policy.[51] Pella thought that Italy could link ratification of the EDC treaty with renewed British and American support for Rome's aspiration over Trieste. Neither Washington nor London had any intention of yielding to Italian diplomatic blackmail. The American administration, on the contrary, put further pressure on the Italian government to have the Paris treaty ratified. The growing difficulties between Rome and Belgrade, Pella's nationalist bombast, the opportunist use of the EDC issue and the ensuing strain on the relationship with Washington, led the Italian government also to play down the EPC scheme.[52] In late 1953 the fulfilment of both the EDC and the EPC still appeared as a remote goal and the setting up of a European army was becoming an element in a complex international debate.

Pella's policy met with complete failure and he was compelled to resign. In February 1954 a new government was formed under the leadership of the Christian Democrat Mario Scelba, who appointed as Foreign Minister Attilio Piccioni, a leading representative of the Christian Democrat party. Both Scelba and Piccioni seemed eager to come back to De Gasperi's traditions as far as foreign policy was concerned.[53] The Scelba government was, however, in a weak position. At first the Italian authorities aimed at renewing close, friendly relations with Washington but the ratification of the EDC treaty still represented a serious obstacle. Italian diplomats and politicians clearly understood the serious risks involved for the whole Western system in a complete failure of the EDC scheme. In particular some Italian foreign-policy makers feared that the crisis of the European army plan could lead to a breaking-up of NATO and to a new American 'isolationism'. While some diplomats believed Italian ratification of the Paris treaty could influence the French attitude,[54] other diplomatic representatives had no confidence whatsoever in such an initiative.[55] The latter would have preferred the Italian government to try to strengthen its ties with Washington, as, in their opinion, only a close bilateral relationship with the United States could give Italy a steady guarantee for the political and military future of the peninsula.

The diplomats' contrasting opinions were carefully examined by the Italian Foreign Ministry, but Scelba and Piccioni also had to take into consideration the internal consequences of possible ratification of the EDC treaty. So the Italian authorities publicly stated their allegiance to both the EDC and the EPC. They also started the parliamentary process for the ratification of the Paris treaty, even if they chose a complex procedure that was often regarded as a postponement of the question. Scelba doubted early Italian ratification could really influence the attitude of the French authorities and the Italian Foreign Ministry focused its attention on the yet unsolved Trieste question.[56] But the major Western powers probably paid little attention to Italy's doubts and waverings as the future of the EDC was in the hands of the French parliament; even in Washington the lack of Italian ratification was regarded as a minor nuisance in comparison with increasing French opposition to a European army.[57]

In the spring of 1954 the dramatic worsening of the military situation in Indo-China led to a sudden political development in Paris. The Radical Socialist Pierre Mendès-France was appointed Prime Minister. His first foreign-policy aims were to disentangle France from the Indo-China war and to achieve a definite solution of the EDC problem. As for the Far East crisis, within a few weeks Mendès-France had signed the Geneva agreements that put an end to France's involvement in Indo-China. On the basis of this diplomatic achievement, the French Prime Minister focused his attention on the EDC. He had never concealed his lack of enthusiasm for the Pleven Plan, in particular for its supranational implications. He also knew there was no clear-cut majority in favour of the EDC treaty in the *Assemblée Nationale*, but he felt bound to save some aspects of the EDC scheme. He worked out further proposals, which, if accepted by France's European partners, would have led to the setting-up of an international organization with few, if any, characters of supranationality.[58]

Italian political and diplomatic circles, which had appreciated Mendès-France's firmness on his accession to power, now feared that his plan, if implemented, could lead, as an obvious consequence, to the failure of the EPC projects – and of Italy's hopes of political and economic integration.[59] In spite of Italy's fears the Rome authorities felt themselves unable to develop any effective diplomatic initiative. They still wished to see the EPC implemented but its creation was linked to the setting up of the European Defence Community. The Scelba government, because of its weakness and strong internal opposition, was in no position to hasten the procedure for the ratification of the treaty, whose future was in the hands of more powerful international 'actors'. Piccioni was about to resign from office and Italian public opinion was more interested in the solution to the Trieste question than the future of the European Defence Community.

In late August 1954 the Foreign Ministers of the Six met in Brussels. Mendès-France expounded France's new proposals for the EDC future. The French plan was firmly rejected. The Italian delegates opposed the French scheme but they chose to adopt a low-profile attitude as they realized the weakness of Italy's diplomatic position.[60]

At the end of August the French *Assemblée Nationale* rejected the EDC treaty. Even if Mendès-France had neither supported nor opposed the ratification of the Paris treaty, the French parliament's decision meant a serious blow to the Western political and military system based on NATO and on American involvement in European affairs. In particular the Eisenhower administration appeared on the eve of developing a 'peripheral strategy', implementing Foster Dulles' 'agonizing reappraisal'. A British initiative, based on the hypothesis of reviving the Brussels Treaty organization through Italy's and West Germany's accession to the European alliance, quickly served to mend the breach in the relationship between the United States and western Europe. Between September and October 1954 the London and Paris agreements paved the way for a solution to the EDC crisis. The Brussels Treaty was transformed into Western European Union (WEU); West Germany and Italy became full members of this political-military alliance; and the German Federal Republic was granted complete freedom in both internal and international affairs. In 1955, as an obvious consequence of these developments, and with France's consent, Bonn became a member of NATO.[61]

Italy's role in the process was, once again, a minor one. The French rejection of the EDC had been no surprise for Italian diplomats and politicians and there was no reaction on the part of the Rome government. The Italian authorities were worried about the future of NATO, as well as that of European integration; they feared an American 'agonizing reappraisal', but in their contacts with United States diplomats they confined themselves to stressing Italy's allegiance to 'Atlantic' ideals and Rome's confidence in a friendly American attitude towards the peninsula. They made every effort to convince the American administration that, even if the Italian parliament had not ratified the EDC treaty, the Scelba government still regarded the European Defence Community as a viable scheme.[62] When the British cabinet worked out its plan, Italy's early reaction to Eden's initiative was influenced by some suspicion. The Palazzo Chigi feared the emergence of a close French-British partnership, which would have left Italy scant room for manoeuvre in the European context; moreover the Italian authorities quickly realized that any hope for the setting-up of the European Political Community was fading.[63] In spite of these suspicions, on the occasion of Eden's mission to Rome in September 1954, Scelba stated his government's agreement with the British plan.[64] Italy's fears of an American disentanglement from European affairs overcame the Palazzo Chigi's doubts about British and French ambitions. But Italy badly needed United States and British support in the negotiations over Trieste, which in that same period had reached their final stage. During the London and Paris conferences, which led to the agreement on the setting-up of the western European union, the Italian delegates seemed mainly interested in defending minor economic interests.[65]

In early 1955 Italy's ambitions and hopes had been disappointed. In their analyses some Italian diplomats outlined a sombre picture of Rome's international role.[66] Europe appeared influenced by a renewed French-British entente cordiale. As for the American attitude towards the old continent, the Eisenhower administration seemed to regard West Germany as the most important and faithful partner. The French rejection of the EDC had led to the end of the EPC project. Italy had been unable to achieve either a major role in the European continent or the economic benefits that she hoped to get through the use of the political integration issue.

In a few months, however, the objective of European integration returned to the limelight. Benelux and French plans for the creation of a common market and an atomic energy community, Monnet's initiatives and the success of the Messina conference gave new impetus to the process of cooperation among the Six. It was a new chance for Italy's hopes. Furthermore the fading of the cold war and the survival of NATO allowed the Italian authorities to pay far less attention to defence needs and military problems, while the Suez crisis was definite proof of British and French decline as great powers. Even if the Italian government did not play the most relevant role in the negotiations leading to the establishment of the EEC and of EURATOM, Italy seemed able to achieve most of her objectives.[67] It is likely, however, that it was the sudden and extraordinary growth of the Italian economy, rather than Rome's political plans or diplomatic initiatives, which gave the peninsula a right to be a leading protagonist in the renewed process of European integration.

11 Attempting an Unlikely Union: the British Steel Industry and the European Coal and Steel Community 1950-54

Ruggero Ranieri

As is well known the British government did not accept the terms of the Schuman Plan and did not, therefore, participate in the negotiations among the Six which eventually resulted in the foundation of the European Coal and Steel Community (ECSC). In fact many regard this as the crucial break that was to leave Britain tottering at the margins of the European Communities. Trade in coal and steel between the Six and the United Kingdom remained extremely limited throughout the 1950s. When eventually negotiations were opened up between the two parties in 1954, they led to only a limited agreement. So at first sight the theme of this essay would appear to be little more than a non-event in the broader shaping of postwar Europe: a view that most of the literature seems to share. There is one exception, however, which is Duncan Burn's book on the postwar steel industry. Although it only gives a brief account of the actual negotiations with the ECSC, it chooses to look at every single issue affecting the steel markets, be it investment, prices or protection, in a comparative perspective, in the belief that this is the best way to trace the roots of what Burn perceived to be serious long-term problems affecting British industry.[1] My own examination of the records has reached broadly the same conclusions; the account of the British steel industry's relationship with the Six has proved to be an interesting enquiry into a case of mistaken identity, shedding helpful new light on British attitudes towards Europe. This chapter seeks to examine the issue first by rapidly reassessing the British response to the Schuman Plan between 1950 and the end of 1952 in the light of a few of the economic issues involved, and then by focusing on the discussions held inside the British government in 1953, designed to thrash out a satisfactory negotiating position with which to approach the ECSC in the forthcoming round of talks. It was in the course of these consultations that the positions obtaining inside the economic ministries as well as inside the steel industry had a chance to emerge most clearly.

A few points have been firmly established about the position taken by the

United Kingdom in response to the French initiative of 9 May 1950. The British Government did not wish to commit itself to what it perceived as a leap into the unknown, one marked by the undesired stigma of European 'federalism'. More important still was the fact that Monnet was so keen to achieve supranationality to control Germany's heavy industry that he discarded any suggestion of a more conventional negotiating framework; nor, for that matter, was he prepared to grant Britain a kind of supervisory role in his dealings with Bonn.[2] To this picture must be added, however, the great importance attached on the British side to the emergence of a continental cartel, and the mixture of fear, concern and anxiety this prospect elicited. The basic outlook was generally defensive and the Ministers were confronted with the widely held belief among both coal and steel experts that 'the consequences of our having to compete with a powerful, integrated group of European industries formed without our participation' were indeed alarming.[3] It was, in fact, a widely shared belief that a block of steel producers, presumably under German leadership, was bound to benefit from long-term advantages in terms of integration and specialization that eventually the United Kingdom would find it impossible to match. Nor would it have been possible merely to resort to protection, for this would have clearly damaged the prospects of the British engineering industry, which featured, among other things, as the country's largest export earner. In the shorter term, moreover, there was a general feeling of a movement towards a period of surplus production, and that this was bound to give an edge to a larger cartelized grouping because of its likely readiness to engage in aggressive selling. In this light, participating to some extent in the new arrangements might well have been the only way to 'protect British steel from dumping and price-cutting'.[4] The working party (WP) set up in May 1950, comprising mainly officials of the economic ministries and representatives of the industries concerned, produced a number of reports that clearly exhibited a favourable disposition towards the Schuman Plan arrangements.[5]

What was remarkable about the first of such reports, submitted in June 1950, was that it covered much the same ground that the French technocrats were independently considering as a basis for their submission to the Six by way of the so-called 'Document de Travail'.[6] It called for an 'authority' to be set up with a number of mandatory powers, covering, among other things, investment policies; tariffs, subsidies and quotas in the common area were to be removed; and a common set of rules governing price policies was to be adhered to. The report also examined the case in which the United Kingdom was not to participate in the pool and found that prospect most uninviting, especially in the long term.[7] The second report, appearing one year later when negotiations among the Six had already reached a conclusion, persisted, nevertheless, in recommending a step towards the new arrangement, leading to something very short of participation: 'partial membership' as it was called, entailing the acceptance of 'most of the Treaty's provisions'.[8]

In reaching these conclusions the WP was heavily influenced by the favour displayed by some of the economic officials (Treasury, Economic Section, Ministry of Supply) towards a liberalization of the steel market, whereas the steel industrialists from the BISF, as we shall see, showed a predisposition to argue in terms of a cartel arrangement, similar to the one that had been struck during the interwar period.[9] The most radical conclusions of the WP came under attack at ministerial level. However, this position of guarded attention on the part of the steel industry still represented the bottom line, beyond which the government did not dare to go in its rejection of the Community. Indeed, during the course of an important meeting of the Economic Steering Committee (ESC) in May 1951, it was recognized that the steel industry needed to strike 'some kind of friendly association with the Community'.[10] It might therefore be argued that the concept of an association with the Six was firmly rooted in the country's economic interest.

On the other hand, it is clear that the Schuman Plan was surrounded by many reservations and much distrust. Nobody, it is true, directly challenged the WP's conclusions; what happened instead was that they were gradually whittled down, becoming, as a result, ineffective as a possible blueprint for action. Clearly some of this resistance proceeded from the sectors of the government that had a vested interest in protection, such as the National Coal Board, but most of the opposition seems to have been of a more general nature, rooted in domestic and foreign-policy perceptions. Thus the higher the level of discussion, the firmer the resolve not to act upon any of the WP's recommendations.[11] Moreover, there seems to have been little difference between the Labour and Conservative administrations. Thus, for example, the minutes of the Cabinet discussion in June 1950 can be seen as expressing the deepest reservations towards any international authority in coal and steel, which was altogether a different view from the one expressed by the WP. There was a voicing of fears that the expansion of the two industries would be halted; concern was expressed about the reaction of the trade unions, and cartel arrangements were rejected; all this was rounded up by a decision not to do anything but presumably wait and see, hoping that the French initiative would ultimately fail.[12] Two years later, after more reports by the officials saying it was crucial to reach an agreement on a common investment policy, Foreign Secretary Eden was to announce that the British government entertained deep-seated reservations towards the Community and that 'we shall be most unwilling to enter into any commitments towards the Community which would give the latter the right to interfere in our own coal and steel plans.'[13]

In the course of 1952 with the ratification of the treaty on its course, anxiety among British industrialists had clearly grown stronger. The formal decision of the government to appoint a delegation to the High Authority (HA) and to seek an association with the Six, accompanied by more positive noises from the Foreign Office (FO), was not enough to dispel these apprehensions.[14] Monnet himself seemed to take the matter to heart during his explanatory journey to London in the summer of 1952, just as his HA was taking office, for he reassured his British counterparts that one of the first things which he had in mind was to chair a joint UK/HA committee, which should issue a statement 'with the object of reassuring the coal and steel industries of the United Kingdom as to the intentions and objectives of the Community'.[15] Soon afterwards he seemed to forget about the matter, pressed by the more immediate concern of setting in place the Community's institutions. The first reports from Luxemburg by Sir Cecil Weir, head of the newly appointed British delegation, clearly indicated that Monnet was uncertain about his next moves towards the United Kingdom, except for his general utterances about the need to establish 'common principles'.[16] There was no doubt, however, that both parties were thinking seriously about their relationship: the ECSC treaty itself induced hasty negotiations with Britain, and the WP, before being wound up in July 1952, had produced a list of practical points of mutual concern.[17] Yet because the Common Market for coal and steel still needed to be practically established and regulated, there was little imperative for immediate action. It was felt necessary, especially on the British side, to engage in yet another round of painstaking self-appraisal.

In July 1952, the British cabinet had decided that the ultimate responsibility for ECSC matters would rest with the FO, albeit in consultation with a committee – the SPC (Schuman Plan Committee) – in which the Treasury, the Board of Trade (BoT), the Ministry of Fuel and Power and the Ministries of Supply and of Labour would be represented. A few months later this committee set up a new Working Party to examine the implications of a possible Treaty of Association between Britain and the Community. It started meeting in February 1953, chaired by an official from the Treasury, and it proceeded, in the same way as the preceding WP had done but more extensively, to consult with the representatives of both the coal and the steel industries.[18] After having held about thirty sessions and produced a voluminous body of documents it finally drafted a substantial report, meant to constitute the basis of further decision-making by the British government. The conclusions of the report were, not surprisingly, slanted in favour of Britain forging a close relationship with the Six; but once again it did not prove influential. However, what provides a number of fascinating clues is the way in which the different issues were argued during the Working Party's sessions.

Opinions were divided, especially in relation to steel. There was a group of free-traders, coming mainly from the Treasury, although not without some support from other quarters such as the Ministry of Supply, who argued in favour of more competition and thought that developing close links with the Community would be instrumental in achieving it. There were the protectionists, among whom the BoT officials were, at this stage, the most outspoken, who feared the Community, and stood by the tightly regulated arrangements under which the steel market had been reorganized after 1945; somewhere in the middle stood the British Iron and Steel Federation (BISF) in an attempt to enjoy the best of all possible worlds. Finally the FO seemed to be looking with considerable favour at the prospect of an association with the ECSC, an attitude possibly originated, at this stage, by the conviction that the drive towards European unity was irreversible and that it was essential that the United Kingdom remain in touch with it.[19]

In order to better follow the discussion it is useful to examine briefly the context in which previous agreements had been reached with the Continental steel cartel. The history of the relationship of British and European steel was a troubled one. Without wishing to enter into the question of the origins of the competitive decline of British steelmaking, there seems to be agreement on the fact that by 1913 the industry was already experiencing some problems in facing its major competitors across the Channel: the Germans. Expansion during the First World War took place at high capital costs and often in the worst locations; the industry fell further behind during the 1920s, a period referred to by the literature as a 'black decade'.[20] In the second half of the 1920s there was a tendency to move away from basic steel production; the most successful firms were non-integrated ones, using imported semifinished products as low-priced inputs. Because of the high prices of the British firms, continental producers became increasingly able to compete in the British home market. In 1931, with domestic production badly affected by the depression, imports from Europe reached 53 per cent of total domestic output; this finally convinced the government to grant the industry a protective tariff.

A new body, the Import Advisory Committee (IAC) was appointed with the aim of ensuring the public interest in the industry's tariff policy, while, at the same time, out of the negotiations conducted between the IAC and the newly constituted BISF, a wholly new framework for the industry was created, according to which 'systematic' planning was to be achieved and competition on the domestic market eliminated. The tariff, on the other hand, was intended to give the industry some leverage in its dealings with Europe, which was all the more necessary because European exporters, taking the lead from the Belgians, were committed to price-cutting on a grand scale. In 1933 when continental producers established a new cartel with the declared aim of carving up export markets, Sir William Larke, Director of the National Federation, is reported as saying: 'there is no doubt I think that British industry cannot stand alone and fight a combination of this character with any success . . . it is essential that we enter into a measure of special cooperation'.[21] It was in fact a matter of life and death for the beleaguered British industry to be able to reach a truce with its partners across the Channel. The trick was partly performed in 1935 by raising a tariff of about 50 per cent that finally convinced the European cartel to mitigate its demands. This was the prelude to a set of tight market-sharing arrangements.

These events unquestionably marked a watershed for the steel industry in Britain, turning it towards centralization and government supervision, features which were rendered even more stringent during the War. Nobody, however, seemed to complain, be it the industrialists or the experts from the ministries; the discussions held on the future of the industry between 1943 and 1945 ended on a note of general agreement as to the necessity to perpetuate such a cosy state of affairs. According to Duncan Burn, who himself played a part in the shaping of the postwar industry, the choice in favour of protection and price-fixing was mainly intended to defer the inevitable 'day of reckoning . . . when British steel would have to meet either American or continental competition'.[22]

As it turned out that day came later than expected, although it did finally arrive. In the meantime the industry was offered a strong incentive to achieve further concentration and rationalization in the form of massive investment plans designed, among other things, to increase pig-iron capacity.[23] All imports and exports remained strictly subject to quotas. Prices were rigidly fixed, and, what is more, kept low on the domestic market by a combination of subsidies and compensation schemes, meant to cushion the cost of imported semis and raw materials, especially iron-ore. Profits, therefore, were tied to the higher prices charged for exports, about 60 per cent of which were shipped to colonial and Commonwealth markets where British steel still enjoyed preferential treatment. Under such circumstances, however advantageous they might have been regarded both by domestic producers and by exporters of metal manufactured goods, who enjoyed the benefit of low-cost steel inputs, any guess about the true competitive position of the industry was bound to be haphazard indeed.

Given these premises, to contemplate forming an association with the Six might have appeared completely beside the point, since the result of such a move could only have been the attainment of a greater degree of liberalization. Also, steel trade with the ECSC countries had fallen to a low level and was mainly composed of exports to The Netherlands and to a modest degree of purchases of Belgian and French semi-finished products. Purchases of German scrap, which had been considerable in the early postwar years, had lately been sharply declining.[24] As it turned out, however, the industry's self-assurance was not high and the prospect of stepping up trade with the highly industrialised west European markets was not one that could be easily dismissed. The isolation in which the industry had cornered itself was perceived as a source of weakness.[25] The unspoken assumption was that, if it was going to be permanently cut-off from the new European cartel embodied in the ECSC, British steel did not stand much of a chance. The crucial question was that of price fluctuations. It was in order to protect the home market from underpriced steel imports in times of surplus that tariffs had been imposed in the first place, shortly followed by government-fixed prices. It was recognized, however, that such a radical cure, which amounted to sheltering the industry from whatever price fluctuations might have taken place on the continent, carried with it some undesirable consequences, especially as steel is, in most cases, an intermediate good. In the event of another sharp decline in steel prices, therefore, continental engineering industries would have enjoyed an undue advantage over their British counterparts. In other words, no matter how many protectionist barriers were raised, the interdependent nature of steel markets was bound to reassert itself. This was why the ECSC offered an enticing prospect.

The chief hope was that an association with the Community would result in a less-artificially founded, and therefore more assured, price stability. As Sir Robert Shone of the BISF put it: 'some form of association might help to influence them and would also give an opportunity for us to achieve the main objective of averting dumping by the Community in this country'.[26]

Opinions differed, however, as to the exact nature of that association and how close the relationship should become. A group of officials comprising the representatives in the WP from the Ministry of Supply, from the Treasury and from the United Kingdom Delegation in Luxemburg, were prepared to go the whole way; in fact their opinion prevailed in the final report.[27] Their assumption was that the best way of influencing the development of the Community and making the market more stable was to allow British steel to associate closely with the industries of the Six, short of joining the Common Market. Reciprocal tariffs and quotas were to be removed and United Kingdom producers were to abide by the pricing regulations of the ECSC, which would have meant in the first place giving up the double pricing of exports, while at the same time allowing firms a greater degree of flexibility to set and align their price schedules. The more liberal-minded elements on the British side were prepared to subscribe to the pricing system of the Community, thus relinquishing their own, rigidly regulated, domestic one. A certain amount of joint decision-making would then have taken place in times of shortage and surplus; more precisely in times of surplus, a voluntary mutual agreement to restrict output was foreseen, since this was considered to be the best way to prevent price-cutting.[28] In times of steel shortage, on the other hand, it was hoped that Britain could still enjoy access to a certain amount of Community steel, a desire that seemed to run in the face of the often-proclaimed objective of self-sufficiency.

What can be said about these conclusions emerging from the WP? They were broadly consistent with previous assessments made on the question by similar bodies in 1950 and 1951. Since there is no reason to suspect that a group of government officials, mainly from the economic ministries, had contracted an enduring commitment to federalism, their suggestions are probably best under-stood as a reflection of the many unspoken taboos underlying British steel postwar policy. There were others in the WP who were not prepared to contemplate such a radical change. Burns from the BoT, for example, pointed out the fact that allowing freer competition would mean an increase in steel prices at home as well as the abandonment of the long-term investment strategy, initiated in 1945. He also questioned the wisdom of entering into any pact with the continentals, given their unfair pricing record. Moreover he thought it would have been impossible to liberalize trade on a partial basis, for this would have meant incurring the opposition of GATT.[29] The question of the waiver eventually to be obtained from GATT to join a preferential arrangement played some part in the discussion and it deserves a few more comments. BoT officials argued that such a concession on the part of GATT was extremely unlikely. In fact, they added, it would have been more easily obtained if Britain had decided to join the Common Market altogether, for in that case she could have relied on full American backing. By giving a partial adhesion to the ECSC, she would, on the other hand, arouse the opposition of practically everybody, consumer countries as well as producer countries. In view of this Burns summed up his case by remarking:

only two alternatives were possible, the first was to embrace full membership which would enable us to claim the waiver, the second was to be prepared to make this a breaking point in our membership of GATT.[30]

In fact a third possibility had been canvassed in the course of the discussion, consisting of a move to abolish tariffs and quotas entirely, although it must be said that this had aroused much hostility from the industrialists, who, among other things, did not wish to see the British market exposed to the competition of American steel, now increasingly produced on the East Coast, nor to Japanese exports, which were beginning to feel their way into European markets and were thought to be unfairly low-priced.[31] But even ruling out this third more radical solution, given the previous record of that organization when dealing with preferential arrangements, it seemed reasonable to expect some degree of flexibility on the part of GATT, if Britain were to decide to liberalize her trade with the Six. This was clearly pointed out by a report of the ESC reviewing the issue later in the course of 1953.[32]

Some of the arguments deployed by the BoT and other officials defending the existing state of affairs inside the British steel market and arguing, from that basis, for the rejection of any overture towards the continent, were, therefore, rather simplistic and their protectionist bias made them a fairly easy target. Self-confidence in the industry, after all, was not running high. It fell to an industrialist to explain to the people from the government 'that it was not to be expected that the UK producers would enjoy a competitive margin for long'[33] and that therefore a certain increase in competition was to be welcomed as a beneficial stimulus. What the industrialists had in mind was a more guarded approach towards the ECSC than that envisaged by the more liberal-minded officials, commanding the majority of the Working Party, and one which would have enabled them to hang on to what they considered to be their major assets without foregoing the opportunity to shed some of the more burdensome controls to which they were subjected.[34] Clearly they did not like to take part in the Community's price regulations as this would have required them to charge a single published price inside the new jointly regulated area and would therefore have spelt an end to their current authorized practice of export premium pricing, at least on most continental markets (though it would have made it difficult for them to then discriminate against their Commonwealth buyers).[35]

In any case the basis of the deal the British industrialists would have preferred were clear enough: they wanted a resumption of the interwar cartel agreement. This would have entailed the Community committing itself not to dump on the British market, while British industrialists undertook not to undercut producers in Europe. In keeping with this, they also seemed to think there were other ways to achieve price stability than rigid government price-fixing as it was currently practised in the United Kingdom. They would have much preferred a system of fixed minimum prices, leaving them free to settle the actual price level.[36] Finally, it would have been a matter of trade-offs: so much British steel in Europe in exchange for that many imports into the United Kingdom, granted by lowering tariffs, or, better, opening quota ceilings. In addition, although they had no intention of sharing with the Six the preferential arrangements they enjoyed in the Commonwealth, they thought some kind of understanding on exports to third countries to be desirable, at least in the long term, for it was recognized that the Community exporters were bound to form a powerful cartel.[37] Market sharing was to be extended in their view to raw-material supplies: they regarded it as particularly desirable in the case of Swedish and Algerian iron-ore, although in the latter case they soon discovered that their long-term purchasing contracts with the French government had not been put at risk. The French had obtained Algeria's exclusion from the Community and shown, moreover, little willingness to accommodate the requests of potential large-scale buyers of the ore, such as the Italians.[38]

The argument of the British industrialists was altogether weaker, or rather extremely short-term, in the high value it put on the Commonwealth connection. This came out clearly during the Working Party's discussion.[39] There were four important markets in which British steel still enjoyed some preferential tariff treatment: Australia, Canada, New Zealand and South Africa. It soon became apparent that Australia had embarked on a massive build-up of her steel capacity, so that not only would she soon be able to provide her own needs but would presumably be able to outbid the British in New Zealand. In the other two countries preferential duties had been whittled down to practically nothing and, in face of strong competition in Canada from American producers and in South Africa mainly from European ones, British steel was just managing to hold on to particular market niches, such as to the one for rail products. The dilemma was aptly summarized by one official who:

thought that the Commonwealth system was bound to break up sooner or later in any case:

it was difficult to say whether action on our part in the context of an Association with the
Community would precipitate a breakup.[40]

The case put forward by the industrialists for a businesslike approach to the
ECSC, although recorded as just a minority view inside the Working Party,
gained considerable ground in the following months. The proposal for forming a
common steel market brought into light sharp divisions inside the Cabinet, which
were ultimately resolved in favour of the side that was less committed to a
positive approach towards the European Communities. By the time they were
submitted to the Cabinet in January 1954, however, the conclusions of the WP
seemed to be in a strong position since they had been officially endorsed by the
FO, keen to make a positive gesture towards the Six, and had also gained the
enthusiastic backing of the ESC, chaired by the Treasury.[41] Moreover, Monnet's
recent official letter, inviting the United Kingdom to negotiate, seemed to be
contemplating an association not far removed from the WP's suggestions.[42]
Nevertheless, the official consultation of the coal and steel industries, which the
Cabinet decided to entrust to the Ministries of Supply and of Fuel and Power, was
to prove an unsurmountable stumbling block.[43] At the next Cabinet meeting in
which the issue was considered, the Minister of Supply, Duncan Sandys, felt
comfortable enough to rebuke all the pro-European argument by bluntly stating
that there was no question of grafting the 'principle' of a common market on an
unwilling steel industry.[44]

The matter then had to be deferred to a Ministerial Committee chaired by the
Secretary of State for Commonwealth Relations, Lord Swindon, in which the
voices of the Ministries closest to the industries soon appeared to be prominent.
Leaving aside the role played in these events by the newly appointed Iron and
Steel Board (ISB), which seemed to regard the defence of the existing situation
within the industry as its main purpose, clearly the good disposition of Sandys
towards his steel industrialists must ultimately be explained on political
grounds.[45] In fact it soon appeared that, outside of a common market, there was
little room for an agreement between British steel and the ECSC. The two pricing
systems were quite irreconcilable, so the search for a 'half-way' solution, carried
out between April and May 1954, by yet another group of officials in consultation
with the industry, was forced to concentrate on the reduction of barriers.[46]

Two ideas were mooted: one to allow a quota of imports from the Six at a
nominal rate of duty – in other words, free trade under licence. This would have
posed all sorts of administrative problems; moreover, when the industry looked at
it and compared it to the similar arrangement struck with the European cartel in
the 1930s it found it lacked one vital ingredient: the allotment of export quotas on
third markets.[47] This hardly seemed a feasible proposition to make to a High
Authority committed to curbing cartels. Attention, therefore, focused on tariffs
and a new proposal was drafted that envisaged the United Kingdom reducing its
tariff by about two-thirds to a level close to the Community one in exchange for a
commitment on the part of the industries of the Six not to undercut British
prices. This was a scaled-down version of the previous WP's idea and was based
on the same premises, such as the need to open up the United Kingdom's market
to competition and make price levels more responsive to conditions in demand.[48]

Yet it was open to severe objections on two counts. Firstly tariff reductions, because of GATT, would have had to have been extended and this might have unnecessarily exposed the British market; also it was not clear whether a meaningful reduction in protection was ultimately compatible with the system of maximum fixed prices (the ISB clearly thought it was not). However for the BISF this was by no means the bottom line. For them the ultimate test would have been the extent of the price fluctuations to which the British market would be exposed. Although recognizing it would be difficult to secure a binding commitment to price stability from the ECSC exporters, they found some comfort in the fact that the Common Market seemed able, because of its very existence, to curb the unruly practices of producers such as the Belgians and Luxemburgers. Why, however, take risks? For the BISF the best way to enter into any talks was to raise the British tariff to the level at which it had originally been set in 1935 by bringing the value brackets and specific duties in line with the rise in prices which had since occurred.[49]

In the last resort, the government was ready to concur with the methods outlined by the steel industry. The decisive step was taken during a meeting of the Ministerial Committee in May, in which Sandys carried the day with a motion rejecting any proposals for a preordained 'half-way' approach towards the Six and confining the agenda of the imminent talks with Monnet to the setting-up of a Council of Association, on whose subcommittees, it was said, representatives of the coal and steel industries from the two sides could concern themselves with the issue of substance.[50] Objections by the BoT against giving corporate bodies the mandate to settle tariff levels were put on the record but a few days later the Cabinet entrusted the Minister of Supply with the task of negotiating with the Europeans.[51]

Looking at the preparations on the other side of the Channel, however, we find that posture was not altogether different. Originally Monnet had spoken of a broad agreement involving a 'joint formulation of policies' on investment and prices that would lead to an 'association based on common rules and regulations'.[52] However, at the beginning of 1954, when the representatives of the Six national governments were brought in to thrash out the final position, such high-minded intentions were replaced by more practical considerations.[53] In the discussion among the Six, everybody appeared concerned about the extremely low level of British prices. Nobody, among the experts of the Six, was quite sure of how much of this differential was due to artificial pricing and government subsidies, and how far instead it was a result of a greater level of productivity on the part of British firms. With the benefit of hindsight, we might therefore say that the British bluff had paid off handsomely.[54]

The HA had suggested a three-stage operation: during the first the United Kingdom was to lower its tariffs immediately to the Franco-German level; then both the United Kingdom, France, Germany and Italy would lower tariffs to the Benelux level increased by about two points. For the Six this was bound to happen anyway in the context of the so-called 'external harmonization'. Finally the United Kingdom and the Six would eliminate reciprocal tariffs, leaving a single external one (for this, permission from GATT would have been required).[55] The French, however, were afraid of being flooded with British steel and therefore opposed the third stage in the HA agenda; they would also have preferred to postpone the second one indefinitely. In particular, before acting to reduce barriers, they wanted to see further cost-structure harmonization.[56] The Dutch on the contrary were afraid of too long a delay in the reduction of barriers and wanted a clear timetable to meet the third stage. The Belgians, Italians and Luxemburgers seemed to share the French fears on the third phase and the Italians urged caution particularly on special steels. The Belgians, who accounted for the largest share of exports to the United Kingdom, appeared resigned to losing the British market altogether, because of price differentials and British investment plans, so they were not prepared to open up their domestic market to British exports if they could avoid it. The Germans seemed reserved.

The result was agreement: even asking for a release of all barriers to reciprocal trade was going too far and as a first step they should try to put an end to double pricing and work out some arrangement for times of scarcity and overproduction. Further liberalization both for coal and steel was to be phased out, pending that ominous catchword of 'harmonization'. As for third markets it was agreed that topic should not be raised at the beginning of the talks but only at a convenient moment. The French and the Germans would have liked to attack the Commonwealth's preferential system, while the Belgians, whose pricing was notoriously more flexible, would have been content with a measure of liberalization.[57] All this made the Dutch extremely uneasy since they feared, wrongly as it appears, that any request by the Community on third-market sharing would lead the British to abandon the talks. In fact it seems the British were expecting just that very request and were preparing to meet it. On the whole we may say that, in addition to some considerable misunderstanding of the true British position, there was also on the part of the Six a certain amount of grasping deviousness; on the part of the HA there was mainly uncertainty, for they knew they did not really wield the power to control the exporters' cartel.

The actual talks between the Minister of Supply Duncan Sandys and Monnet, an account of whose progress lies beyond the scope of this chapter, took place in the autumn of 1954.[58] Given the narrowness of their agenda it is hardly surprising that the outcome was so disappointing. From the point of view, however, of the disposition of British steel, backed by the Ministry of Supply, success could not have been greater. Monnet, especially after the failure of the European Defence Community, was under pressure from the French government; fearing the collapse of his entire edifice he desperately wished to show that the HA was somehow still alive. He was happy therefore to settle for very little. In retrospect we might agree that from the British side this was truly a missed opportunity: surely they could have easily secured an agreement to match the longer-term interests of their industry. The case for liberalization, however, had been lost. What was eventually signed in December 1954 was a Treaty of Association establishing a council on which HA members and British Ministers, as well as representatives of the ISB and the National Coal Board, were to sit and discuss barriers to trade and other matters. In other words, no more was done than to establish a framework for further talks.[59] The latter's major result proved to be an agreement on tariffs, which came into effect at the end of 1958. The British tariff fell for the first time since the 1930s to a maximum rate of 10 per cent but the significance of this was greatly diminished by the fact that the British steel market remained firmly regulated. By the end of the 1950s trade betwen the United Kingdom and the Six had fallen to its lowest ever level.[60]

Some of the questions about the ability to compete on the part of British steel, however, began to find rather disquieting answers. By the end of 1957 continental producers not only enjoyed a clear superiority in all Bessemer converter-produced steel but were also producing a number of shapes of open-hearth steel more cheaply than British firms.[61] The advantage of the Six was enhanced by their more flexible pricing system, based on multiple basing points and a certain measure of price alignment, which allowed average prices to fall by more than quoted ones.[62] Furthermore, during the 1958 slump, continental firms turned once again to cutting their export prices so that their export prices fell well below British domestic ones. This was hardly in itself remarkable; in fact it might have been taken as bolstering the argument on the British side for protection and stability. The fact, however, was that a rigidly controlled steel market with fixed prices at the point of delivery, such as the one erected in Britain, was not conducive to flexibility. In the long-run it was bound to erode firms' ability to compete, especially since it appears to have squeezed profit margins. Moreover the privileged position enjoyed by British steel in Commonwealth markets was rapidly coming to an end. The argument could therefore be made that British steel would have greatly benefited by joining a larger trading area like the ECSC, and that, not having done so, it was bound to lose ground. This would have happened irrespective of the industry's productivity performance as compared to its competitors. All the evidence shows that at this time productivity in the United Kingdom was growing substantially, so that the difference with the continent could not have been particularly great.[63]

Protection had been a response to the difficulty of competing with European steel in the 1920s and 1930s.[64] From this first choice, a chain of others derived: in the first place low prices were set, to be maintained by subsidizing coal and cushioning firms against the higher prices of imported scrap and iron-ore through a central compensation mechanism funded by levies on the entire production of ingots. This in turn had to be balanced by a rigid system of centrally determined regional prices, with the further provision that each region should have the same price level to avoid interregional dumping. The rationale behind these measures was the need to attain self-sufficiency, with the implication that large investment plans had to be launched and again that prices had to be kept low. The system, on the whole, was quite coherent but the premises on which it had been built were, to a large extent, defensive ones. Breaking out of this pattern would have required radical solutions of the kind advocated by the reports of the Working Parties. It is doubtful, however, whether the countries of the Community would have been prepared to accommodate British steel in their preferential arrangements, not least because they perceived it, no doubt with much exaggeration, as an ominous rival. The cartel-like solution advocated by the BISF proved an easier one to push through but in reality it had little to offer. Conditions had altered radically since the interwar period: playing with tariff barriers had become only a limited part of the game. The really crucial issue was the balance between competitive pricing and national and international claims for the regulation of prices and investment. Arguably in the British case inflexibility went hand-in-hand with attempted autarchy but in the long-term this could only increase the attractiveness of competing by the rules of a wider market.

12 Resisting Integration: Aerospace National Champions

Vicki L. Golich

Introduction

The evolution of civil aviation in Europe is in many ways representative of the political and economic forces impelling European integration in the 1990s. Since the beginning of aviation, states[1] have struggled with the choice between dichotomous strategies – unilateral domination or transnational collaboration – for achieving a goal each held in common: maintaining a strong presence in the industry.

This examination of civil aircraft manufacturing within Europe from 1945 through the signing of the Rome Treaties in 1957 begins with a discussion of the industry's evolution and the underlying European philosophy of appropriate state-economy relationships to facilitate an understanding of state and corporate behaviour during the postwar era. Next, different approaches to rebuilding commercial aviation after the war are analysed. Finally, initial attempts at joint production are explored to gain further insights into the forces behind regional cooperation.

Philosophy and history of national champions

Most modern European states emerged as political units during the era of economic mercantilism, when wealth and power were each considered proper ultimate ends of national policy.[2] Governments were obligated to intervene in domestic economies. The introduction of *laissez faire* economics challenged some aspects of this close state-economy relationship; nevertheless, governments were still responsible for providing infrastructures that facilitated trade.[3] Since commerce was 'regarded as an instrument of national policy',[4] firms within strategic industries were selected to be 'national champions'. They received special support; they monopolized production and sales. Virtually all states had a 'national champion' airline,[5] while aircraft manufacturers generally received less conspicuous public support.[6]

Acceptance of government as a partner in the economy was underscored in civil aviation by its synergy with national security. From the first attempts at conquering air travel, state élites[7] recognized its military potential. Several attempts to establish an international air-law code based on Grotius' freedom-of-the-seas principle failed because government élites were unwilling to yield sovereignty over this strategic industry.[8]

The First World War cemented the perceived synergy between aviation and military power. Direct development of civil aviation was temporarily halted during the War; however, both military and commercial aviation benefited from advances in aircraft design and production technology because their needs coincided: reliable, fast delivery of important dispatches, goods and people.[9] War-devastated ground transportation and communications' systems in Europe provided a strong incentive for the development of an efficient air transport system. By late 1917, regular air-mail service was in place.

By the late 1930s, the United States had gained supremacy in civil aircraft manufacturing and European airlines were buying American aircraft. Europe's early lead was undermined by myopic perceptions of aircraft performance requirements and the events of 1938. From 1929–39, European airlines were consciously used to link empires, which required short-to-medium range and relatively primitive landing and take-off technologies.[10] By 1938, the British, French and Germans shifted their focus to the production of military aircraft.

During the Second World War, changes in technology and public attitude increased the potential significance of commercial air transport. Aircraft reliability and efficiency were enhanced by advances in design and construction, including improved radio communications, navigational aids and increased speeds, range and capacity performance. Prewar grassy landing fields were transformed into asphalt or concrete runway systems facilitating greater size and performance sophistication. The new comforts of flying resulted in the general public becoming 'air-minded', more frequently choosing air transportation when travel distances exceeded 200 miles.[11]

By 1945, everyone realized that commercial aviation was likely to expand.[12] Its prestige, its potential for generating revenues and jobs and its national security synergy meant each state wanted to participate significantly in the industry. European aircraft manufacturers faced the monumental task of resurrecting a moribund capacity to build commercial-class aircraft. Many of their factories had been destroyed during the War; their technological expertise lay in building war-fighting aircraft rather than transport aircraft; and they faced overwhelming competition from American manufacturers.

Most importantly, the technological advances that increased the potential rewards to be derived from commercial aviation also increased its costs and risks. Aircraft and engines were larger and more complicated; longer lead times were required between gestation, production and revenue-earning. Attempting to incorporate increasingly sophisticated technology into aircraft design and produc-tion made the pay-offs uncertain. Research, development and production (RD&P) costs increased so dramatically that a single manufacturer could no longer privately finance a civil aircraft (see Table 12.1). Higher costs meant

Table 12.1 Aircraft Development Costs, 1933–74
(millions of 1974 US dollars)

Plane[a]	Time period	Development costs
DC 1/2/3	1933–6	1.5
Canberra (UK military)	1945–51	50
Caravelle	1953–9	140
Douglas DC8	1955–9	200–300
Concorde (Anglo-French) (including engine)	1962–74	2,400
Boeing 747	1965–9	1,000
Airbus A-300 (Franco-German)	1969–74	500

[a]Excludes engines except where indicated.

Source: M. S. Hochmuth (1974) 'Aerospace', in Raymond Vernon (ed.), *Big Business and the State: Changing Relations in Western Europe*. Cambridge, MA: Harvard University Press, p. 150.

higher prices, which meant airlines could not easily afford to replace or increase their fleets (see Figure 12.1). These new industry dynamics increased the cash-flow needs of the manufacturer and 'put a premium on accurate technical and commercial judgments'. With 'longer replacement cycles, the price of market failure rose; it became more difficult, and certainly more expensive for a firm missing out on one generation of aircraft to challenge for success in the next'.[13] Aircraft manufacturers needed larger markets[14] so they could sell more planes, lower production costs through the achievement of economies of scale, and eventually lower prices facilitating the sale of even more aircraft. Europe suffered from compartmentalized national markets. The United Kingdom, France and Germany[15] each harboured at least two major aircraft manufacturers, 'all much smaller than the leading US firms'.[16] National champion airlines became captive markets for domestically produced aircraft, so European aircraft firms were unable to access a global market.

Three possible sources of financial support for rebuilding the industry existed: (1) government treasuries; (2) private assets – either from other corporations or from market-investment opportunities; and (3) international collaboration, which would allow for the pooling of resources. Depending on the prospective foreign collaborator, the last was either rejected or closely monitored; it was definitely a last choice among policy options. Private assets had been drained as a result of the War effort. Therefore government support became a *sine qua non* of the industry. While this did not present an ideological hurdle, each European state had to determine which intervention instruments it would use to maintain a competitive presence in the industry. Policy options included military and commercial airline procurement,[17] direct and indirect subsidies, favourable loan terms, direct and indirect protection against imports and financing civil aerospace exports.[18]

Government decisions to intervene created new problems. Domestically, the 'intervention dilemma' sometimes conflicted with democratic political structures.

Once established, commitments to technically complex, large-scale, long-lead-time projects may serve to limit the Government's real freedom to control events. Advanced

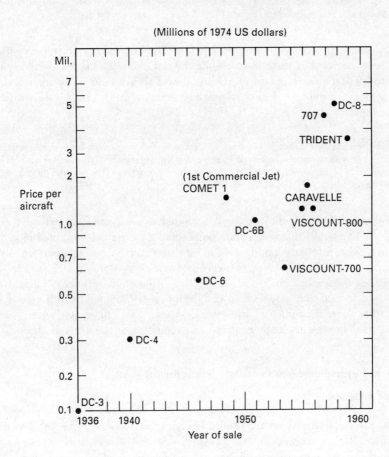

(Millions of 1974 US dollars)

Figure 12.1 Commercial Aircraft Prices, 1936–60
(millions of 1974 US Dollars)

Source: M. S. Hochmuth (1974) 'Aerospace', in Raymond Vernon (ed.), *Big Business and the State: Changing Relations in Western Europe*. Cambridge, MA: Harvard University Press, p. 151.

technologies generate powerful, technically fluent and articulate lobbies within Government and industry, shaping both the specialist and policy advice offered to Ministers. With projects spanning many ministerial careers, requiring the acquisition of a high level of knowledge to form an independent judgement, and with, perhaps, politically sensitive issues like unemployment dependent on decisions, the tendency is often to rely on the specialist or to postpone any decision which would fundamentally alter the course of development. Similarly, the emergence of a major commitment may be incremental, with no obvious point for a single definitive decision. Ministers wake up suddenly to a large, perhaps irrevocable, demand for further resources. Responsibility becomes attenuated over the years, and momentum rather than choice determines events.[19]

Furthermore, to achieve economic efficiency, policy-makers must resolve the 'independence-control dichotomy': while the state may assume responsibility for directing a particular programme, it must almost always yield authority over day-to-day progress and technical or commercial decision-making to private actors. It is not easy:

to find the optimum balance between control and independence; one which provides Government with adequate supervision and sufficient information to monitor and review progress without superseding, undermining or obstructing the authority and judgement of the [private] agent.[20]

At the global level, policy-makers confronted an emerging consensus that free trade would prevent the destructive competition that had twice erupted in global conflict. The international dimension of the intervention dilemma involves attempts to achieve a balance between protectionism, which could destroy the political-economic régime, and ineffective promotion of those industries perceived as vital to a state's survival.[21] Each country adopted its own unique set of intervention instruments; between 1945 and 1957, aircraft manufacturers throughout Europe gradually rationalized production at the domestic level.

National approaches to industry development

United Kingdom

It was particularly difficult for the United Kingdom to resolve the 'intervention dilemma'. Perhaps because Britain has survived as both a mercantilist state in the fifteenth to seventeenth centuries and a free-trade advocate following the Industrial Revolution and the introduction of *laissez faire* economics, these competing ideologies never merged in a coherent or compatible fashion. Britain's intervention strategies have been 'marred by a series of shuddering starts and stops'.[22] The goal of industry dominance remained constant; the means of achieving it ranged from detailed involvement to more market-oriented incentives.

Initially, Britain rejected state ownership but promoted civil aviation via procurement from a 'magic circle' of existing manufacturers.[23] By 1938, confronted with increasing competition from the continent and across the Atlantic, an internal committee was created to review British Air Policy; it recommended greater public support of the industry. Although the Second World

Table 12.2 The Brabazon Types

Type no.	Designation	Comments
1A	Bristol Brabazon	Long-range, piston-engined; first flight 4 Sept 1949; cancelled 1952.
11A	Airspeed Ambassador	Short-range, piston-engined; first flight 10 July 1947; 20 built for BEA.
11B	Vickers Viscount	Short-range, turbo-prop; most successful postwar British airliner.
11B	Armstrong Whitworth	Short-range, turbo-prop; insurance for ApolloViscount; only 2 aircraft built.
111A	Avro 693	Medium-range, turbo-prop/jet; cancelled 1947 in design stage.
111B	Avro Tudor II	Developed from interim type; unsuccessful.
IV	Comet	World's first jet airliner; fatal crashes 1953.
VA	Miles Marathon	Piston-engined feederliner; first flight 19 May 1947; small batch sold to Royal Air Force.
VB	De Haviland Dove	Charter/executive type, twin-piston engines; first flight 25 Sept 1945; 500 sold; evolved into equally successful Heron.

Source: Keith Hayward (1983) *Government and British Civil Aerospace: A Case Study in Post-War Technology Policy*. Manchester, Manchester University Press, p. 257.

War intervened, the precedent for peacetime government involvement was established.

During the War, hoping to exploit the British advantage in jet-engine technology,[24] another committee, chaired by Lord Brabazon, developed a plan based on two assumptions: first, the extant industry structure of a 'strategic reserve' of small, competitive companies would be maintained. Secondly, airlines would be the conduit through which government money would be funnelled to manufacturers. Despite a bias against detailed government involvement in the civilian economy, the committee literally designed nine transports, known as 'Brabazon Types', to be produced (see Table 12.2). The option of pursuing licenced construction of American aircraft, preferred by many manufacturers, was consistently rejected.[25]

After the War, the perceived need for government support of civil aerospace was intensified by four factors: (1) the persistent belief that civil aviation was critical to both national security and economic recovery; (2) a sense of inferiority vis-à-vis the United States related to Britain's heavy economic indebtedness to its Atlantic Ally,[26] coupled with the conviction that a revitalized commercial aircraft industry could represent a resurgent and autonomous Britain, less dependent on its former colony; (3) a large aerospace labour pool;[27] and (4) the postwar Labour government's ideological commitment to 'a planned, centrally directed industrial and economic recovery'.[28]

As work began on the transition from a military to a civilian economy, government officials were insufficiently sensitive to changes in industry dynamics and the importance of consumer (the flying public) preference. They introduced 'interim designs' – derivatives of old military aircraft (see Table 12.3) – believing that 'even if this would not result in particularly advanced aircraft, firms would have something to sell and British airlines a domestic product to buy,

Table 12.3 The Interim Designs

Type	Comments
Vickers Viking	Wellington Derivative; 600 built.
Avro Tudor	Britain's first pressurized airliner.
Handley Page Hermes	Halifax derivative.
Bristol 170	Civil and military freight aircraft.

Source: Keith Hayward (1983) *Government and British Civil Aerospace: A Case Study in Post-War Technology Policy*. Manchester, Manchester University Press, p. 258.

while the more ambitious Brabazon Types were being developed'.[29] British airlines were caught in a double bind: they could not compete in the international air-transport-services market with interim designs but they were required to 'Buy British' as an 'honourable legacy of the war'.[30] Revenues flattened, exacerbating their inability to purchase new aircraft. Manufacturers also had little manoeuvrability: they could only produce Brabazon and interim aircraft but were dependent on airline purchases for financial support. Experimentation with innovative technology was virtually impossible. The Vickers Viking was the only successful interim type produced.

By the late 1940s, universal dissatisfaction with the government's intervention policies led to an internal inquiry, which concluded 'that the customer [defined as the airline] was likely to be the best judge of what it wanted from an airliner'. Therefore, 'direct and unhindered collaboration' between manufacturers and airlines should be allowed and the 'centrally directed, programmatic approach' to civil aircraft production should be abandoned.[31] The government would provide direct financial support to aircraft manufacturers but only after substantial orders from a major airline had been placed. Still missing was a sensitivity to the tremendous costs incurred in the early stages of aircraft development. Furthermore, the government continued to influence airline-procurement decisions via financial control and airlines were still expected to 'Buy British'. By 1950, the government had invested over $300 million in the Brabazon programme and was unwilling to concede its failure. This approach yielded technical and market successes in the Vickers Viscount and the de Haviland Comet and Dove aircraft; however, of the eleven aircraft finally produced, none was competitive with US-built aircraft.[32]

Eventually, British policy-makers realized the 'strategic reserve' concept was not working. Too many projects and the wide distribution of contracts had fragmented the industry.[33] Between 1944 and 1959, twenty-five different commercial transports were launched by twelve different firms, competing for the same government funds and success in a world market, over half of which was in the United States.[34]

Rhetoric notwithstanding, when the Conservatives came to power in 1951 close government involvement in commercial aviation continued. The primary means of support remained the 'Buy British' principle. One government official commented that airline fleet purchases would determine 'whether we ultimately make or mar this [aircraft] industry'.[35] The British European Airways (BEA) Chair agreed, noting that 'one of the most important of BEA's special obligations is to assist development of British transport aircraft', while the British Overseas

Airways Corporation (BOAC) Chair asserted airlines did not need to make money, but should 'support the British aircraft industry . . . develop routes around the world, and so on'.[36]

The Conservatives decided airline management should not be asked to commit large sums of money toward the purchase of unproven aircraft.[37] The 'cost of developing new aircraft at present appears to fall too heavily on the Air Corporations, and places them at a disadvantage compared with the foreign competitors who use . . . American aircraft'.[38] Thus, airlines gained the right to 'tailor' aircraft to their demands. After the Comet failure management grew cautious, preferring the old reliable turbo-prop over the speed and risk of jet transports.[39] Meanwhile, America's Boeing and Douglas pursued jet aircraft development and launched the 707 in 1952 and the DC8 in 1953. In spite of private investment approaching £4 million, the absence of public support for speculative development doomed potential market successes, such as the Vickers V1000.

Furthermore, the government continued to influence design and production decisions. Vickers' Viscount success was 'rewarded' in 1957 with the impossible task of developing the VC10 two years after the market had been saturated with the 707. Similarly, the government forced de Haviland to develop its tri-jet Trident according to BEA specifications, which bore 'little reference to wider export market requirements'.[40]

By 1956 'the majority of British firms lacked the financial strength to carry the cost of private ventures or to survive a period of general increase in R&D costs and declining demand for military aircraft'.[41] A 1957 White Paper announced there would be 'no long range bombers after the "V" bombers and no high performance fighters beyond the Lightning',[42] which eliminated future military aircraft development as an adjunct to civil aircraft production. Policy-makers were finally convinced consolidation was the solution. Still unwilling to let the market dictate how, the government directed the process (see Figure 12.2).

Britain's civil-aviation development was characterized by a situation in which 'responsibility for project choice, monitoring and control was left in limbo between a full, free-market private-enterprise system and state interventionism'.[43] The intervention tools of indirect subsidy and *ad hoc* government involvement in design and production combined with myopic perceptions about the similarities between British domestic flying needs and global requirements, the refusal to produce under licence with US manufacturers, and the fragmented nature of firms in the manufacturing sector to create a weak, though surviving, industry.

France

The French tradition of a strong civil service actively engaged in promoting and protecting particular enterprises dates back to the Bourbons. Thus it was expected that the government would support industrial redevelopment after the Second World War.

France dominated world aviation until the 1930s, when its supremacy was challenged by Britain's 'interest and strength, Germany's new and superior technology, and the growing United States market'.[44] As in Britain, the industry's initial progress was facilitated by small, privately owned firms but eventually this

132   VICKI L. GOLICH

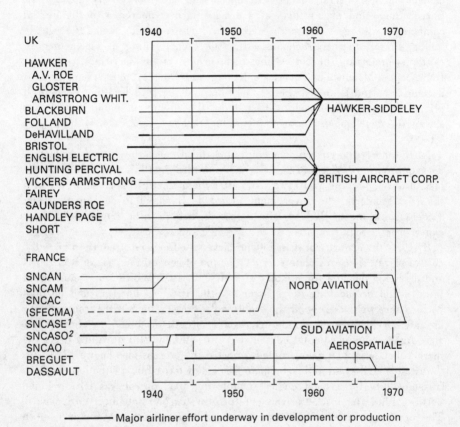

Figure 12.2 Major British and French Aircraft Manufacturers, 1936–71

Notes: (1) SNCASE stands for Société Nationale de Constructions Aéro-nautiques du Sud-Est, commonly known as Sud-Est.
(2) SNCASO stands for Société Nationale de Constructions Aéronautiques du Sud-Oest, commonly known as Sud-Oest.
Source: M. S. Hochmuth (1974) 'Aerospace', in Raymond Vernon (ed.) *Big Business and the State: Changing Relations in Western Europe*. Cambridge, MA: Harvard University Press, p. 156; Keith Hayward (1983) *Government and British Civil Aerospace: A Case Study in Post-War Technology Policy*. Manchester, Manchester University Press.

fragmentation hampered further development. In an early attempt to coordinate aircraft-production efforts and avoid wasteful duplication of talent and money, Léon Blum's Popular Front nationalized the industry in 1936. Several small firms merged to form larger combines and two prominent engineer-entrepreneurs, Bréguet and Dassault, lost their factories. During the War, the industry languished under German occupation.

After the War, the French felt economically and militarily inferior *vis-à-vis* the United States and other European states. Policy-makers believed 'a strong and independent aircraft industry was an important element in its quest to regain its position as a great power and as the most important country in Western Europe'.[45] The industry was nationalized again and, between 1945 and 1955, government élites designed a plan to revitalize aviation using intervention instruments such as access to low-cost credit, direct subsidy, import protection, government procurement[46] and investment financing.[47] Firms were 'required to subcontract extensively with one another in order to utilize all production resources',[48] which facilitated the reincorporation of Bréguet and Dassault.

Eventually, a unique management dialogue between government bureaucrats and industrialists 'became the symbol . . . of French industrial policy'.[49] Aircraft design and development was left to the engineers who enjoyed guaranteed government support. Engineer-entrepreneurs learned fairly early the potential gains associated with taking calculated risks. They incorporated technological advances into aircraft design, developed aircraft quickly, flew prototypes in a minimum amount of time and at a minimum cost, and avoided head-on competition with United States manufacturers. Reflecting government concern for national security, research and development efforts generally focused on military aircraft such as Dassault's Mystère and Mirage fighter aircraft.

Not all production decisions were successful. In 1946, George Héreil, a lawyer and bankruptcy trustee, was named by Charles Tillon, the Communist Air Minister, to be president of Société Nationale de Constructions Aéronautiques du Sud-Est (SNCASE or Sud-Est). The company was struggling to produce the government's first large order for commercial transports – a 1939 vintage aircraft. Héreil obtained further government backing for the development of a larger, equally unsuccessful airliner, which had to be cancelled in 1950. To keep Sud-Est alive, the government awarded it the licence to produce the British Vampire. By 1947, the French realized that changes in industry dynamics meant corporate policy-makers had to be 'masters not only of bureaucracy and politics but of business as well'.[50] A two-year 'housecleaning' replaced political appointees with business people.

When the airlines indicated they needed an intermediate range jet, the production cycle for the successful Caravelle began.[51] Interesting because its production involved collaborative work with the British, the Caravelle used Rolls-Royce Avon engines and the first section of the Comet fuselage, built under licence from de Haviland.[52] French government officials believed that 'to maintain broadly based and independent aerospace capabilities France had to seek out some form of collaboration with foreign powers'.[53] Whereas Britain had refused collaboration with the United States, it was willing to extend the possibility to France.[54]

French willingness to pursue collaborative work with the British was partially motivated by a growing disenchantment with United States' leadership within the

North Atlantic Treaty Organization (NATO). In the mid-1950s, NATO officials sought to increase production and operations efficiency by implementing a programme of weapons rationalization, standardization and interoperability (RSI), which required the use of common weapons and collaborative production of weapons systems. The first cooperative NATO procurement project began in 1953 and the first collaborative production effort in 1956; each ended in failure.[55] After several false starts, European members complained that 'NATO collaboration usually implied adopting American aircraft'.[56] All NATO members have used collaborative means to achieve unilateral ends. 'French, British, and US aerospace nationalism doomed [the RSI] programme from the beginning . . . and assured that no follow-up projects in the early 1960s would survive beyond the planning stage.'[57]

The French selection of transnational collaboration as a survival strategy was also motivated by several other factors: the Algerian War had drained the French treasury and the aircraft industry was suffering from the loss of government financial support; foreign sales and investment were needed. Germany was emerging as the most powerful industrial state in Europe and France wanted to tap into its technological expertise. Collaboration was viewed as a means of driving a wedge between the United States and the United Kingdom. Finally, the French collaborated to avoid European rationalization, which might have relegated manufacturers to the production of components. A continental alliance, under French leadership and with Germany at the core (in a subordinate position), was created and cemented through extensive military, technological and economic cooperation[58] to develop 'a powerbase for more independent European and world policies'.[59]

French civil aerospace benefited from several factors peculiar to its history and environment, including a long tradition of public support of technological industries.[60] The nationalized industry facilitated the adoption of an informal corporatist structure – a triumvirate of government, corporation and consumer-managing industry development. Government provided financial support and protected the industry from foreign competition; manufacturers combined engineering and entrepreneurial talents to develop innovative and marketable aircraft; airline management, sensitive to global market needs and financially secure, provided meaningful purchase-support to manufacturers. This triumvirate successfully rationalized its industry and chose to participate in joint ventures with foreign partners when it served their interests. In the end, French policy resulted in the creation of a single major manufacturer of commercial transports.

Germany and other European states

Throughout the early 1900s, Belgium, Germany, Holland, Italy, Russia, Spain and Sweden all developed fledgling aviation industries. (Table 12.4 lists a sample of airplanes and manufacturers from 1919 to 1960.) Eventually Germany and Holland challenged France for aviation leadership. As in France and the United Kingdom, aviation in these countries was directly and indirectly subsidized by individual governments.[61] Eventually, all except the Soviet Union were forced to pursue transnational production strategies because their home markets were so small. Following the Second World War, the Soviet Union isolated its production to its own political bloc.

Germany faced a different set of constraints and opportunities than other European states in 1945. A strong tradition of government involvement had begun with Frederick the Great; subsequent German governments supported scientific and technical education and research.[62] While Germany's aerospace industry boasted many fine domestic firms, it also benefited from early collaboration with Holland's Anthony Fokker. In 1912 and 1913, the Dutch aerospace engineer-entrepreneur tried unsuccessfully to sell his aircraft to the British or the Dutch, but only the German Navy was interested. Germany supported his projects because they were important to its war effort.[63] Initially, Germany concentrated on lighter-than-air flight capabilities, first with dirigibles, then gliders.[64]

From 1919 to 1926, when virtually every other aviation power was utilizing converted military airplanes for commercial transports, German commercial aviation benefited from their Treaty of Versailles prohibition on building airplanes of more than 100 horsepower. 'Teutonic flying interest turned to gliders, and . . . valuable new lessons in aerodynamic structure were learned that later served in designing their aircraft.'[65] Germany also circumvented the intent of the Treaty by establishing firms to work on transports in other countries.[66] Thus in 1925, when finally permitted to conduct passenger operations, Germany was the only country with 'true, unconverted air transports'.[67] Once treaty restrictions were dropped, Germany's aviation industry, like Italy's, became a 'thinly disguised military machine'.[68]

Between 1945 and 1955 Germany's aircraft-manufacturing sector virtually ceased to exist, although it was clear that Germany would regain its status as an industrial nation. Temporarily prohibited from 'flying even model airplanes, much less gliders',[69] considerable outside technological help was a prerequisite to the rebirth of commercial aviation. Both domestic and international political constraints prevented Germany from unilaterally pursuing aerospace development. Transnational collaboration and 'extensive domestic rationalization' enabled Germany to compete with larger manufacturers in neighbouring states.[70] Germany accepted a subordinate partner relationship with France.[71]

Germany, more so than other European states, was compelled to pursue a collaborative strategy of industry development for political reasons. The same market forces that supported transnational-cooperation efforts throughout the continent were also effective incentives, as were similar political motivations of prestige and power. However, domestic self-consciousness and international suspicions required Germany to work with foreign partners if its products were to be successful in the marketplace.

The birth of internationalized production

Internationalized production is not new. Known as the 'Golden Age of Aviation', 1927–32 was marked by the widespread practice of licenced production of foreign aircraft. In the 1930s Fokker built DC2s under licence. The USSR produced their version of the DC-3/C-47, the Li-2. Peru helped build the Faucett-Stinson single-

Table 12.4 Commercial aircraft by country of origin, date of first service, and first airline to use, 1919–60

Maker	AIRCRAFT Type	Country of origin	Date of first service		First airline
Junkers	F.13	Germany	July	1919	Junkers Luftverkehr
de Havilland	D.H.4A	UK	25 Aug	1919	AT & T
Handley Page	W/8B	UK	16 May	1922	Handley Page Air Tpt.
Fokker	F.VIIb/3m	Netherlands	Mid	1926[1]	KLM
Ford	'Tri-Motor' 5-AT	US	11 June	1926[2]	Stout Air Services
Handley Page	Heracles H.P. 42	UK	11 June	1931	Imperial Airways
Junkers	Ju. 52/3m[3]	Germany	May	1933	DLH
Boeing	247D	US	April	1933	United Air Lines
Douglas	DC-2	US	18 May	1934	TWA
Lockheed	L.10 'Electra'	US	11 Aug	1934	Northwest Airlines
de Havilland	D.H. 89A 'Rapide'	UK	July	1934	Hillman's Airways
Savoia-Marchetti	S.M.73P	Italy	Mid	1935	SABENA
Douglas	DC-3[4]	US	25 June	1936	American Airlines
Short	S-23 'Empire Boat'	UK	30 Oct	1936	Imperial Airways
Focke-Wulf	FW200A 'Condor'	Germany	Late	1938	DLH
Savoia-Marchetti	S.M.83	Italy	6 Nov	1938	SABENA
Boeing	307 'Stratoliner'	US	8 July	1940	TWA
Curtiss	C-46 'Commando'	US		1942[5]	BOAC[5]
Savoia-Marchetti	S.M.95	Italy		1945	Alitalia
Sud-Est	Languedoc	France		1945	Air France
Lockheed	L.049 'Constellation'	US	1Mar	1946	TWA
Douglas	DC-4	US	7 Mar	1946	American Airlines
Vickers	'Viking'	UK	1 Sept	1946	B.E.A.
SAAB[6]	Scandia	Sweden		1946	AB Aerotransport[7]
de Havilland	'Dove'	UK	9 Dec	1946	CAA
Short	Solent	UK		1946	BOAC
Douglas	DC-6	US	27 April	1947	United Air Lines
Martin	4-0-4	US	Oct	1947[8]	LAN, Chile[8]
Convair	CV.240	US	1 June	1948	American Airlines
Ilyushin	IL-12	USSR	Early	1948	Aeroflot
Boeing	377 'Stratocruiser'	US	7 Sept	1948	United Air Lines
Douglas	DC-6B	US	11 April	1951	Western Air Lines
Lockheed	L.1049G 'Super Constellation'	US	Nov	1951[9]	Eastern Air Lines[9]
de Haviland	'Comet' 1A	UK	2 May	1952[10]	BOAC
Vickers	'Viscount' 700	UK	16 April	1953	BEA
Breguet	Provence	France		1953	Air France
Douglas	DC-7c	US	May	1956	Pan American
Ilyushin	IL-14M	USSR		1956	Aeroflot
Tupolev	Tu 104A	USSR	15 Sept	1956[11]	Aeroflot
Bristol	'Britannia' 310	UK	1 Feb	1957[12]	BOAC
Vickers	'Viscount' 810	UK	13 Feb	1957[13]	BEA
Fokker	F27 'Friendship'	Netherlands	28 Sept	1958	West Coast Airlines
de Havilland	'Comet' 4	UK	4 Oct	1958	BOAC
Boeing	707-120	US	26 Oct	1958	Pan American

Fairchild[14]	'Friendship' F-27	US/ Netherlands[14]	Sept	1958	West Coast Airlines
Canadair	Forty-four	Canada	Dec	1958	Air Lingus Airlines Flying Tiger
Lockheed	'Electra'	US	12 Jan	1959	Eastern Airlines
Ilyushin	H-18	USSR	20 April	1959	Aeroflot
Sud	'Caravelle' 1	France	6 May	1959	Air France
Boeing	707-320	US	26 Aug	1959	Pan American
Douglas	DC-8-30	US	18 Sept	1959[15]	Delta & United Air Lines
de Havilland	'Comet' 4B	UK	1 April	1960	BEA
Boeing	720B	US	5 July	1960[16]	United Air Lines
Sud Aviation	'Caravelle' 6R	France	18 Feb	1961	SABENA
Traders Ltd.	Carvair	UK		1962	Air Charter
Nord	Nord 262	France		1963	Air Inter
Hawker Siddeley[17]	Trident	UK		1964	BEA
Nihon Aeroplane Manufacturing Company (NAMC)	YS-11	Japan		1965[18]	TOA Airways
Potez 841	Potez	France		1965	Aero Dienst GMBH
British Aircraft Co.	One-eleven	UK		1965	BUA
Fokker[19]	'Fellowship' F-28	Netherlands		1965	LTU

Source: Davies, 1964, pp. 536–7; Munson, 1967; Winter, et al., 1969.

Notes: This table was derived primarily from R.E.G. Davies' seminal work *A History of The World's Airlines* (1964). He selected aircraft according to 'the relative importance of each aircraft in its lifetime and the contribution made to airline progress'. Using Kenneth Munson's *Civil Airliners Since 1946* (1967) and *Airplanes of the World, 1490–1969*, by William Winter, William Byshyn and Hank Clark (1969) I have added several aircraft because they are representative of European manufacturers after the Second World War. Some aircraft are included because they were the products of initial attempts at international collaborative production.

1. Fokker F.VIIa/3m; Fokker VIIb/3m in April 1928.
2. Type 4-AT; type 5-AT in September 1928.
3. Approximately 5000 total were built: 170 by CASA of Spain and over 400 by the French Ateliers Aéronautiques de Colombes.
4. Two thousand were built under licence with the Soviet Union as the Lisunov (Li-2) and 450 in Japan as the L2D2.
5. CW-20 prototype.
6. Only 17 produced, 11 by SAAB and 6 with Aviolanda, de Schelde, and Fokker factories in the Netherlands.
7. In 1948, ABA became part of Scandinavian Airlines System (SAS).
8. M.2-0-2. Only 31 of original series built; first M.4-0-4 entered service with T.W.A. 5 October 1951.
9. L.1049; L. 1049c in June 1953; L1049G in January 1955.
10. Comet 1; but excludes two military Comet 1 is and fifteen military Comet 2s.
11. Tu 104.
12. Britannia 102; Britannia 310 on 19 December 1957.
13. Viscount series 801.
14. This was the first Fokker airliner since the 1930s; design began in the 1950s. In 1956, the Dutch manufacturer signed an agreement with Fairchild, which had been building Fokker trainers in the US for several years, to build and market the Friendship on the US side of the Atlantic.
15. DC-8-10; DC-8-30 on 27 April 1960.
16. Boeing 720; variant listed is the fan-engined development.
17. De Haviland became a part of Hawker-Siddeley in 1960.
18. The Japanese Ministry of International Trade and Industry (MITI) first established a Transport Aircraft Development Association consisting of six of the major producers in the country in May 1957. Its purpose was to design and produce an indigenous medium-range commercial transport.
19. In 1964 The Netherlands government promised financial support, and agreements were signed with three other European aircraft manufacturers to collaborate on production. Short Brothers and Harland of the UK would be responsible for outer wing and landing gear assemblies. Germany's Hamburger Flugzeugbau and Vereinigte Flugtechnische Werke (VFW) would build the front and rear fuselage sections, tail units and engine installations. Fokker would produce the front and center fuselage sections and the wing center sections.

engine aircraft that operated on Faucett routes for years after the Second World War.[72]

In an effort to decrease tension and instill a more cooperative spirit, internationalized production was formally extended to other industry sectors after the War. France and Germany began the process in 1951 with the European Coal and Steel Community (ECSC). Four years later final plans for the European Economic Community (EEC) were made at the Messina conference. On 25 March 1957, the original Six members of the EEC – Belgium, the Federal Republic of Germany, France, Italy, Luxemburg and The Netherlands – signed the Treaties of Rome.[73]

Although nationalist sentiments reigned supreme, market forces were clearly compelling. In civil aviation, the list of unsuccessful aircraft built by individual countries was growing: the French Languedoc, Bretagne, Armagnac, Potez 840 (feeder liner) and Dassault Mercure; the Swedish Saab Scandia (32 passenger twin-engine DC-3 'replacement'); the German VFW614; and the British Avro Tudor, Airspeed Ambassador, Bristol Wayfarer 170 and Britannia, de Haviland Comet, Vickers Vanguard and VC10, Handley Page Herald, and Hawker Siddeley Trident. Only four of these even achieved three-figure sales. The few successes, modest by US standards, included the Sud Caravelle, Vickers Viscount, BAC111, HS 748 and 125, Dassault Falcon and the Fokker F27 and F28. In 1957 as in 1945, the industry structure and dynamics meant European national markets were too small.[74]

The 1950s and 1960s were marked by several aborted attempts at cooperation. Boeing held discussions with de Haviland Aircraft Company about production of the Trident but returned home to build the 727 instead. Douglas began negotiations on marketing rights and production of the Sud Aviation Caravelle, but decided to produce the DC9 alone. Early joint-venture failures can be attributed to the fact that 'each of the firms involved nurtured the hope of acquiring ultimate ascendancy over national and international competitors'.[75] Cooperative efforts were motivated by parochial desires to resume a dominant position in the industry sector, achieve and maintain a competitive position vis-à-vis the United States, or prevent another European competitor from becoming the dominant producer on the continent.

Conclusion

Historically, political units have struggled to find the optimum balance between control and autonomy over the development of domestic economies. Generally speaking, politics shapes the framework within which economic activity takes place. Private actors, operating with varying degrees of autonomy to achieve their corporate goal of survival, often restructure the constraints and opportunities for political behaviour. Eventually a new framework for economic activity emerges and the state-corporate dance for control and autonomy begins again.

This dance may change the nature of control and involvement by the state in the economy. For example, the introduction of paper money and usury was first resisted by political élites. Their use proved so beneficial to private actors that the state acquiesced, adopting a new set of rules and regulations that returned control to the state.

Sometimes the dance results in political economic revolutions, such as the Industrial Revolution. An explosion of innovative production techniques restructured state-society, state-economy and state-state relations. The Revolution was facilitated by a unique convergence of changes in physical conditions, technology, intellectual thought, economic relationships and political organization.

Since 1750, the dominant world political-economy has operated according to capitalist dictates. A continuing debate among political élites has been about how much state involvement in the economy is appropriate. Political entities seek to survive just as corporate actors do. Survival is related to protection from external attack and internal subversion. Survival has also been defined in economic terms – whether because a healthy economy is deemed critical to survival in its own right or only as a means to pay for military protection from external enemies. Just as tactics and strategies for military combat have changed as a result of changes in the five factors noted above, so have the political instruments of economic intervention. Similarly, just as ideas about when military action is appropriate have changed over time, so have notions regarding when and how much state intervention in the economy is proper. By the end of the Second World War, state and corporate actors confronted a new aspect of the intervention dilemma – the consequences of state involvement for their own domestic economies *and* the international system as a whole.[76] It was clear in 1945 that a dynamic relationship existed between society, the state and the international system. Thus the dilemma became one of how

to engineer a competitive presence in a full range of industrial activities with instruments of public intervention that are not necessarily very effective and that threaten the well-being of the international economic system.[77]

Finally, states were confronted with dramatic changes in the structure and dynamics in several industry sectors. States were particularly concerned about maintaining a presence in those sectors they perceived to be vital to their national survival, such as civil aviation. This intensifies the intervention dilemma.

Between 1945 and 1957, the development of civil aviation followed a path of gradual consolidation throughout Europe, albeit a path unique to each country. A single major manufacturer of commercial-class aircraft emerged in France following a 'route of entrepreneurial success in an environment characterized by competition and skimpy funding'.[78] American conventional wisdom to the contrary, the nationalization of the industry in France proved to be an important part of its success story. The British commercial aerospace industry entered the postwar period 'with the advantages of size, technical superiority, the opportunity to plan strategically, and a government willing to finance airliner ventures'.[79] By all rights, this British industry sector should have dominated significantly. Industry participants suffered from indecisive government involvement and dependence on captive domestic airline markets. The British industry failed to force a real, well-timed consolidation of the fragmented industry.[80] Germany was motivated to seek transnational partners not only as a result of market forces but also because of painful political factors.

An important aspect of this consolidation process deserves more attention and may be particularly revealing about the future evolution of the international political economy. Large transportation and communication systems are natural monopolies if private actors are allowed to act 'freely' in the market place.[81] As industry dynamics force corporations to service an expanding market to be profitable, preferred corporate strategy will be to rationalize production.[82] Given the political economic culture of a particular state, such consolidation may be viewed positively or negatively. As this analysis reveals, the United Kingdom consciously attempted to preserve a fairly large number of firms because decision-makers believed the resulting competition would be beneficial to the industry. In contrast, the French initiated rationalization. Eventually, however, the firms in each country consolidated their production structures.

A more difficult concern arises in the context of a global market. When market dynamics and structure require transnational rationalization, state élites must struggle with a new situation. Between 1945 and 1957, European-state élites sought to dominate civil aviation unilaterally because of its perceived strategic value; they pursued the goal with heavy state involvement. Eventually, market forces coerced state and corporate élites to participate in joint ventures with foreign producers. This was the only viable means of matching market realities with productive capabilities. Ironically, industry domination required foreign collaboration. Still, collaboration was externally coerced and viewed only as a means to the old goal of unilateral domination; the latter remained one way of achieving power and autonomy in the international system.

Another irony occurs once private-sector cooperation achieves marginal successes. To facilitate further private-sector growth by making transnational ventures even more efficient and effective, state officials must coordinate government functions such as standards' certification, which can lead to the creation of supranational government authorities.[83] Eventually the network of private and public activity becomes so complex and intertwined that the beginnings of a new political organization emerge.[84] Without suggesting that a 'United States of Europe' will replace a loose confederation of states cooperating in the market in 1992, a return to national level production is unlikely.

13 The Council for Mutual Economic Assistance: 1949-57

G. Izik-Hedri

The economic policy of the Socialist countries and economic cooperation between them has always been plagued by the fact that the changes inaugurating Socialist régimes did not take place under the anticipated conditions. Marxist theory envisaged that the advent of Socialism would be a global phenomenon, but in 1917 Socialism was victorious only in Soviet Russia. Similarly the spread of Socialist régimes at the end of the Second World War, in 1948-9, remained limited to what came to be known as eastern Europe. The conditions under which these revolutions occurred was no more consonant with the theoretical criteria than their geographic extent. The classic Marxian model assumed a well-organized, efficient economy and political democracy. Yet the Socialist régimes inherited societies burdened by paternalist and even feudal traditions. Whereas the model expected change to be driven forward by the internal imperatives of the old societies, in the case of the People's Republics external pressure was responsible for the imitation of a Stalinist state-Socialism. Expectation and outcome diverged just as sharply in the development of the Socialist régimes. Whereas a temporary dictatorship was supposed to give way to the withering away of the state – a kind of social deregulation – the Socialist régimes witnessed the monstrous growth of the state that was compounded by the claims of the 'party'.

The eastern European countries had barely begun to come to terms with these problems when they were confronted by the prospects of economic integration in the postwar world. Both Marxists and non-Marxists agreed that lasting economic cooperation was only possible between countries of a similar social structure. This meant, in practice, that integration embracing the whole of the European continent was unrealistic. In the West the industrially developed countries, strengthened by the Marshall Plan, were moving towards integration along lines that had been laid down in theory for some time. In the East theories of regional integration had scarcely been formulated when the new régimes were obliged to respond to developments in the West. Their response came in the Proclamation issued at a meeting of the Communist and Worker's Parties of the Socialist countries in January 1949:

The conference established further that the governments of the United States of America, Britain and of certain other countries of western European countries, had been, as a matter of fact, boycotting trade relations with the countries of peoples's democracy and with the USSR, since these countries did not consider it possible to submit to the Marshall Plan dictate, as this plan violated the sovereignty of the countries and the interests of their national economies . . . The conference decided that in order to establish still broader economic cooperation among the countries of people's democracy and the USSR it was necessary to institute a Council for Economic Mutual Assistance, comprising representatives of countries taking part in the conference, on the basis of equal representation.[1]

This cold war proclamation not only betrays the feeling of being under threat but also the positive intent to tie central and eastern Europe to the Soviet Union politically and economically. The emphasis on sovereignty arose from both international and domestic considerations. It was intended to suggest that the new régimes were a reflection of popular desires and wishes and not an external imposition that might lead to the possibility of later annexation. It was, then, political will that underlay the foundation of the Council for Mutual Economic Assistance (CMEA).

The CMEA was formally established by Bulgaria, Hungary, Poland, Romania, the Soviet Union and Czechoslovakia in Moscow in April 1949.[2] Its avowed intent was to promote a new type of international division of labour among countries with identical social systems and a common ideology. The assumption was that this cooperation would be mutually advantageous and would later facilitate an efficient integration into the world economy. In the atmosphere of the cold war, however, it was generally accepted that multilateral cooperation would assist

the countries grouped in the CMEA in strengthening the socialist economic order, developing socialist industrialization, on the one hand, and in fighting off the discrimination manifested by the capitalist countries, eliminating the economic dependence on the imperialist powers, on the other.[3]

The economy of the majority of the member countries was backward. Intraregional trade had been of modest dimensions, varying between 7 and 18 per cent before the Second World War. International cooperation at the level of individual enterprises was practically non-existent. This was the less than promising background for the pursuit of rapid economic development, the elimination of differences in levels of development between member states and consequently the rapid extension of trade within the CMEA. The main mechanism of development was to be the supply of raw materials and energy by the Soviet Union in return for which the other member states were to expand their own exports to the Soviet Union. In practice this entailed the complete orientation of their economies to Soviet requirements and the development of a radial pattern of trade (see Table 13.1).

The fact that one state stands out as a predominant trading partner within a region is not in the least unusual. The Federal Republic of Germany enjoys such a role within the European Community, for example. Within the CMEA, however, slow technological development meant the benefits of increasing specialization

Table 13.1 Percentage of Total Foreign Trade

Country	Year	Exports to		Imports from	
		USSR	Other CMEA countries	USSR	Other CMEA countries
Bulgaria	1950	57	35	75	10
	1958	55	27	55	27
Hungary	1950	25	41	40	16
	1958	24	33	33	31
Poland	1950	33	23	36	25
	1958	25	23	31	22
GDR	1950	39	29	40	36
	1958	43	25	47	15
Romania	1950	66	24	47	31
	1958	50	19	53	22
Czechoslovakia	1950	26	28	34	20
	1958	34	26	33	29

did not adequately compensate for the costs of investment. This continued to be a problem as the rigid system of planning directives contributed to retarding the rate of technological development.

At the founding session of the CMEA in 1949 only the basic principles of cooperation were set down. The CMEA was to facilitate the harmonization of planned development of the member countries, the continuous growth of labour productivity, the constant improvement in the welfare of peoples, and the industrialization of the less well-developed member states. Member states were to implement the agreed policies of the Council and to report back upon the implementation of policies. Following the Soviet model of the time, member states formulated three- and then five-year national plans. As part of the planning process they concluded long-term trade agreements that were broken down into annual targets. The whole process was governed by directives that flowed from the top downwards. The basic decisions were taken by members of the Council and Secretary Generals and First Secretaries of the parties. The agreements they reached formed the basis of directives to competent national authorities, the ministries and planning offices, who, in turn, set targets for subordinate management structures. At the end of the process individual state companies and cooperatives received their own instructions. The intent was that each country would be assured of an adequate supply of raw materials, machinery and other products necessary for its development while its export markets would be equally reliable.

According to the ideology of planning, the process was supposed to be two-way. Draft plans at company level were to be passed up to the ministries which would coordinate these plans. Subsequently, these summaries were to be compared with the detailed national plans formulated by the central-planning agencies. In practice a multilevel system of bargaining developed. Planned targets were vital at company level for they determined levels of remuneration. At higher levels commitment to development issued in a different set of targets. The central-planning authorities, who were concerned to maintain some coherence and balance in the national economy as a whole, intervened, modifying the agree-

Table 13.2 Growth of Industrial Production (1950=100)

	1955	1960
Bulgaria	190	397
Hungary	170	267
Poland	220	330
Rumania	202	340
Soviet Union	185	304
Czechoslovakia	167	273

ments worked out at lower levels. Finally, national economic plans were enacted by parliaments. This cumbersome process could not always be completed before the start of the planning period and was further complicated by the decisions of CMEA partners, especially the Soviet Union, who acted on the basis of preliminary figures.

The neglect of market forces led to extensive disproportionalities. Quality and technological development were pushed into the background in the pursuit of quantitative targets. Since achievement was assessed annually enterprises could fail to meet delivery dates within the year without suffering any adverse consequences. The disruption caused by belated delivery necessitated frequent revision of the plans. In particularly severe cases the leaders of CMEA countries would have to be brought in to resolve such problems on an international basis. The Soviet Union, as the main supplier of raw materials and fuels, played a vital role in these adjustments. The commitment of the Soviet Union to maintaining social stability in other CMEA countries often lay behind the decision to fill raw-material and fuel shortfalls. Yet there were also disadvantages to the asymmetrical relationship of the CMEA. Adherence to the Stalinist model meant that all states were supposed to develop heavy industry, but this led to excess and parallel capacities. Khruschev's attempt to break this cycle in 1959, by encouraging the development of complementary economic relationships, did not meet with much enthusiasm from his partners. The Rumanian leaders, in particular, reacted strongly to the humiliation of being consigned to the role of supplying foodstuffs and raw materials.

Despite these difficulties the 1950s witnessed a boom in the CMEA economies. The utilization of extensive labour reserves in conditions of guaranteed markets and supplies issued in spectacular growth (see Table 13.2).

During the same period the development of the CMEA was hesitant. The Second Session of the CMEA Council, held in Sofia in August 1949, dealt primarily with technical considerations and patents. The agreement that inventions and innovations should be freely available among members was later to be revealed as an impediment to growth. The Fourth Session, in Moscow in March 1954, dwelt on the problems of harmonizing national plans. This was to be a perennial concern and only recently, in the wake of Gorbachev's reforms, was the impossibility of harmonization finally accepted. In May 1956 the Seventh Session, in Bucharest, founded eight permanent commissions (subsequently increased only to be reduced again) with the aim of assisting multilateral economic, scientific and technical cooperation among members. The Ninth Session of June 1958, again in Bucharest, adopted the so-called Bucharest price principle and also adopted measures for product specialization. It also considered more wide-ranging five-year agreements, intended to extend cooperation beyond trade agreements. The construction of a new pipeline for oil and gas supplies from the Soviet Union was agreed at the Tenth Session held in Prague in December 1958. On the tenth anniversary of the CMEA two Sessions took place. The first of these, the Eleventh Session, held in Tirana in May, returned to the themes of product specialization and broad-based economic cooperation. More significantly it also adopted measures concerning the unification of energy systems. At the Twelfth Session, in Sofia on 14 December 1959, the CMEA finally adopted a Charter that drew heavily upon the preceding Sessions. Despite the earlier groundwork the Charter consisted of only seventeen articles in comparison to the 248 of the Treaty of Rome, which established the European Economic Community. Subsequent amendments of the Charter, which occurred on three occasions, set out from agreements reached at Sofia, concerned, for example, multilateral agreements on rail and sea transport and cooperation in the fields of health-care, quarantine restrictions and the control of agricultural pests and diseases.[4]

Between 1949 and 1957, however, the focus of the CMEA was intraregional trade. This was analogous to developments in other regional frameworks. Both the EEC and the EFTA achieved a rapid expansion of intraregional trade by reducing tariffs and other barriers to trade in their early years. All three organizations looked, at the outset, to the growth of intraregional trade as a proportion of total trade as their immediate goal. All of them protested against the accusation that they were promoting 'closed' economies. In the West advocates of integration argued that trade creation far exceeded trade diversion. In the East the CMEA followed Lenin's thesis that differences in social systems would not hinder the international division of labour. In Lenin's words, 'There is a force which is greater than the wish, will and determination of any enemy government or class, and this force is the general relationship in the world economy which forces them to embark upon relationships with us.'[5] This much-quoted thesis had been advanced by Lenin at the Pan-Russian Congress of 1921 when he gave an account of the initial – though very modest – results of the Soviet Union's foreign-trade policy. As evidence he pointed to the fact that the industrially developed capitalist powers, which had applied an economic blockade in the hope of undermining the Soviet Union, were entering into a trading relationship with it. Lenin's thesis had been prefigured by Marx's theories on the internationalization of the economy and was subsequently to be adopted by Stalin. It is reflected in the preamble to the CMEA Charter according to which the governments confirmed their 'readiness to develop economic relations with all other states – irrespective of their social and state systems – on the principles of equality, mutual advantage and non-interference in domestic affairs.'[6]

In the meantime, however, Stalin had put forward the concept of 'two world economies': the Socialist economy based upon the principles of mutual cooperation and the Capitalist economy based upon market competition. This was probably necessary to justify the autarchic trend exhibited by the CMEA. It was also appropriate for the cold war atmosphere. The Soviet Union, moreover, had emerged from the Second World War in a severely weakened economic condition, while its opponent, the United States, was stronger than ever before. Despite Soviet military power Stalin's country lagged far behind the United States in terms of economic development. The United States sought to utilize its economic and technological advantage to exert pressure on the Soviet Union, restricting trade through the COCOM. While these restrictions did not seriously impair the Soviet defence industry, they did hit the civilian industries of the CMEA. In this framework of mutual suspicion and recrimination East-West trade amounted to a mere $2 billion in the first half of 1950, which in turn constituted scarcely 1 per cent of world trade.

The impact upon the countries of east-central Europe was substantial. Trade relations dating back several centuries tapered away because one partner was 'eastern' and the other 'western'. However, there were exceptions. A distinct and different trade régime existed between the two parts of occupied Germany and subsequently between the two German states. Within certain limits their mutual trade was not subject to the constraints facing other members of the respective alliances. Because of their peculiar geostrategic position Finland and Austria both enjoyed unusually extensive relations with the Soviet Union.

It was not easy to repress the force of objective market relationships, despite the political pressures of the day. The CMEA countries demanded increasing quantities of Western goods: high-quality goods that they would receive within specified delivery dates. The Western position was also changing. It had become apparent by the mid-1950s that the trade restrictions had not seriously impeded either the Soviet Union's military potential or the rapid industrialization of the CMEA states. Moreover, west European countries were loath to abandon potential, and past, export markets. They were more willing to restrict imports from the CMEA states. The reasons given for this were in the first place that Western countries risked becoming economically dependent upon the East if they failed to restrict imports and, in the second place, that the foreign-trade monopolies of the CMEA states might flood Western markets with underpriced goods. Neither argument was very convincing at a time when imports from Socialist countries amounted to a mere 2 per cent of total OECD imports.

During this period the CMEA states continued to seek long-term trade agreements, though they did not mean thereby to give up their policies of import substitution. The Western states were not inclined to enter into such agreements, partly for the political reasons mentioned above and partly simply because they felt that such agreements would be unduly advantageous to the CMEA countries.

The CMEA itself encountered several problems from the outset, despite its initial limitation to the regulation of trade. The detailed quotas that regulated trade were for the most part quantitative. Yet some mechanism of clearing balances was still required. The solution was to use roubles with the exchange rate of the national currencies to the rouble being centrally determined. The problem was that national price levels differed considerably and could, indeed, scarcely be determined amid the complicated maze of subsidies and taxes. Once again the reality was that prices were set at the end of a long and complicated process of bargaining. It might be thought that the economic interest of the strongest CMEA member, the Soviet Union, would automatically prevail in these negotiations, but this was not the case. The economic interest of the Soviet Union was counterbalanced by its interest in the social stability of the other members of the CMEA.

An attempt to improve pricing mechanisms was, however, made in 1958 when recourse was had to world-market prices. The 'Bucharest price principle' endorsed the use of modified world-market prices. According to this principle, world-market prices, purified of the fluctuations generated by booms and monopolistic distortions, were to serve as the basis for trade within the CMEA. Yet this did not fully resolve the problem. The prolonged bargaining continued, this time over the degree of 'purification' required. The process was further complicated by the lack of any world-market referent for some goods.

Another characteristic of CMEA trade was that it was highly restricted. The introduction of specialization did little to alter this fact, especially in the 1950s when genuine specialization was a distant aim. CMEA specialization, moreover, tended to neglect the possibility of direct international contact between production units. The undesirability of this restriction was soon recognized and the permanent branch commissions of the CMEA were established, in 1956, precisely to develop such links. At the same time economic experts were also given a greater role within the system. The final decisions, however, remained firmly within the control of the political authorities.

It was evident to many economists that this form of international cooperation led to neither efficiency nor to a higher level of complementarity. It was also evident that significant improvements in the system could only be brought about by a fundamental transformation of the economic policies of member states. The restrictive factor was ultimately the international political situation. Hence, it was not until 1968 that the 'New Economic Management', which broke with the system of planning by directives, could be introduced in Hungary. Even then lack of political reform meant the desired results were not achieved. In the Soviet Union which, after all, played the decisive role within the CMEA, reform had to wait until the mid-1980s and the emergence of Secretary-General Gorbachev.

In the period 1949–57 CMEA ideology prescribed cooperation between central authorities. Compulsory quotas and planning directives served as the basis of the system. The goal was the harmonization of national economic plans. All that clashed with the objective laws of the economy. It should be noted, however, that there are basic discrepancies in the periodization of postwar history depending upon whether one is considering developments in the West or the East. The Treaty of Rome may mark a turning point in the history of the West, but 1957 has no analogous significance for the CMEA. The CMEA Charter was not finalized until later. The most important body of the CMEA, after the Council, was the Executive Committee, and this was not even established until the Fourteenth Session of the Council in Moscow in June 1962. There are then both parallels and significant differences in the trajectories of integration in East and West.

14 The Political Economy of International Economic Security: Retrospect and Prospect

David Willis

Introduction

Economic forces are in fact political forces. Economics can be treated neither as a minor accessory of history, nor as an independent science in the light of which history can be interpreted. Much confusion would be saved by a general return to the term 'political economy' which was given the new science by Adam Smith himself and not abandoned in favour of the abstract 'economics' . . . till the closing years of the nineteenth century. E. H. Carr (1939) *The Twenty Years Crisis.*[1]

Although there has been a great deal of scholarly controversy regarding the origins, and to a lesser extent, the economic and political impact of postwar economic agreements between the superpowers, there has remained a virtual consensus among historians and political scientists concerned with the evolution of international relations in this period on at least two aspects of the postwar economic order: the primacy of the balance of economic and military power in shaping postwar economic reconstruction in Europe, and the dominant power position of the United States in accounting for the development of the international economy. In this view, the pattern of European economic integration, and also its deep division between East and West, is to be viewed as a consequence of Great Power rivalries, polarized between American hegemony in the western European economies, and in eastern Europe, Soviet military power supporting the development of Communist-Party-dominated centrally planned economies. Thus according to a commonly accepted view, the present unities and disunities in Europe owe much to external influences, notably American foreign-policy concerns.[2]

This chapter does not intend to dispute the importance of power struggles between the American and Soviet systems in shaping the postwar economy. However, it advances some grounds for questioning the adequacy of a model of international economic relations from the late 1940s which views international economic régimes, including the regional trade régimes of eastern and western Europe, as adequately accounted for in terms of the preponderance of economic and military power in the postwar system. There is little quarrel with the idea that American economic and political power in the postwar period became deeply implicated in the remapping and reshaping of Europe. European economic reconstruction involved not only American financial aid and technology to western Europe, but also deliberate efforts to promote a culture of mass-production and consumption. Outside Europe, American foreign policy strove to 'make the world safe' for American capitalism. American foreign-policy concerns thus provided a major impetus towards the development of international 'free trade' régimes in the early postwar period.[3]

However, a problem with the bipolarism in historical work in this period, and the preoccupation with 'Great Power' influences, is that these have tended to detract attention away from the equal (if not by economic measures the greater) successes of the smaller 'neutral' powers, such as Belgium, Denmark, Sweden and Finland, adopting policies that ran counter to American 'cold war' ideologies, and in eastern Europe, the economic and policy divergencies among the CMEA countries.[4] The view is taken in this chapter that the conflation of military and economic power within the hegemonic model of national economic dependencies has tended to detract attention away from the analytical significance of a number of developments in interstate economic relations that remain anomalous within a realist model of the international economy. The argument will be presented in three parts: first, a brief overview will be presented of conceptions of international economic relations in the early postwar period, and some reasons suggested for the appeal of an hegemonic interpretation of the political character and role of international financial and trading regimes. Secondly, some of the basic assumptions of a preponderance of power model of interstate relations will be established, and against this, some trends in the postwar period that appear anomalous and hard to explain within the terms of this model. Finally, an alternative model is proposed that seeks to take into account the different logics of and incentives to the formation and maintenance of international economic régimes for the regulation of interstate economic relations. This points the way to the need for greater attention to factors, both in interstate relations and in the international economy, that have contributed, for want of a better phrase, to the 'relative autonomy' of international régimes, including the emergence of Pan-European political institutions.[5]

Retrospective

At the risk of over-simplification, there appear in essence to be at least two distinctive literatures on the development of the postwar international economic system that have few points of connection. According to the dominant political perspective, this order was shaped primarily in the establishment of spheres of economic interest by the superpowers, which between them effectively shaped the international political economy, with the conflict of rival and mutually incompatible ideologies of the United States and the Soviet Union dominating the political agenda.[6] What is at heart a 'realist' model of international economic relations and international law, views the institutions created in this period as largely instrumental to the foreign-policy interests of the superpowers.[7] In this view, a reconstructed Europe was to become an important, but largely subordinate, interest in America's concerns to stem the threat to its economic trading interests and security posed by Soviet Communism.[8] The west European states have thus converged under American tutelage and support to social democratic goals, while the Soviet Union responded to its own strategic needs by subordinating the economic development of the weakened east European states, lacking the protection of the Atlantic Alliance. Thus the latent economic nationalism of the east European states were bound by an iron corset,[9] cut off from the possibility of full participation in the international economic system both by the deliberate exclusion by the United States of the east European states from full membership of the new trade régimes such as GATT and IMF, and the early antagonism of the Soviet Union towards these institutions.[10]

Effectively underpinned by what might be termed a geopolitical and 'state-centric' model of the international economic system, the so-called 'hegemonic' model of the distribution of interstate power in the international economy has itself enjoyed a virtual hegemony in accounts of international economic relations. The victory of the one system over the other in the long-run was recognized as depending on success in shaping the emergent framework of international rules governing international trade and finance. For the economically and politically weak, the economically and militarily dependent and the vanquished alike, the unfolding dramaturgy of a divisive superpower hegemony not only in Europe, but wider afield in South East Asia and the Pacific Rim,[11] were events of epic proportions in which smaller states could play only a diminutive role. The world of superpowers and supergames had arrived, and was rapidly seen to evolve around cold-war confrontations between the rival ideologies of the Soviet Union and United States, and the ability of the US to exclude nation-states that did not conform to the Western 'rules of the game' from full membership of international trade associations.[12]

Although this view of the postwar international economic order has been widely shared by historians of the period, and some of the main protagonists, there has persisted an alternative version of the postwar economic system emphasizing principles of universalism, reciprocity and voluntary exchange which also found its advocates in the early postwar period.[13] Thus the early designs for the international regulation of trade and finance emphasized the value of universalism, mutual interests in the achievement of a stable and competitive economic order, and in the reduction of barriers to international trade: a perception that was, moreover, shared by Soviet economists during the early phases of the Bretton Wood negotiations.[14] In short, postwar economic régimes were conditioned by conflicting geopolitical interests but were widely perceived as a bulwark against renewed international conflict. This conception was again clearly expressed in hopes for a new international economic order, with provisions for free-trade standing centrally as an alternative base to the military in provisions for security.

Clair Wilcox, writing in 1949, provides a reasonable statement of this alternative vision:

The Charter (of the ITO) is an integral part of the world economic reconstruction. If the loans extended by the International Bank for reconstruction and development are to be repaid, goods must be permitted to move freely among nations. If the International Monetary Fund is to succeed in stabilising currencies, steps must be taken to restore balance in the World's trade. If the Fund's efforts to remove exchange regulations are to have any meaning, quantitative restrictions must be subjected to international controls.[15]

One concern of this chapter is to establish how well this more placatory and accommodatory role of international régimes fits the complex geopolitical conflicts and issue-linkages emerging in the postwar negotiations on economic security.

The economic contradictions of hegemony

One reason for the persuasiveness of the hegemonic theory of the international economic system lies in its ability to go at least some of the way to reconciling realist observations with the conflicting sentiments of reparation and appeasement. As developed in the work of Gilpin, Kindleberger and Krasner,[16] the theory of hegemonic stability holds that the stable, open, international economic structures that emerged in the postwar period were largely determined by the existence of an hegemonic distribution of state power: that is, 'one in which there is a single state that is much larger and relatively more advanced than its trading partners'.[17] Students concerned to explain the period of postwar stability in the face of disequillibriating economic pressures and continuing interstate rivalries and competition for power have emphasized a number of factors. But above all has been the happy coincidence of the interests of the United States as an 'awakened superpower' in committing its superior economic and military resources to backing a liberal international trade régime.[18] The emergence of a liberal trading régime is thus to be explained by the fortuitous preponderance of power (both military, and by the time of the bombing of Hiroshima, of military power) in the hands of political leaders of a state whose principal values were liberal democratic, and whose economic interests lay, because of their already-leading economic position, in the maintenance of an open and competitive system of international trade.[19] The GATT and IMF were to promote American corporate interests abroad, while financial aid to the reconstruction of the western European economies under the Marshall Plan, the reform under Allied government of the economies of West Germany and Japan[20] and support to friendly political régimes everywhere, are seen as complimentary aspects of American foreign policy, sharing much the same roots – a fear that economic regression would threaten political instability and American trading interests. Thus restrictions under the Morgenthau plan to 'pastoralize' Germany were progressively relaxed and offset by positive Allied support to West German infrastructure. Elsewhere, notably in South East Asia and Latin America development became a strategy of containment.[21]

A major consequence of the identification of these initiatives with a liberal hegemony, has been the depiction of American support for the return to individual private enterprise and liberal democracy – seen as complimentary 'freedoms' – as the foundation of the later prosperity of western Europe. The image of America acting as a benevolent dictator has persisted in accounts of the development of institutions such as the IMF. The crisis precipitated by the rejection of Keynsian economics in America, the 'productionist' ideologies underpinning the Marshall Plan for the economic reconstruction of Europe, the imposition of American corporate and liberal democratic values on Japan, and finally, a self-conscious effort by American foreign-policy staff to use aid as a point of leverage wherever weaknesses were detected in the Communist power bloc, all neatly dovetail in the new economic theories and fit the overall thrust of the hegemonic model of the postwar order.[22] In these arrangements, supportive economic theories of managed trade emerged, heavily backed by the United States and unveiled for the enlightenment of a grateful Europe. It is an approach that allows scope for the interplay of great with minor state powers and international diplomacy, the ideological as well as the material interests of America, and suggests the grand design of American strategic thinkers, aided and abetted by British diplomacy, in seeking to subordinate short-term economic interests of European federalists and American isolationists to more long-term foreign policy objectives.[23] Realism and idealism converged in the postwar realities of defending the economic freedoms of international capitalism and the civil liberties of liberal democracy.

A major claim advanced for the hegemonic model has been its usefulness in accounting for the unusual period of stability in the face of interstate rivalries and tensions.[24] Above all, the hegemonic model proposes the centrality of the conflict between America and the Soviet Union in shaping the pattern of European economic development and disunity, and the substantial interests of the former in shaping European reconstruction in accordance with American interests – along international, multilateral and universalistic, rather than along federalist or Pan-European lines.[25] In all this, the essential facts explaining the development of the international economy and the emergent pattern of Europe are the hegemony of the United States and the development of international régimes such as the IMF and GATT as instruments of American foreign policy and as essentially predatory instruments.[26]

A number of influential scholars have viewed the postwar economic order as both hegemonic in character, and as shaped principally by the interests and economic resources of the United States.[27] Susan Strange follows a long line of scholars in arguing that the Bretton Woods system was determined principally by the demands and wishes of the United States.[28] Parbonni casts the United States largely in the role of benevolent despot *vis-à-vis* the international economy, though critical of the United States in giving simultaneous support to systems of free international trade and international flow of capital, while at the same time deliberately subverting the internationalization of Bretton Woods where it threatened to undermine the dollar.[29]

Viewed from the vantage point of both major and minor powers with an interest in the rapid resumption of international trade, the idea that peace could not be secured without the re-establishment of a new world economic order appeared beyond dispute. The idea that a competitive free-for-all of *laissez-faire* provided a basis for international peace and prosperity had clearly suffered from the experience of the depression and the protectionism of the 1930s. Keynes had already reached the conclusion that the exercise of state power would be necessary after the War to restore equilibrium.[30] In 1940, Isiah Bowman, a geographer, lecturing to the territorial study group of the influential Council on Foreign Relations, saw the threat posed by Germany as essentially 'an economic question', suggesting that Hitler's 'lebens traum' might be 'lebens traum for all' rather than 'lebens traum for one'. Yet Britain, with its crumbling colonial empire and a war-devastated economy, was hardly in a position to maintain this role. A year later, the editor of *Life*, Henry Luce, captured the optimism of the American public when he announced that the United States was about to 'assume a leadership role in the world', thus initiating the 'American century'.[31]

Observation of a strong link in the American imagination between defences against the Communist threat (galvanized into action by Churchill's famous 'iron curtain' speech) has been regarded as particularly crucial in the proponents of hegemonic models of international régimes. From this perspective ideological antagonisms and threats to capitalist systems help to explain both the ability of American policy-makers committed to a more active international policy to overcome isolationist tendencies at home. The Council of Economic Advisers, for example, stated in its annual report for 1955 that:

our own interest clearly calls for a policy that will in time extend into the international field those principles of competitive enterprise which have brought our people great prosperity with freedom. Against the Communist ideology of the omnipotent state, owning all means of production, and dominating all economic activity, the United States holds forth the ideals of personal freedom, private property, individual enterprise and open markets. In the long run, other countries are far more likely to rally to liberal values if we take the steps within our own power to encourage them to join in mutually beneficial economic intercourse. Hence our trade and investment policies affect our ability to increase the solidarity of the free world.[32]

According to one view, American economic superiority in the postwar period freed foreign policy from domestic constraints, giving rise to a 'no limits' stance on the cost of achieving foreign-policy goals.[33] This is seen as extending well beyond the writing of the rules of international trade and finance that were to prevail in the postwar period, to the deliberate subversion of European moves towards federalism. Thus for Hirschman writing as early as 1945, and for later writers, a central feature of the new American hegemony was its defeat of the axis powers, whose trade was conspicuously organized into closed regional systems under extensive state direction. American leaders were convinced of a profound connection between the cartelization of world trade in the 1930s and the origins of the Second World War, as well as its own economic depression; they aimed to prevent its recurrence. The Bretton Woods agreements thus represented a victory for this policy, attaching Germany and Japan to a liberal economic order based on market principles, restricted state intervention, multilateral and non-discriminatory, and above all cutting off the eastern European states from any prospects of participation in the international economy so long as they remained committed to Communist doctrines.[34]

Economists and historians have been able to cite some impressive evidence in support of this interpretation for the development of international régimes, though the approach to explanation of the patterning of postwar Europe arguably over-emphasizes both the novelty of the use of trade asymmetries to establish spheres of influence, and the importance of American and Soviet actions in this respect.

The deliberate creation and use of trade asymmetries to create spheres of influence is an important feature of both the Soviet (CMEA) in eastern Europe and American foreign policy in western and southern Europe but its novelty and force can be easily overstated, and in any case has depended on 'consensus' between the great powers on what constitutes defensible economic space. The consequences of the lukewarm response of the British government to the growth of southern and eastern European dependence on German trade is a good case in point.[35] Up until the early 1960s, the United States continued to make a considerable and disproportionate contribution to the reduction of tariffs in order to induce greater tariff reductions and to incorporate a wider grouping of states within the GATT, a fact that has been seen as contributing to America's economic decline.[36] Crucially for the pattern of European economic and political integration in the early postwar period, the United States was able to offer substantial financial and technological aid to its allies in western Europe in return for support for its foreign-policy objectives both in Europe and globally. But this transfer of technology and resources was forced on a reluctant public and business community and arguably contributed to the erosion of the United States' comparative advantage in high-technology production.[37] Historians may thus be on firm ground in depicting the shaping of markets in this period, and the economic reconstruction of western Europe, as heavily conditioned by, if not direct extensions of the security concerns of the United States – for example, the Mutual Defence Export Control Act 1951 that stipulated that aid would be curtailed to all countries exporting strategic, including non-military, goods to Communist nations.[38] However, it is on less firm ground in assuming that this heavily influenced patterns of European trade and economic development.[39]

The economic divisions of Europe also seem at first glance consistent with hegemonic theory, if, that is, the economies of the EFTA group of countries, which maintained a neutral stance towards the east European economies, are left out of western Europe, and the actual pattern of trade and economic relations occurring within this period is ignored. While the rapid recovery and growth of the west European economies, and a world boom in trade, suggest the success of programmes of managed trade, increasing tensions between America and west Europe, and (at least by 1955) the lukewarm support in western Europe for American policies of economic containment of the Soviet Union and eastern European centrally planned economies, do not readily fit a theory of American hegemony. There are certainly patterns of dependence but these are by no means as clearly divided between the centrally planned economies and western European economies as geopolitical theories would maintain. West Germany, helped by the special constitutional status of eastern Germany before unification, has maintained extensive trade links with eastern Europe, including foreign direct investment. The neutral states of northern Europe have also nurtured extensive trade links from the beginning, partly as an extension of 'security' interests. However, the concentrated nature of these economies also facilitates trade with countries in which prices are 'negotiated' or 'bargained' centrally, rather than through markets.[40] If anything, east European dependence in trade terms on the Soviet Union has become the most intractable obstacle to Pan-Europeanism but owes more to systemic factors, notably the incompatibility of divergent economic systems, than the force of cold war constraints on East-West trade and foreign direct investment. The incompatibility of 'central planning' and Western-style capitalism can again be easily exaggerated if the 'corporatist' economies of the EFTA group of countries are left out of account. Again, recent studies suggest a considerable amount of East-West economic interdependence through barter-trade and non-market price-fixing agreements.[41]

A number of observations on the influence of the 'minor' powers and eventually the rise of new economic superpowers (Japan, West Germany and the EEC), remain anomalous within a model emphasizing the decisive role of American and Soviet Union's external ambitions. First, there is some disagree-ment on the nature of the United States' strategic role and the strength of the underlying imperatives towards the creation of a multilateral trade system. A major weakness of the argument of a coincidence between commercial and military interests is historical evidence of a conflict between foreign-policy aims and economic or commercial logic.[42] The dominant assumption concerning government subsidies to foreign direct investment in this period has been that increased capital exports were encouraged through a variety of incentives because of a perceived coincidence of American economic welfare, American domestic expansion and national power. In Packenham's characterization of American foreign aid, 'all good things go together'.[43] While American diplomatic consider-ations have favoured a global pattern of investment, particularly directed in favour of areas of political instability, American manufacturers have tended to identify their interests in high-income areas.[44] In fact, what emerged from these cross-cutting pressures between foreign policy and economic policy was a 'trade not aid' strategy, or at least aid in support of trade, in which the main interests of business appeared to be to limit large governmental capital flows and offset the emergence of a public economy in the developing countries – at least in so far as these were seen as detrimental to American interests – but above all in which increased congressional pressures to limit American commitments of aid to Europe were beginning to be felt.[45] This reflected a general corporate bias against extensive public programmes that increased the level of interference with and fiscal burdens on business. These were by no means distinctively American business concerns.

Nor is it clear that the United States was acting in the interests of American big business in efforts to promote American investment abroad. Although this might be an accurate depiction of Eisenhower's vision of the United States' interests in the postwar economic order, again there is some historical evidence that this may have been overstated. First, there was major internal dissent on the assumption that export of capital was in the national interest.[46] The role of foreign direct investment (FDI) in securing supplies of materials from overseas, frequently cited as a reason for foreign aid, was similarly hardly an issue after the end of the Korean War. Moreover, American foreign investment constituted a surprisingly small part of American wealth in this period.[47] An examination of the saliency of an outward-going foreign-policy orientation during this period suggests somewhat similar conclusions on the overstatement of American interest in promoting the internationalization of economies in this time, at least through governmental auspices.[48] Despite the claims of Eisenhower that tax incentives were 'one of the foundation stones of his administration's foreign policy', there is a great deal of evidence that the administration did not consider either tax incentives or the expansion of American multinationals to be vitally important policy objectives.[49] Moreover, despite Krasner's claims[50] about the ideological nature of these commitments there is some evidence to suggest that the United States administration had a fairly realistic grasp of a lack of coincidence between the pattern of investment dictated abroad by commercial and diplomatic considerations.[51] This did not dictate an increase in FDI in support of United States' security interests, but a freeing of multinationals to commercial logic in their investment decisions.[52] Despite well-publicized cases of American military and diplomatic actions in defence of national interests abroad and the clear pre-occupation with the securing of strategic resources supplies,[53] what stands out in many less-publicized cases is the unwillingness of the American administration to contravene international codes in defence of particularistic interests, and the integrative force of these concerns in terms of the development of international agreements where supplies become seriously threatened by economic or political predation, or by more direct forms of expropriation.[54] Finally, the counter-productive consequences of 'external ambitions' for the economic development of both the United States and the Soviet Union, and the destabilizing consequences of great power rivalries, have increasingly become a focus of attention.[55]

These inconsistencies in the evidence on the constraints on United States' external ambitions and involvements are far from satisfactory from the standpoint of the theory of hegemonic stability; moreover they point in another direction: that America was drawn into the service of multilateralism by a broader consensus, shared in Europe, which had its origins not in economic nationalism, but a repulsion from this rooted in the wartime experience, and a retreat to more limited concerns of national economic security.[56] Countries with widely differing 'dominant' political ideologies thus entered the postwar negotiations with an interest in creating a framework of international rules capable of re-establishing an open trading system as a first line defence of national economic security.[57]

Various explanations have been offered for Soviet repudiation of this course in 1946.[58] However, the most plausible explanation is that the outbreak of the cold war altered the pay-offs from international economic cooperation on both sides. The Soviet Union thus came to view these institutions as a 'Pax Americana', and as peripheral to the real interests of the United States in Europe, particularly with the announcement of the Marshall Plan.[59] In so far as the United States and Soviet Union were in apparent accord in this respect in the early stages of discussions, much greater attention needs to be paid to conflicting west European influences in fomenting great power rivalries. Great Britain's self-image as a superpower with international responsibilities and interests, and the antagonism until the late 1950s and beyond to entanglement with more 'narrowly' conceived European integrationist movements, has emerged as a particularly important factor shaping postwar international economic relations, suggesting a 'pull' rather than a 'push' theory of American involvement in Europe, particularly the pull supplied by Anglo-American diplomacy. For example, Pelling charts the difficulties encountered by Britain in reconciling the demands of the Commonwealth, Europe and its 'special relationship' to America, noting American sensitivity to Britain's resentment of its treatment as 'just another European power' as one American diplomat put it, writing in 1950.[60] Unfortunately, this does not square well with the idea of the United States as either hegemonic or 'prime mover', or as the mainstay of international economic stability. Indeed, it is equally consistent with a more reactive theory of American involvement in Europe and beyond. Taylor, for example,[61] has recently established the pivotal role of Britain in the tripolar politics of the late 1940s. In effect, Britain was able to set the agenda, despite her economic weakness, by playing on American fears of Soviet aggression. Other studies have also revealed the extent of cyclical fluctuations in the salience of these issues in American politics.

Another rather unsatisfactory feature of the predictions of the hegemonic model is the evidence for a disproportionate 'small power' influence on international agreements and some, albeit accidental, redistribution of power in the international economy (or the limitations placed on the scope for manoeuvre of its own policy-makers) resulting from consequences of American efforts to encourage multilateralism and economic cooperation, particularly against the quiet rise to economic supremacy of West Germany and Japan, relatively unencumbered by military commitments.[62] According to one view, supported by dependence theorists, multilateral trade régimes such as the GATT and the IMF acted as instruments to maintain the privileged position of the hegemony. Soviet perceptions of the IMF as essentially instrumental to the interests of the United States have been reinforced by the changing, cycling attitude of the United States towards the utility of these institutions.[63] However, American financial and technical assistance, though self-interested and politically slanted, was also contradictory, both in detaching the strength of the dollar and its role in the international economy from American-policy influence. Triffin referred to the 'dilemma' of the American position in this respect in which deflationary effects result from United States correction of its balance-of-payments deficits, or else the international monetary standard collapses if it failed to do this because American foreign liabilities exceeded its ability to convert dollars into gold.[64] On the one hand, fears of reactions to American economic superiority contributed to increasing dissatisfaction with the system, a countervailing move towards regional economic integration in Europe, the rise of medium and small state coalitions and the ultimate collapse of American hegemony.[65]

These observations bring to the fore the pivotal role of the postwar international political economy: the IMF and parallel provisions in the Marshall Plan. Most arguments concerning the role of United States financial supremacy and global economic interests in the immediate postwar period make considerable play on American economic self-interests in structuring the development race between eastern and western Europe. These included the establishment of international credit mechanisms (through the IMF) and, more directly relevant to western Europe, Marshall aid to economic reconstruction and modernization that has been seen as massively favouring dependency on United States capital goods and technology, as well as serving critical policy objectives in countering the growth of Socialism and Communism in Europe. However, this analysis is from the 'neorealist' perspective of the cold-war period; it fails to take account of earlier optimism on the scope for reconciling differing economic ideologies within a framework of multilateral trade.[66] Moreover, the model of interstate power implicit in this is a 'basic forces' model that conflates economic and political power and authority.[67] The United States may have gained in economic superiority, but did this contribute to political clout in the international economy in proportion to the financial costs? Whitman observes, for example, that the Bretton Woods' system 'from its beginning drifted away from its original concept of equality towards reliance on a single key currency, the US dollar'. While the system embodied in the IMF's Articles of Agreement vested substantial discretionary decision-making powers in the IMF, and provided, after a transitional period, for a legal symmetry or equality of rights and obligations on member countries, America was left carrying the bill.[68] Secondly, Britain, by this time a great power only in the self-image of policy-makers, was successful in limiting intrusions into the domain of domestic policy in the arrangements made for the Fund itself[69] (for example, it was written in that the Fund could not oppose any exchange-rate change on the grounds that the domestic social and political policies of the country requesting the change were in question).[70] It seems fair to conclude with Ruggie that what emerged with the IMF was not an hegemonic institution but a security community reflecting a shared set of values. Moreover, this consensus was brought about not only as a response to a common fear of unemployment and its politically destabilizing effects, but also as a common aversion to external interference in domestic affairs, or what Ruggie has termed 'socially embedded liberalism', following Polanyi's distinction between 'embedded' and 'disembedded' social orders.[71]

Taking all these considerations together, it is not surprising that the monetary régime that finally emerged in the 1950s was different in several important respects to the intent of Bretton Woods, and that both the IMF orthodoxy and the GATT contained major exception clauses giving a footing for the growth of regional economic interests that were anything but favourable to the American conception of international free trade. The postwar agreements had effectively put in motion a set of multilateral economic institutions that could be used both to consolidate regional interests in Europe and to provide an alternative motor to economic regeneration and integration independent of both military and United States economic resources; and that could also be used later to counter American protectionist turns against west European imports and to create a bridgehead to the economic cooperation of eastern and western Europe. The most convincing explanation, ironically, rests in the reluctance of the United States to be drawn into further financial support for European economic reconstruction. This it achieved partly through securing the location of the IMF headquarters. At the inaugural meeting of the Board of Governors of the IMF and IBRD at Savanna, Georgia, the United States succeeded in having both institutions located in Washington and hence close to the day-to-day influence of Congress – a move that has readily been given a hegemonic gloss. However, in actuality, this rendered the IMF increasingly sensitive to Congress which was in turn sensitive to the costs of postwar reconstruction falling on the American exchequer. More importantly perhaps, the opportunity was provided for the United States to overstep the mark. At a meeting of the executive committee of the IMF in May 1947 (a committee consisting of full-time officials paid by the United States), the Fund was given authority to 'postpone or reject . . . a request or accept it subject to conditions' in overcoming payments' difficulties. IMF conditionality was further extended in 1952 to include 'policies the members will pursue'.[72]

Subsequently, the United States succeeded in excluding recipients of aid from the Marshall Plan from drawing aid from the IMF, effectively limiting the latter to the developing countries – where assistance rapidly evolved (under the conditionality principle) to include domestic austerity measures and reduced public spending. Not surprisingly, the total drawings on the Fund had dropped to zero by 1950, while the European reconstruction programme took over most of west European needs. At the same time, the IMF began to be widely viewed, particularly in eastern Europe and the Soviet Union, as an instrument of American foreign policy and hegemony. Thus in attempting to extend its foreign-policy reach through economic means, the United States administration also guaranteed that the IMF would become a major focus of international conflict, in which issues of national economic sovereignty and the need to establish either the representativeness or the autonomy of international institutions and to place these on a more cooperative basis have remained prominent.[73]

Prospects: beyond realism?

Viewed from the vantage point of the 1980s and 1990s realist theories that conflate economic and military power seem over-predictive if not deterministic. Hegemonic theory is both more subtle and more complex than realist theory, moving, as Krasner notes, well beyond a simple 'billiard ball' model of international relations. But it still shares a realist conception of the relationship between economic and political power that has proved anything but realistic.

The myth of national power and wealth as mutually assuring has done much to ossify the economic geography of Europe, pushing it toward the false re-assurances and risky logic of 'MAD' and, perhaps more insidiously, towards a belief in national autarchy in the name of national economic interest.[74] It is not difficult to see why the development of the postwar international régimes has been figured largely in the language of interstate relations, power politics and military defence, while critiques have rested more ambivalently on the importance of the economic base for international security and the rationality of cooperative solutions to international trade tensions, in efforts to move away from all of these.[75] The postwar trade and finance régimes and the move towards western European economic federalism were established at a time when national sensibilities were shocked, shattered and without exception open to new concepts of internationalism defined by an overwhelming preoccupation with regional economic security and protection against overweening territorial ambitions. Moreover, the settlements that emerged, and from which international guarantees were sought, were rooted for the most part in a renewed concern to protect national integrity from the uncertainties of the international economic system. From this perspective, then, it becomes necessary to see the development of postwar divisions into different regional trading blocs in terms of conflicting attitudes towards nationalism and the ideal of national economic sovereignty. This implicates nation-building and state-formation at the root of the régime phenomenon in international economic relations, but suggests that interstate power in itself fails to account for the nature and direction of their influence or their relative stability, despite significant fluxes in the pattern of state power. What stands in danger of being overlooked by a geopolitical or preponderance of power model is that historically, such régimes have gained much of their authority and legitimacy from the scope of membership, functional[76] and even 'moral' authority in the form of international consensus, rather than from their ability to wield substantial coercive powers or economic incentives. Wars of words in the winning of alliances have not infrequently replaced or given direction to both military coercion and economic warfare.

So where does all this take us? One possibility is that it takes us back to the economists' perspective on the internationalization of the European economy, viewing the expanding and permeable boundaries of Europe broadening as the result of competitive forces and the search for economies of scale, favouring in turn voluntaristic agreements to suspend the narrowing scope of nationalistic interests and the growth of international norms based on principles of exchange and interdependence, rather than power relations.[77] Internationalization of economies is the main force released by the postwar agreements; this force has been seen as working particularly against Socialist political systems, if not against the nation-state.[78] However, this idea is clearly counterfactual. A more tractable thesis is that the experience of 'economic warfare',[79] born of economic austerity and a retreat to national autarchy and contributing to a miserable and destructive conflict, turned national interest inward to a concern with national economic security.

More than half a century ago, Eugene Staley sought to establish a connection between the outbreak of war and neomercantilist ambitions.[80] Many realists went on to conclude that the use of trade and economic resources by the already-economically strong as a means of securing their position in the world was an inescapable fact of life and must inevitably involve a marriage of military and economic superiority. The prescription and warning may be correct; but 'realist' conclusions that have flowed from the observation of the dependency of international régimes for trade and finance on foreign-policy interests of the dominating kind may lack realism as well as the essential motivating forces of idealism. What this overview demonstrates is the apparent failure of attempts to manage the new and emergent tensions in international economic relations in the postwar period. As in the nineteenth century, the map of Europe, if not the entire globe, was marked out, particularly in the cold-war period, into general responsibilities for security refined into more solidly defined spheres of interest – most visibly in the partitioning of eastern and western Europe and the establishment of the 'iron curtain'.

However, the result was certainly not in this period, and rarely has been, mutual accommodation, a successful management of economic relations, but on the contrary the exacerbation of tensions and economic warfare. The argument is thus not so much against the hegemonic model of great-power dominance of economic development of postwar Europe, though these have been shown to be both weak and inconsistent. Rather, the argument is against the realism and lack of idealism of the underlying model of international economic relations – notably a geopolitical conception of state-defined economic interests and rivalries and a power-preponderance theory of the basis of international economic order. A connection drawn in the early postwar period between economic security and economic growth through trade, and the spectacle of east European failures under Soviet hegemony and cold-war confrontations with the United States, helped to shift European political economy irrevocably away from a belief in the centralized military state as a secure base for national economic security, at least in western Europe, replacing this with economic security itself and a deliberate building-up of international economic interdependencies.

If this analysis is correct and hindsight has any value, the continuing volition to a larger European economic space faces all the dangers of national economic rivalries and a retreat to narrow regional interests. However, the underlying strength of European cooperation in the wider global context has emerged from the ineffectiveness of states in responding to the changes and challenge in the international economy, but also the increasing costs, both military and economic, of maintaining exclusive territorial jurisdictions over economic exchange.[81] Rather than being a temporary set-back to the classical balance of power between nation-states, the wartime experience of interstate conflict and the perception of a relationship between economic insecurity and economic nationalism had irrevocably crippled both the ideological and political coherence of great-power solutions to problems of international economic order, at the same time creating a space within which smaller powers gained in their influence over the rules of the game in the international economy. The struggle of the rival hegemonies of the United States and the Soviet Union to secure regional economic advantage on the basis of military advantage may turn out to have played an important but misperceived role in the development of European economic cooperation. Their failures may also have helped to sharpen the perceptions of 'the commons',[82] caught up in this tragi-comedy, of the virtues of economic cooperation divested of xenophobic instincts. In the process, the state had become both too 'big' from the standpoint of evolving social democratic and corporatist norms and 'too small' either to deal with the costs of adjustment to changes or to manage satisfactorily international economic relations. A more relevant context for the study of European regional economic integration than that of United States economic hegemony and the preponderance of state power in the international system may thus be the economic and political conditions favourable to the development of regional unities that have helped to shape and support the development of new concepts of economic security based on international economic cooperation.

Notes

1 Introduction: shaping postwar Europe

1 The standard work on this is Alan S. Milward (1984) *The Reconstruction of Western Europe 1945–51*, London, Methuen.
2 A. W. de Porte (1979) *Europe between the Superpowers*, Newhaven, Yale University Press.
3 The relationship between economic cooperation and hegemony has spawned an extensive debate. See, for example, Robert O. Keohane (1984) *After Hegemony: Cooperation and Discord in the World Political Economy*, Princeton, Princeton University Press. The issue is dealt with in this volume by D. Willis.
4 The recent calls for an 'Eastern Marshall Plan', that is, a repetition of the Marshall Plan oriented this time to the reconstruction of eastern Europe, are testimony to the perceived significance of the Plan.
5 This is developed in William Wallace (1990) *The Transformation of Western Europe*, London, Pinter.

2 Innocents abroad: federalism and the resistance between party and movement 1945-47

1 For a recent discussion of this literature, see M. Burgess (1988) 'Visions of a Federal Europe in the Resistance: A Comparative Analysis'. Paper presented at the International Conference on 'European Unity in Context: Making the New Europe – the problem of European Unity and the World War', University of Hull, (September), pp. 1–20.
2 This point has been underlined in W. Lipgens (1968) 'European Federation in the Political Thought of Resistance Movements during World War II', *Central European History*, Vol. 1, pp. 5–19.
3 Quoted in J. D. Wilkinson (1981) *The Intellectual Resistance in Europe*, London, Harvard University Press, p. 226.
4 Probably the best contemporary example of this suspicion of political parties is the West German Greens. See, for example, G. O. Kvistad (1987) 'Between State and Society: Green Political Ideology in the mid-1980s', *West European Politics*, Vol. 10, pp. 211–28.
5 For a detailed analysis of the MFE, see W. Lipgens (1982) *A History of European*

Integration, 1945–1947, Vol. 1, Clarendon Press, Oxford, pp. 103–17, 274–8 and 628–33.

6 Ibid. p. 109. See also M. Burgess (1984) 'Federal Ideas in the European Community: Altiero Spinelli and European Union, 1981–1984', *Government and Opposition*, Vol. 19, pp. 339–47. For further information on Spinelli and the origins of his federal ideas, see M. Burgess, 'Altiero Spinelli, Federalism and the EUT', Chap. 9 in J. Lodge (ed.) (1986) *European Union: The European Community in Search of a Future*, London, Macmillan, and (1989) *Federalism and European Union: Political Ideas, Influences and Strategies in the European Community, 1972–1987*, London, Routledge.

7 C. F. Delzell (1974) *Mussolini's Enemies: The Italian Anti-Fascist Resistance*, New York, Princeton University Press, p. 192, and C. F. Delzell (1960) 'The European Federalist Movement in Italy: First Phase, 1918–1947', *Journal of Modern History*, Vol. 32, p. 243.

8 Lipgens, *European Integration*, op. cit., p. 111.

9 Lipgens, ibid., p. 114.

10 Lipgens, ibid., p. 114.

11 Lipgens, ibid., p. 117.

12 Lipgens, ibid., p. 275.

13 Lipgens, ibid., p. 278.

14 N. Kogan (1983) *A Political History of Italy: The Postwar Years*, New York, Praeger, p. 16.

15 See J. Pinder (1989) 'Federalism in Britain and Italy: Radicals and the English Liberal Tradition', Chap. 12, in P. M. R. Stirk (ed.), *European Unity in Context: The Interwar Period*, London, Pinter Publishers.

16 For the Action Party's European programme, see Lipgens, *European Integration*, op. cit., pp. 252–3.

17 This meant putting pressure on parties and governments to support federalist solutions to contemporary problems, but their main purpose at this time was to concentrate on the struggle for a republican form of government.

18 J. D. Wilkinson, *Intellectual Resistance*, op. cit., Chap. 8.

19 F. Roy Willis (1971) *Italy Chooses Europe*, Oxford, Oxford University Press, p. 11.

20 Wilkinson, *Intellectual Resistance*, op. cit., p. 224.

21 D. Urwin (1982) *Western Europe Since 1945*, London, Longman.

22 Wilkinson, *Intellectual Resistance*, op. cit., p. 223.

23 Lipgens, *European Integration*, op. cit., p. 272.

24 Willis, *Italy Chooses Europe*, op. cit., pp. 15–16.

25 Wilkinson, *Intellectual Resistance*, op. cit., p. 228.

26 Urwin, *Western Europe Since 1945*, op. cit., p. 12.

27 Willis, *Italy Chooses Europe*, op. cit., p. 11.

28 Wilkinson, *Intellectual Resistance*, op. cit., p. 225.

29 Wilkinson, *Intellectual Resistance*, op. cit., p. 227.

30 Lipgens, *European Integration*, op. cit., p. 272.

31 Willis, *Italy Chooses Europe*, op. cit., p. 11.

32 Quoted in Wilkinson, *Intellectual Resistance*, op. cit., p. 227.

3 The Marshall Plan and the politics of growth

1 D. Ellwood (1990) 'The American Challenge and the Origins of the Politics of Growth', in M. L. Smith and Peter M. R. Stirk (eds) *Making the New Europe*, London, Pinter, pp. 184–99.

2 W. Abelshauser 'The Role of the ERP in German Recovery and Growth: A Macroeconomic Perspective', in Charles S. Maier (ed.) *The Marshall Plan in Germany*, forthcoming; V. Sorensen (1987) 'Social Democratic Government in Denmark under the Marshall Plan'. Ph.D. thesis, European University Institute, Florence, March; P. P. D'Attorre (1985) 'Anche Noi Possiamo Essere Prosperi: Aiuti ERP e politiche della produttivita negli anni cinquanta', in *Quaderni storici*, No. 58, pp. 55–93; Henry Pelling (1988) *Britain and the Marshall Plan*, London, Macmillan.

3 Harriman's comment at Ambassadors' meeting in Paris, 22–24 March 1950. Report in *Foreign Relations of the United States, 1950*, Vol. III, p. 800.

4 For the Italian case, Vera Zamagni, 'L'economia italiana fra ricostruzione e sviluppo'. Paper presented at the Milan conference: 'La nascita di due repubbliche. Italia e Germania dopo la seconda guerra mondiale', May 1989.

5 This is the theme of Michael J. Hogan (1987) *The Marshall Plan: America, Britain and the Reconstruction of Western Europe 1947–1952*, Cambridge, Cambridge University Press. Alan Milward has suggested that the European powers were politically and economically strong enough to follow an alternative course; but while the economic evidence for this hypothesis is debatable, the political facts point in almost all cases in quite the opposite direction: cf. Alan Milward (1989) 'Was the Marshall Plan Necessary?', a review essay centring on the Hogan book in *Diplomatic History*, Vol. 1, pp. 231–53.

6 'Communist activities were not at the root of Europe's difficulties,' said the State Department's Policy Planning Staff in May 1947. They were attributable to war, physical destruction and 'the profound exhaustion of spiritual vigor': 'Policy With Respect to American Aid to Western Europe: Views of the Policy Planning Staff', in *Foreign Relations of the United States 1947*, Vol. III, p. 225.

7 Memo from F. V. Norall to Roscoe Drummond, Director European Information Division, Paris, 9 August 1950, in National Archives, Washington D.C. (NA), Record Group (RG) 286, Office of Special Representative (OSR), Central Secretariat, Information Division, Retired Subject File.*

8 Memo from Waldemar A. Nielsen to Secretary Harriman, 26 April 1948, in NA, RG 286, OSR Information Division, Office of Director, General Subject Files 1948–9, 'Publicity and Information 1948' sub-file.

9 *Documents on American Foreign Relations (1948)*, Princeton, 1950, p. 235.

10 'Principles on Guaranties for Information Media', 13 September 1948, in NA, RG 286, OSR Information Division, Office of Director, General Subject Files 1948–49, 'Huse (Personal File)'.

11 Monthly Report, Information Division, ECA Mission to Italy, 1 September 1948, in NA, RG 286, OSR Information Division, Mission files, 'Italy 1948–9' sub-file.*

12 Notes dictated by Berding for use in Congressional presentation, 16 January 1950, in NA, RG 286, OSR Information Division, Information Subject File, 'Previous Testimony' sub-file.*

13 Ltr. F. R. Shea, Chief, Field Branch, European Information Division, to Berding, 24 February 1949, in NA, RG 286, OSR Administrative Services Division, Communications and Records Section, Country Files 1948–9, Italy 'Publicity and Information: Radio-Film' sub-file.*

14 Both sides of the question are discussed in Joseph B. Phillips 'Italy: Making the ECA Visible', *Newsweek*, 10 October 1949; labelling debate in *Congressional Record-Senate*, April 1949, pp. 4209–13.

15 Comment by Robert Mullen, Director, Office of Information, in 'Budget Estimate, Fiscal 1950', in NA, RG 286, ECA Washington, Information Division, Information Subject File, 'Previous Testimony' sub-file.

16 Copy of pamphlet 'ERP in Italy' in NA, RG 286, ECA Washington, Information Division, Office of Director, Informational Country File, 'Italy', sub-file.*

17 Memo on 'Labor Information', 19 December 1949, in NA, RG 286, OSR Information Division, Mission files, 'Italy: Publicity and Information' sub-file.

18 Anthony Carew (1987) *Labour Under the Marshall Plan*, Manchester, Manchester University Press. Paul Addison (1985) *Now the War is Over: A Social History of Britain, 1945–51*, London, BBC, pp. 193–9.

19 These were frequently portrayed in the monthly newsreels, 'ERP in Action', of which 13 editions were made, and in the documentary series 'The Marshall Plan at Work in . . .', dedicated to activities in 12 of the participating countries. A number of these films are viewable in the National Archives, Washington D.C., Motion Picture Branch.

20 Graham Hutton (1953) *We Too Can Prosper*, London, Allen and Unwin, pp. 150–1 and p. 202; citation from p. 5.

NOTES   165

21 'Radio Address by M. Raymond Aron of *Le Figaro*', in NA, RG 286, OSR Information Division, Office of Director, General Subject File, 1948-9, 'Publicity and Information 1949' sub-file.

22 Ltr. Friendly to C. Houston, Director of Information, ECA Washington, 31 August 1948, in NA, RG 286, OSR Information Division, Office of Director, General Subject Files 1948-9, 'Huse (Personal File)'.

23 Report, 'ECA in Action' by Alexander S. Keller, 13 October 1950, in NA, RG 286, ECA Washington, Office of Information, Office of Director, Country Subject Files, 'Netherlands'.

24 Memo from T. Wilson, Information Chief, UK Mission to R. Drummond, 18 October 1948, in NA, RG 286, OSR Information Division, Office of Director, General Subject Files 1948-9, 'Policy 1949' sub-file.

25 Correspondence between F. R. Shea and R. Drummond, November 1949, in NA, RG 286, OSR Information Division, Office of Director, General Subject File, 1948-9, 'Publicity and Information 1949' sub-file.

26 Minutes, Conference of Information Officers, Paris, 28 August 1950, in NA, RG 286, OSR Information Division, Office of Director, General Subject Files 1949-50, 'Information Officers' sub-file. The OEEC Secretariat admitted it could do little to help on the publicity front, and endorsed the approach used by ECA based on bilateral arrangements with individual countries; correspondence of February 1949 in NA, RG 269, OSR Information Division, Office of Director, 'Publicity and Information 1948-9' sub-file.

27 See discussion of Hogan, *Marshall Plan*, op. cit., in Ellwood, 'The Impact of the Marshall Plan, Review essay', *History*, forthcoming.

28 *Newsweek*, 10 October 1949, No. 14.

29 Memo from Henry S. Reuss to A. Friendly, 25 February 1949, in NA, RG 286, OSR Information Division, Office of Director, 'Publicity and Information 1949' sub-file.

30 Ibid.

31 Memo from Thomas K. Hodges, Editorial Research Analysis Section, to R. Drummond, 19 October 1949, in NA, RG 286, OSR Information Division, Office of Director, 'Policy 1949' sub-file.

32 Report of the O. S. Advisory Commission on Information, 30 October 1949, in NA, RG 286, OSR Information Division, Office of Director, 'Publicity and Information 1949' sub-file.

33 Ibid.

34 Report in telegram. London Mission, to OSR, 25 November 1948, in NA, RG 286, OSR Information Division, Office of Director, General Subject Files 1948-9, 'Public Opinion Polls (Publicity and Information 1948-9)', sub-file.

35 Common Council for American Unity (1950) *European Beliefs Regarding the United States 1949*, New York. Hollywood was a great source of concern to the Council, since its products left a poor impression on the minds of the interviewees and were thought to convey a deplorable image of the US generally; discussion in Ellwood, 'Cinema and the Projection of America', Proceedings of the Fiesole Conference, 'Hollywood in Europe 1945-60', March 1989, forthcoming.

36 Ellwood, 'The Impact of the Marshall Plan', op. cit.

37 'Notes for Ambassador Katz Regarding Information', no date but end 1950, in NA, RG 286, Central Secretariat, Subject Files 1948-52, 'Public Relations' sub-file.

38 Ellwood, 'The Impact of the Marshall Plan', op. cit.

39 Ibid.

40 'Some Notes on Information Policy', summary of comments by Tom Wilson, ECA London, 14 November 1950, in NA, RG 286, OSR Central Secretariat, Subject Files 1948-52, 'Public Relations' sub-file.

41 Report 'Productivity trip to Italy', 11-16 June 1950, in NA, RG, 286, OSR Labor Information Office of Economic Advisers Country Subject Files 1949-50, 'Italy Productivity (General)' sub-file.

42 Italian case in ECA, 'Italy Country Study 1950'; for British experience, Pelling, *Britain and the Marshall Plan*, op. cit., pp. 34-37.

43 Telegram from OSR to ECA Rome, 19 August 1950, in NA, RG 469, Mission to Italy, Office of Director, Subject Files (Central Files), 1948–52, 'Program Long-Term' sub-file.

44 Memo from F. V. Norall to R. Drummond, 1 August 1950, in NA, RG 286, OSR Information Division, Retired Subject File (Information), 'Mission Memoranda' sub-file.

45 Paul G. Hoffmann (1951) *Peace Can Be Won*, New York, Doubleday, p. 53.

46 Council of Economic Advisers cited in Charles S. Maier, 'The two postwar eras and the conditions of stability in twentieth century Europe', *American Historical Review*, 1981, p. 346; Cleveland cited in Alan. S. Milward (1985) *The Reconstruction of Western Europe 1948–52*, London, Methuen.

47 OECD Convention, 14 December 1960.

48 *New York Times*, 7 June 1949.

49 W. W. Rostow (1978) *The World Economy – History and Prospect*, Austin & London, University of Texas, Chapter 17, esp. pp. 261–70.

50 M. M. Postan (1967) *An Economic History of Western Europe, 1945–1967*, London, Methuen, pp. 22, 25 and 48–9.
  *This material has been examined further in Ellwood, 'From Re-Education to the Selling of the Marshall Plan in Italy', in N. Pronay and K. Wilson (eds) (1985) *The Political Re-Education of Germany and Her Allies after World War II*, London, Croom Helm.

4 Americanism and anti-Americanism in British and German responses to the Marshall Plan

1 A. S. Milward (1984) *The Reconstruction of Western Europe*, London, Methuen.

2 The most careful consideration is Volker R. Berghahn (1986) *The Americanisation of West German Industry 1945–1973*, Leamington Spa, Berg. Less-restrained is Kees van der Pijl (1984) *The Making of an Atlantic Ruling Class*, London, Verso.

3 Paul Sering (Richard Lowenthal) (1946) *Jenseits des Kapitalismus*, Nuremberg, Nest-Verlag. Werner Sombart (1906) *Warum gibt es in den Vereinigten Staaten keinen Sozialismus?* Tübingen, Siebeck.

4 Robert M. Collins (1981) *The Business Response to Keynes, 1929–1964*, New York, Columbia University Press, p. 141. The idea of American neocapitalism as the decisive feature of the Marshall Plan has been most consistently emphasized by Michael Hogan: see (1987) *The Marshall Plan*, Cambridge, Cambridge University Press.

5 For examples of Communist Party rhetoric see Ilja Ehrenburg (1948) *Anschlag auf Europa*, Berlin, Tägliche Rundschau, and Derek Kartun (1948) *The Marshall Plan*, London, Communist Party.

6 See the 1949 review of H. Laski's *The American Democracy* in *Labour*, September, p. 252 and the comments of Fritz Baade, 'Die Vereinigten Staaten von Amerika in ihrer Stellung zu der Westeuropäischen Wirtschaftsunion', in Fritz Baade et al. *Die Wirtschaftsunion in ihrer Stellung zu den Nationalwirtschaften and zur Weltwirtschaft*, Münster, Runge, n.d., p. 81.

7 Anthony Carew (1987) *Labour under the Marshall Plan*, Manchester University Press, p. 2.

8 On the Third Way see Hans-Peter Schwarz (1980) *Vom Reich zur Bundesrepublik*, Stuttgart, Klett Cota; Wilfried Loth (1977) *Sozialismus und Internationalismus*, Stuttgart, D. V. A.; and Walter Lipgens (1983) *A History of European Integration. Volume 1 1945–1947*, Oxford, Clarendon.

9 It is worth noting Kenneth O. Morgan's 1984 observation that if Labour was suspicious of American capital the Foreign Office was suspicious of everything American: *Labour in Power 1945–1951*, Oxford, Oxford University Press, p. 263.

10 Alan Sked, 'Die britische Arbeiterbewegung und der Marshall Plan', in O. K. Haberl and L. Niethammer (eds) (1986) *Der Marshall-Plan und die europäische Linke*, Frankfurt am Main, E. V. A., pp. 407–22. For broader accounts see Henry Pelling (1988), *Britain and the Marshall Plan*, London, Macmillan, and Allan Bullock (1983) *Ernest Bevin, Foreign Secretary 1945–1951*, London, Heinemann.

11 *Labour Party Annual Conference 1949*, p. 197.
12 *Labour Party Annual Conference 1947*, p. 173, See also the contribution of Lucy
   Hainsworth, ibid., p. 172.
13 Ibid., p. 160. For the views of Zilliacus see Chapter 3, 'Uncle Sam Steps Out', in (1947)
   Mirror of the Present, London, Meridian.
14 Towards the end of Labour's period in office this claim had worn thin, as J. Hammond
   (National Union of Mineworkers) pointed out: 'We keep raising ghosts and believing
   they are real . . . We have not got a planned economy in Britain.' *Annual Trades Union
   Congress 1951*, p. 529. On the confusion over what planning actually meant see Alec
   Cairncross (1985) *Years of Recovery: British Economic Policy 1945–51*, London,
   Methuen, especially Chapter 11 and his concluding comment p. 503: 'The balance of
   payments was the focus of the one really determined effort of planning in which the
   Labour government engaged.'
15 *Annual Trades Union Congress 1948*, p. 451.
16 Hogan, *The Marshall Plan*, op. cit., pp. 142–5. For the French case see R. Kuisel (1988)
   'L'American Way of Life et les missions Françaises de productivité', *Vingtieme Siecle*
   No. 17, pp. 21–33. For the Italian case see P. P. D'Attorre (1985) *ERP Aid and the
   Politics of Productivity in Italy during the 1950s*, EUI Working Paper No. 85/159. Badia
   Fiesolana San Domenico, EUI, and David W. Ellwood (1981) 'ERP Propaganda in
   Italy: its History and Impact in an Official Survey', in Ekkehart Krippendorf (ed) *The
   Role of the United States in the Reconstruction of Italy and West Germany 1943–1949*,
   Berlin, Freie Universität Berlin, pp. 274–302.
17 *Annual Trades Union Congress 1947*, p. 80.
18 'Can Americans Help Our Industries?', *Labour*, August 1948, pp. 362–3; 'The First of
   the Fifty', *Labour*, March 1949, pp. 208–9; 'Round-up Report of Industrial Teams
   Seeking Ideas in the United States', *Labour*, August 1949, pp. 384–5.
19 Carew, *Labour under the Marshall Plan*, op. cit., pp. 147–51.
20 It should not be forgotten that Britain was in the midst of a production campaign and
   that Chancellor Cripps was so prone to issuing injunctions for greater effort that the
   United States Ambassador could comment, 'To put the matter cryptically (not
   Cripptically) the only answer to Britain's difficulties is to work harder and, I fear, for
   less.' *Foreign Relations of the United States 1948*, Vol. 3, p. 1116.
21 'Three Big Ss in SucceSS', *Labour*, November 1949, pp. 500–2.
22 *Labour Party Annual Conference 1947*, pp. 174 and 167.
23 'Development of Industry', *Labour*, February 1947, pp. 181–2; 'Structural Plan for the
   Clothing Industry', *Labour*, May 1947, pp. 252–6.
24 *Annual Trades Union Congress 1946*, p. 11.
25 Carl Landauer (1959) sees Karl Kautsky's *Am Tag nach der sozialen Revolution* as,
   though not novel in its ideas, symbolic of both the promise and the danger facing
   Socialists: 'as presented by Kautsky, the postulate that the cake be enlarged and not
   merely cut into more equal slices, exposed the socialist movement to a dangerous
   attack: elimination of obsolete workshops and concentration of production in the most
   efficient plants might not necessarily require socialisation of the instruments of
   production'. *European Socialism*, Vol. 2. Berkeley, University of California Press,
   p. 1611.
26 *Labour Party Annual Conference 1948*, p. 130.
27 *Annual Trades Union Congress 1947*, p. 419.
28 *Labour Party Annual Conference 1948*, p. 136.
29 For Philip's view see Loth, *Sozialismus und Internationalismus*, op. cit., p. 187.
30 *Labour Party Annual Conference 1948*, p. 227. The sections quoted in the memorandum
   are followed in the *Report* by the suggestion that the idea of a customs union may
   nevertheless be fruitful and by a list of various studies, agreements and proclamations.
   Committee for European Economic Cooperation, *General Report*, London, HMSO,
   1947, pp. 19–20.
31 *European Unity*, p. 4. See also the criticism by M. Edwards, *Labour Party Annual
   Conference*, p. 85, and the thorough and persuasive criticisms in A. Philip (1950) *Der
   Sozialismus und die Europäische Einheit*, Gelsenkirchen, Ruhr-Verlag.

32 *Akten der Vorgeschichte der Bundesrepublik Deutschland 1945–1949* (1982) Vol. 3. Munich, Oldenbourg, pp. 206 and 415–16 and Vol. 4, Munich, Oldenbourg, 1983, p. 705.

33 Ulrich Borsdorff, 'In Kauf genommen. Der Marshall-Plan und die Zweiteilung der Einheitsgewerkschaft in Deutschland', in Haberl and Niethammer (eds), *Der Marshall-Plan*, op. cit., p. 204.

34 Ibid., p. 207. On the Recklinghausen Congress see also Theo Pirker (1960) *Die blinde Macht, Erster Teil 1945–1952*, Munich, Mercator, pp. 92–4.

35 Eberhard Schmidt (1975) *Die verhinderte Neuordnung 1945–1952*, Frankfurt-am-Main, E. V. A., pp. 114–18.

36 On the Third Way and Schmidt's views, see Wilfried Loth (1984) 'Deutsche Europa-Konzeptionen in der Eskalation des Ost-West-Konflikts 1945–1949', *Geschichte in Wissenschaft und Unterricht*, Vol. 35, pp. 453–70.

37 *Akten zur Vorgeschichte der Bundesrepublik Deutschland 1945–1949* (1981) Vol. 5, Munich, Oldenbourg, pp. 413 and 477–81.

38 Werner Link (1978) *Deutsche und amerikanische Gewerkschaften und Geschäftsleute 1945–1975*, Düsseldorf, Droste.

39 Erich Ott (1978) *Die Wirtschaftskonzeption der SPD nach 1945*, Marburg, pp. 175–77.

40 Fritz Sternberg (1947) *The Coming Crisis*, London, Gollancz.

41 Peter Blachstein (1947) 'Wirtschaftskrise in USA?', *Geist und Tat*, Vol. 2, November, pp. 15–18. Schwarz, *Vom Reich zur Bundesrepublik*, op. cit., p. 819.

42 Hans-Peter Ehni, 'Die Reaktion der SPD auf den Marshall-Plan', in Haberl and Niethammer (eds), *Der Marshall-Plan*, op. cit., pp. 225–6.

43 Ott, *Wirtschaftskonzeption*, op. cit., p. 173.

44 Max Biehl (1949) *Die Vereinigten Staaten als Wirtschaftsmacht*, Stuttgart, Shwab, p. 128. See also Hans-Jürgen Grabbe (1983) *Unionsparteien, Sozialdemokratie und Vereinigten Staaten von Amerika 1945–1966*, Düsseldorf, Droste, p. 53.

45 E. U. Huster (1978) *Die Politik der SPD 1945–1950*, Frankfurt-am-Main, Campus.

46 Grabbe, *Unionsparteien*, op. cit., pp. 53–4.

47 Heinrich Kronstein (1950) 'Die Politik des Wettbewerbs in den USA' *Ordo*, Vol. 3, pp. 75–104.

48 It should be noted that the call for more production did not necessarily entail the ramifications associated with the 'productivity campaigns' by the Marshall Planners. But by the same token the common rhetoric could, and still can, blur the distinction.

49 Bernd Klemm and Günter J. Trittel (1987) 'Vor dem Wirtschaftswunder: Durchbruch zum Wachstum oder Lähmungskrise?', *Vierteljahreshefte für Zeitgeschichte*, Vol. 35, pp. 614–17. This article forms part of a considerable and often polemical debate about the precise contribution of Marshall Aid to German recovery. After Werner Abelshauser's repeated efforts to prove that the contribution was slight, recent contributions, including the one by Klemm and Trittel, have begun to reassert the role of the aid. For Abelshauser's reply to some of his critics see 'Hilfe und Selbsthilfe', *Vierteljahreshefte für Zeitgeschichte*, Vol. 37, 1989, pp. 89–115.

50 Ulrich Borsdorff (1979) 'Speck oder Sozialisierung? Produktionssteigerungskampagnen im Ruhrbergbau 1945–1947', in Hans Mommsen and Ulrich Borsdorff (eds) *Glück auf Kameraden!* Cologne, Bund, p. 366.

51 Link, *Deutsche und amerikanische Gewerkschaften*, op. cit., p. 54.

52 'Bundesministerium für den Marshall plan', *Fünfter und Sechster Bericht*, Bonn, 1951, p. 69.

53 Berghahn, *Americanisation of West German Industry*, op. cit.

54 *Recovery under the Marshall Plan 1948–1952. Twelfth, Final Report*, Bonn, 1953, p. 62.

55 Viktor Agartz (1953) 'Beiträge zur wirtschaftlichen Entwicklung 1953', *Mitteilungen des Wirtschaftswissenschaftliches Institut der Deutschen Gewerkschaften*, Vol. 6, p. 246. On the adoption of Agartz's position by I. G. Mettal see Anrei S. Markovits (1986) *The Politics of West German Trade Unions*, Cambridge University Press.

56 Peter Berg (1963) *Deutschland und Amerika 1918–1929*, Lubeck, Mattheisen, pp. 117–20.

57 Gerhard Kreyssig (1947) *Wirtschaftliche Organisation oder Untergang Europas*, Offen-bach, Bollwerk.
58 The perceptions of such corporations and the frequency with which they were seen as a mechanism and model for integration is a relatively neglected aspect of the history of European unity.
59 See also G. H. Kreyssig, 'Memorandum zu Problemen und Aufgaben des Nachkriegs Europa', dated 15 July 1942. I am grateful to C. Regin of Gesamthochschule Kassel for supplying me with a copy of this document. Roman Muziol (1947) *Europäische Aussenhandelsverflechtung und Marshallplan*, Kiel, Institut für Weltwirtschaft, November, pp. 70-2, pointed out that the more highly interdependent Marshall Plan countries did not need the less interdependent, predominantly agrarian, eastern countries to the extent that the latter needed the former.
60 R. Lowenthal (1953) 'Die Westeuropäische Wirtschaftseinheit', *Aufbau eines neuen Europas*, Berlin, Grünewald, pp. 32-50.
61 Ibid., p. 61.
62 Ibid., pp. 39 and 46. On Röpke's view of integration see Ludolf Herbst (1983) 'Die Zeitgenössische Integrationstheorie und die Anfänge der europäischen Einigung 1947-1950', *Vierteljahreshefte für Zeitgeschichte*, Vol. 31, pp. 161-205.
63 W. Röpke, 'Europäische Wirtschaftsgemeinschaft', in *Aufbau eines neuen Europas*, op. cit., pp. 16-17.
64 Lowenthal, 'Westeuropäische Wirtschaftseinheit', op. cit., pp. 38-41. By now criticisms of the role of productivity were beginning to mount. In one leading journal, *The Review of Economics and Statistics*, the following articles can be found: Peter O. Steiner, 'The Productivity Ratio', Vol. 32, 1950, pp. 321-8, which criticizes the assumption that productivity is an analytically useful independent variable; E. M. Bernstein, 'American Productivity and the Dollar Payments Problem', Vol. 37, 1955, pp. 101-9, which denies that higher American productivity *vis-à-vis* America's trading partners was necessarily problematic; and G. D. A. McDougall, 'Does Productivity Rise Faster in the US?', Vol. 38, 1956, pp. 155-76, which denies that it did.

5 Americanism and anti-Americanism in Italy

1 For a general approach see T. Bonazzi (ed.) (1980) *America-Europa. La circolazione delle idee*, Bologna, Il Mulino; J. Evans (1976) *America, The View from Europe*, New York, Norton; H. Honour (1976) *The New Golden Land, European Images of America from the Discoveries to the Present Time*, New York, Pantheon; and A. Gerbi (1983) *La disputa del nuovo Mondo. Storia di una polemica, 1750-1900*, Milan, Ricciardi.
2 There is no general analysis for the period before the First World War. The most interesting text is A. Rossi (1883) *Gli Stati Uniti e la concorrenza americana*, Florence, Barbera. For Socialist perceptions see S. Cognetti de Martiis (1891) *Il socialismo negli Stati Uniti*, Turin, UTET, and, for a more general overview, R. L. Moore (1970) *European Socialists and the American Promised Land*, New York. For aspects of Catholic thought see O. Confessore (1984) *L'Americanismo cattolico in Italia*, Rome; C. Fohlen (1987) 'Catholicisme américain et catholicisme europeen; la convergence de l'america-nisme', *Revue d'histoire moderne et contemporaine*, Vol. 34. Very interesting is the position of U. Ojetti (1899) *L'America vittoriosa*, Milan, Treves, and (1905) *L'America e l'avvenire*, Milan, Treves. For the first Italian studies of American culture see E. Nencioni (1897) *Saggi critici di letteratura inglese*, Florence. For Italian perceptions of American imperialism see A. Aquarone (1973) *Le origini dell'imperialismo americano*, Bologna, Il Mulino, 1973. There are numerous studies of Italian emigration; especially relevant are G. Rosoli, *L'immaginario dell'America nell'emigrazione italiana di massa* (mimeo); E. Franzina (1989) 'Emigrazione transoceanica e ricerca storica in Italia: gli ultimi dieci anni (1978-1988)', *Altre Italie*, Vol. 1, pp. 6-56. An exemplary case of the influence of this phenomenon on the Italian image of the United States is A. A. Bernardy (1911) *America vissuta*, Turin, Bocca. The age of Giolitti is covered by V. Mantegazza (1910) *Agli Stati Uniti. Il pericolo americano*, Milan, Treves. American propaganda in the First World War is discussed by D. H. Lasswell (1938) *Propaganda*

Techniques in the World War, London; O. D. Wannamaker (1923) *With Italy*, New York; A. Lancellotti (1924) *Giornalismo eroico*, Milan, Fiamma. For the role of the YMCA see V. Brizzolesi (1919) *Gli americani italiani alla guerra*, Milan.

3 There are several studies that view Americanization as an aspect of American hegemony: F. Costigliola (1984) *Awkward Dominion. American Political, Economic and Cultural Relations with Europe, 1919-1933*, Ithaca, Cornell University Press; E. Rosenberg (1982) *Spreading the American Dream. American Cultural and Economic Expansion, 1890-1945*, New York; R. Wagenleiter (1986) 'Propagating the Dream: Cultural Policies as a Means of Integration', *American Studies International*, Vol. 1, pp. 60–84. A more limited, but no less important, approach is proposed by N. Ninkovitch (1981) *The Diplomacy of Ideas. United States Foreign Policy and Cultural Relations, 1938-1950*, Cambridge, Cambridge University Press.

4 For relations between Italy and the United States during the Fascist period see J. P. Diggins (1972) *L'America, Mussolini e il fascismo*, Bari, Laterza; G. G. Migone (1980) *Gli Stati Uniti e il fascismo*, Milan, Feltrinelli; M. Vaudagna (1981) *Corporativismo e New Deal*, Turin, Rosenberg. The most recent study of Italian perceptions of America in this period is M. Nacci (1989) *L'antiamericanismo in Italia negli anni '30*, Turin, Bollati. For literary sources see C. Pavese (1951) *La letteratura americana e altri saggi*, Turin, Einaudi; E. Vittorini (1947) *Americana*, Milan, Bompieni; M. Praz (1951) *Cronache letterarie anglosassoni*, Rome; D. Fernandez (1968) *Il mito dell'America negli intellettuali italiani*, Caltanisetta, Scias; N. Carducci (1973) *Gli intellettuali e l'ideologia americana negli anni '30*, Manduria, Lecce; V. Amoruso, 'Cecchi, Vittorini, Pavese e la letteratura americana', in V. Amoruso (1968) *Contraddizioni della realtà*, Bari, De Donato; A. Lombardo, 'La letteratura americana in Italia e l'America di Vittorini', in A. Lombardo (1961) *La ricerca del vero*, Rome, Editioni di Storia e Litteratura.

5 R. De Felice, 'Aspetti politico diplomatici delle relazioni culturali tra Italia e Stati Uniti' in S. Barnes (ed.) (1979) *Italia-USA: giudizi incrociati*, Turin, Fondazione Agnelli, pp. 185–203.

6 Commentaries on the war years and the postwar period emphasize the ideological aspects. See D. Ellwood (1977) *L'alleato nemico. La politica dell'occupazione anglo-americana in Italia*, Milan, Feltrinelli; J. E. Miller (1986) *The United States and Italy, 1940-1950*, Chapel Hill, University of North Carolina Press; J. L. Harper (1986) *L'America e la ricostruzione dell'Italia, 1945-1948*, Bologna, Il Mulino; E. di Nolfo (1986) *La paure e le speranza degli italiani, 1943-1945*, Milan, Mondadori; L. Mercuri (1989) *Guerra psicologica, La propaganda americana in Italia. Stampa, radio, propaganda 1943-1946*, Milan, FIAP.

7 P. Cavallo (1985) 'America sognata, America desiderata. Mito e immagine Usa in Italia dallo sbarco alla fine della guerra (1943-1945)', *Storia contemporaneo*, Vol. 4; E. Vezzosi (1983) *La relazioni Italia-Stati uniti dal 1943 al 1953*, Florence. A book that was widely read in the 1950s still deserves attention: F. Mauro (1944) *Osservazioni di un ingegnere negli Stati Uniti d'America*, Milan, Hoepli.

8 See A. Riccardi (ed.) (1984) *Pio XII*, Bari, Laterza.

9 For the 1950s see 'L'America arriva in Italia', *Quadeni storici* Vol. 58, (1985), and U. Eco and O. Calabrese (eds) (1985) *Italia moderna. Immagini e storia di un'identita nazionale*, Vol. 3, Milan, Electa, pp. 381–94. On the Marshall Plan as a process of Americanization see P. P. D'Attorre (1985) 'Il piano Marshall. Politica, economia, relazioni internazionali nella recostruzione italiana', *Passato e presente*, Vol. 7, pp. 31–63; D. Ellwood (1985) 'La propaganda del Piano Marshall in Italia' *Passato e presente*, Vol. 7, pp. 153–71; E. Aga Rossi (ed.) (1983) *Il piano Marshall e l'Europa*, Rome, Treccani; F. Romero (1989) *Gli Stati Uniti e il sindocalismo europeo, 1944-1951*, Rome, EL. An insight into the broader relationship between Italy and the United States during the postwar period is given by the memoires of ambassador E. Ortona (1984) *Anni d'America*, Bologna, Il Mulino. For the images of America presented to the Italian public in the 1950s see G. Prezzolini (1950) *L'America in pantofole*, Florence, Vallecchi; (1953) *L'America con gli stivali*, Florence, Vallecchi; (1958) *Tutta l'America*, Florence, Vallecchi; V. Pozner (1950) *Paradiso a stelle e strisce*, Milan; E. Enriques Agnoletti (1951) *Idea e realita dell'America*, Rome; L. Barzini (1952) *Gli americani sono*

soli al mondo, Milan, Mondadori; (1978) *Oh America*, Milan, Rizzoli. On Barzini see H. Cristol (1958) 'Un Tocqueville Italien en Amerique? O America de L. Barzini', in *L'Amérique et l'Europe: réalités et représentations*, Marseilles; G. Piovene (1954) *De America*, Milan, Mondadori; G. Triggiani (1957) *Inchiesta sulla gioventù bruciata*, Bari, Laterza; O. Poli (1958) *America in cammino*. Milan, Massimo; and A. Donno (1978) *La cultura americana nelle riviste italiane del dopoguerra, 'Tempo presente', 1956–1968*, Lecce, Millella.

10 For a comparison of the American dream and the Soviet myth see P. P. D'Attorre (ed.) (1990) *Nemici per la pelle: sogno americano e mito sovietico nell'Italia contemporanea*, Milan, Angell. See also S. Lanaro (1988) *L'Italia nuova. Identita e sviluppo, 1861–1988*, Turin, Einaudi; L. Paggi (ed.) (1989) *Americanismo e riformismo*, Turin, Einaudi; and S. Gundle (1986) 'L'americanizzione del quotidiano. Televisione e consumismo nell'Italia degli anni '50', *Quaderni storici*, Vol. 59.

11 G. Bocca (1962) *Miracolo all'italiana*, Milan, Avanti.

12 S. Lanaro, *L'Italia nuovo*, op. cit., p. 82.

13 S. Cundle (1986) 'L'americanizzazione del quotidiano. Televisione e consumismo nell'Italia degli anni '50', *Quaderni Storici*, Vol. 86.

14 For Americanization and anti-Americanism in a different national context, France, see D. Lacorne, J. Rupnik and M. F. Toinet (1986) *L'Amérique dans les têtes: un siècle de fascinations et d'aversions*, Paris, Hachette; D. Strauss (1978) *Menace in the West: the Rise of French Anti-americanism in Modern Times*, Westport, Greenwood Press; J. Thibau (1980) *La France colonisée*, Paris, Flammarion; J. Baudrillard (1987) *L'America*, Milan, Feltrinelli.

15 L. Paggi, *Americanismo e riformismo*, op. cit., p. 20.

16 Ibid.

17 For recent years see W. Porter et al. (1980) 'L'immagine americana in Italia e l'immagine italiana in America', *Comunicazioni di massa*, September-December; U. Eco, P. Ceserani and B. Placido (1984) *La riscoperta dell'America*. Bari, Laterza; E. Galli della Loggia (1986) *Lettera agli amici americani*, Milan; and V. Zucconi (1989) *Si fa presto a dire America*, Milan, Mondadori.

6 Postwar misery in Eastern Europe: glosses on an Hungarian perspective

1 Both texts are included in I. Bibó (1981) *Összegyüjtött Munkái (Collected Works)*, (ed.) I. Kemény and M. Sárközi. Berne, EPMSz; from which all references are taken (see *Collected Works*). The essay on 'Misery' had first been composed during the War, intended as an Introduction to a major work that Bibó was unable to prepare for publication in his lifetime. The full manuscript, 'On European Balance and Peace', is now printed in I. Bibó (1986) *Válogatott Tanulmányok (hereafter, Selected Studies)*, (ed.) I. Vida, and E. Nagy. Budapest, Magvetö, Vol. I. pp. 295–604. The essay on 'Misery', together with a few other substantial pieces by Bibó, appeared in French in 1986, *Misère des petits Etats d'Europe de l'Est*, Paris, L'Harmattan. It is also reprinted in a recent selection, I. Bibó (1991) *Democracy, Revolution, Self-Determination*, New York, Atlantic Research and Publications, pp. 13-89.

2 *Collected Works*, Vol. I. p. 219. (Emphasis in direct quotes is invariably in the original.) The only major work by Bibó that has so far appeared in English (1976) *The Paralysis of International Institutions and the Remedies*, Hassocks, Harvester Press, also firmly asserts the validity of the principle of nationality, drawing a sharp distinction between 'patriotism' and 'nationalism'. See pp. 50-1.

3 *Collected Works*, Vol. I. p. 205.

4 Ibid., p. 207.

5 Ibid., p. 208.

6 Ibid., p. 209. In eastern Europe social changes, again as a correlative of historical distortion, remained petrified in a semi-feudal state. László Németh, playwright, populist political philosopher and an intellectual influence on Bibó, wrote in a memorable piece in 1940: 'Western nations have in the modern age accepted the peasantry also in their midst – so that they have classes but not a part of humanity

shoved underneath the nation. In the East the peasantry and the educated nation not only exist beneath and above – they are in two separate worlds and cultures. In the West there are no people as in the East. And in the East there is no proper nation.' L. Németh (1973) *Európai utas: Tanulmányok*, (*European Traveller: Studies*), Budapest, Magvetö, p. 698.

7 Ibid., p. 213.

8 Ibid., p. 216.

9 'The Causes and History of the German Hysteria' had also been originally part of the manuscript. 'On European Balance and Peace' (see Note 1). A section of it was published in 'Történelmi Szemle' (*Historical Review*), 1980. The whole text is printed in *Collected Works*, Vol. I. pp. 107–84 and *Selected Studies*, Vol. I. pp. 365–483.

10 *Collected Works*, Vol. I. p. 221.

11 Ibid., p. 230.

12 Ibid., p. 231. The same argument is put forward by Bibó in a letter, dated 1978, and published in *Collected Works*, Vol. IV. pp. 1267–74. ('Levél Szalai Pálhoz')

13 S. Balogh (1988) *Magyarország Külpolitikája 1945-1950*, (*Hungary's Foreign Policy 1945-1950*), Budapest, Kossuth, p. 36.

14 Ibid., p. 37.

15 Quoted in I. Vida, 'American Diplomacy and the Hungarian Minority in Czechoslovakia 1945-1947', in T. Takalo, (ed.) (1989) *Finns and Hungarians Between East and West*, Helsinki, SHS, p. 149. It is fair to add, however, that US representative Steinhardt in Prague denied the charge and complained to Washington about the 'audacity of Hungary and Germany, enemy states defeated only a few weeks ago, in criticizing the internal affairs of one of the members of the United Nations'. (Ibid., p. 151.)

16 E. Beneŝ (1946) 'Postwar Czechoslovakia', *Foreign Affairs*, Vol. 24, p. 400.

17 *Collected Works*, Vol. I. p. 192.

18 Bibó's view of the conduct of the Great Powers in the peace negotiations is expressly critical, mainly because of the latter's inattention to and impatience with the affairs of eastern Europe. Concerning the frontier between Hungary and Rumania, for instance, 'a five-minute agreement could only be reached on the basis of the Trianon frontiers only'. A better thought-out settlement, he adds sarcastically, would have required 40–45 minutes. (*Collected Works*, Vol. I. p. 190.) *Cf.* the bitter reminiscences of the exiled Hungarian Prime Minister, Ferenc Nagy: 'After another few days in Paris, I left with the impression that the peace conference was a fiction. The spirit of the Atlantic Charter was not realized, and the great ideals with which humanity had been encouraged during the war, were not brought forth as cornerstones for a better future. The peace conference only blessed the haphazard agreements arrived at between the great powers.' F. Nagy (1948) *The Struggle Behind the Iron Curtain*, New York, Macmillan, p. 273.

19 *Collected Works*, Vol. I. p. 193.

20 Ibid., p. 197. Bibó's views on the Peace Treaty, to be sure, received some sharp criticism from the Left. The Marxist philosopher Georg Lukács, for example, accused Bibó of unwittingly aiding the revival of Hungarian chauvinism with this article. See G. Lukács (1946) 'A *Válasz* elsö száma' (The first number of *Válasz*), *Forum*, October.

21 Ibid., p. 200.

22 Ibid., p. 239. (*Cf. Paralysis*, op. cit., pp. 60–2). It is not certain if Bibó intended to hit out to the Right or to the Left with his sharp denunciation of premature federalism. Any proposal remotely suggesting a revival of the Habsburg Empire (in whatever modernized version) was for him anathema, in 1945-7 and thereafter. But it should be noted that Communist leaders in eastern Europe in this early postwar period, like Tito, Dimitrov, Rákosi and even Stalin himself, as revealed by Djilas in *Conversations with Stalin*, also willingly toyed with the idea of regional federations. Bibó's negative view would then be shared by the American commentator, Robert R. King, arguing that 'the Communist article of faith that creation of a federation eliminates national conflict is erroneous. Boundaries must also be drawn between federal units, and the contested territory can belong to only one unit. The creation of a federation would hardly solve

the problems of national minorities'. (1973) *Minorities under Communism: Nationalities as a Source of Tension among Balkan Communist States*, Cambridge, Mass., Harvard University Press, p. 58.

23 Ibid., p. 240.

24 *Cf.* in a recent work: 'Whatever is happening and will happen in the Soviet Union, undoubtedly one positive side-effect of the Gorbachev-phenomenon already has been the creation of relatively favourable conditions of economic and socio-political transformation in Poland and Hungary, and to a smaller extent in the whole of Eastern Europe.' E. Hankiss (1989) *Kelet-európai alternativàk (East European Alternatives)*, Budapest, K. and J. K., p. 282.

25 In the middle of 1990 it is still too early to judge the longer-term effects, and indeed the stability, of democratizations. Hopefully it would not sound too biased to say that in Romania the anti-Ceausecu Revolution of December 1989 did not appear to have led to the complete supersession of intransigent nationalism and ethnic conflict. One views more optimistically the recent deliberations (Bratislava, April 1990) of Czechoslovak, Hungarian and Polish governmental representatives which included, on the Czechoslovak side, an historic repudiation of the old doctrine of collective war-guilt.

26 *Cf.* J. Szücs (1983) 'The Three Historical Regions of Europe', *Acta Historica Academiae Scientiarium Hungaricae*, Vol. 29, p. 167. This highly influential article was dedicated by its author to the memory of Bibó, and it makes extensive use of Bibó's texts, with particular reference to 'The Misery of the Small States of Eastern Europe'.

27 *Cf.* the excellent article by P. Kende, 'Van-e még esélye és értelme egy közèp-európai államföderációnak?', (Has a Central European federation of states still a chance and meaning?), in *Századvég (Fin de Sièĉle)*, Special Issue, 1989, pp. 7–20, which reaches a similar conclusion.

7 The Hungarian Draft Treaty for the Protection of Minorities

1 New Hungarian Central Archive. Ministry of Foreign Affairs, Peace Treaty Division (NHCA–MFA–PTD). István Kertész, memorandum of 2 July 1945, 'A békétárgyalások elökeszitésének ideológiai alapja', Bé-res (Peace Preparatory Section – Secret Documents), No. 14, 1945.

2 NHCA–MFA–PTD, 14 August 1945, Bé-res, No. 44, 1945.

3 Ministére des Affaires Etrangeres. Archives et Documentation (MAEAD), Serie Z. Europe. Roumanie, Vol. 24. The French position did not change until the summer of 1946. As late as 17 June 1946, Jean-Paul Boncour, French Ambassador to Bucharest, urged recognition of the predominance of the Rumanians but added, 'the system protecting national minorities between the two wars must be restored'. MAEAD, Serie Z, Europe Roumanie, Vol. 24.

4 Memorandum by Pál Sebestyén, dated 1 January 1946, in NHCA–MFA–PTD.

5 See Mihály Fülöp, 'The Sebestyén Mission II', *Világtörténet*, No. 2, 1988.

6 NHCA–MFA–PTD, Bé-res, No. 50, 1946.

7 NHCA–MFA–PTD, Bé-res, No. 130, 1946. The note, dated 8 May 1946, was presented to the British in Budapest on 13 May. On the shift in Hungarian policy towards the protection of minorities, see the memorandum by Fred A. Warner, 30 May 1946, No. 8072/256/21, Public Records Office, FO 371/1.59006.

8 NHCA–MFA–PTD, Bé-res, No. 87 and No. 232.

9 Baranyai's memorandum concerning the Draft Treaty on the Protection of Minorities, dated 11 July 1946, in NHCA–MFA–PTD.

10 NHCA–MFA–PTD, Bé-res, No. 160, dated 20 May 1946.

11 Bevin's telegram to Washington, 7 June 1946, No. SN 5640, FO 371/59024.

12 Lord Inverchapel's telegram to London, 15 June 1946, R 8922, FO 371/5640.

13 *Foreign Relations of the United States 1946*, Vol. 6, pp. 312–13. Barbour's memorandum, 13 June 1946, 711, 64/6-1346, FO 371/59024.

14 FO 371/59024, R 9158/1266/21.

15 James Marjoribanks to W. G. Hayter, 26 June 1946, FO 371/59025.

16 Telegram No. 282 of the British Delegation to the Paris Peace Conference on

discussions between Bevin and the Czechoslovak Minister of Foreign Affairs, Masaryk, on 29 June 1946, FO 371/59038.

17 Stephen D. Kertész (1985) *The Last European Peace Conference*, Lanham, University Press of America, p. 134 and Schoenfeld's telegram No. 312 to Budapest, 10 August 1946, National Archives Box 96, R 6-43.

18 Minutes of the Extraordinary Meeting of the Council of Ministers at 11 a.m. on 6 August 1946, NHCA–MFA–PTD, No. 179, Konf–1046.

19 NHCA–MFA–PTD, No. 106, Konf–1946.

20 See Sandor Balogh (1988), *Hungarian Foreign Policy 1945–1950*, Budapest, Kossuth Könyvkiadó, pp. 229–30.

21 *The Hungarian Peace Treaty and its Interpretation* (1947), Budapest, Documenta Danubiana, p. 13.

22 NHCA–MFA–PTD, No. 363, Konf–1946.

23 *Hungary's International Relations before the Paris Conference* (1947), Budapest, Hungarian Ministry of Foreign Affairs, pp. 133–61.

24 Summary of 17 September 1946 from Paris, in NHCA–MFA–PTD.

25 FO 371/59040 PPC, 46/Hungary PT, 11th Meeting, R 13823/2608/21 and *Hungarian Peace Treaty*, op. cit., p. 14.

26 Gyöngyösi's memorandum of 10 September 1946, NHCA–MFA–PTD 39/Mk. b.

27 Gyöngyösi's memorandum of 27 September 1946, NHCA–MFA–PTD No. 720, Konf–1946.

28 NHCA–MFA–PTD No. 876, Konf–1946.

29 Balogh, *Hungarian Foreign Policy*, op. cit., p. 248.

8 British policy towards western Europe 1945-51

1 See, for example, Lord Gladwyn (1972) *The Memoirs of Lord Gladwyn*, London, Weidenfeld & Nicolson, pp. 114–18.

2 Public Record Office Reference FO 800/493.

3 Raymond Smith and John Zametica (1985) 'The Cold Warrior: Clement Attlee Reconsidered, 1945–7' *International Affairs*, Vol. 61, p. 243.

4 FO 371/49069. See also John Young (1984) *Britain, France and the Unity of Europe, 1945–51*, Leicester, Leicester University Press, p. 14.

5 See FO 371/50912.

6 As early as February 1944, 'It was pretty clear . . . that the COS [Chiefs of Staff] did reject the "Four-Power thesis".' See Lord Gladwyn, *Memoirs*, op. cit., p. 144. See also Margaret Gowing (1974) *Independence and Deterrence 1945–52: Policy Making*, New York, St. Martin's Press, pp. 186–7.

7 See Raymond Smith (1988) 'A Climate of Opinion: British Officials and the Development of British Soviet Policy, 1945–7', *International Affairs*, Vol. 64, p. 63.

8 See Aneurin Bevan's remarks in Cabinet on 11 February 1946, CAB 128/7; and Sir Stafford Cripps' comments on 13 February 1946, FO 371/56780.

9 Joint Intelligence Committee (46) 1 (0) Final Revise 22 February 1946. The paper is referred to in JIC (46) 38 (0) Final revise, 14 June 1946 in DO 35/1604. See also Roy Merrick (1985) 'The Russia Committee of Britain, the Foreign Office and the Cold War 1946–7', *Journal of Contemporary History* Vol. 20, pp. 453–68.

10 FO 371/66546.

11 FO 371/55589.

12 FO 371/55658.

13 FO 371/66546.

14 Quoted in Alan Bullock (1985) *Ernest Bevin. Foreign Secretary*, Oxford, Oxford University Press, pp. 146–7.

15 See FO 800/444.

16 See J. Kent (1990) 'The British Empire and the Origins of the Cold War, 1944–9', in A. Deighton (ed.), *Britain and the Cold War*', London, Macmillan, pp. 165–83.

17 For the debate over dismembering Germany, see FO 371/46872.

18 Unsigned: FO 371/55382. The proposals are filed under FO 371/55381. The draft

treaty is reproduced in B. von Oppen (1955) *Documents on Germany under Occupation 1945-54*, London, Oxford University Press, pp. 130-1.

19 See Cabinet Meeting 73 (46), FO 371/55589; and Cabinet Meeting 56 (46) on 6 June 1946, CAB 129/9.

20 Quoted in V. Rothwell (1982) *Britain and the Cold War 1941-7*, London, Jonathon Cape, p. 329.

21 The text of the speech is reproduced in von Oppen, *Documents on Germany*, op. cit., p. 158.

22 For the changes in American foreign policy see John Lewis Gaddis (1972) *The United States and the Origin of the Cold War 1941-7*, New York, Columbia University Press, pp. 282-315.

23 H. Dalton (1962) *High Tide and After*, London, Muller.

24 See Rothwell, *Britain and the Cold War*, op. cit., p. 331.

25 Playfair telegram Washington; FO 371/55938.

26 See William Cromwell (1982) 'The Marshall Plan, Britain and the Cold War', *Review of International Studies*, Vol. 8, pp. 233-49.

27 Quoted in Michael Hogan (1987) *The Marshall Plan*, Cambridge, Cambridge University Press, p. 49.

28 V. Rothwell (1987) 'Britain and the First Cold War', in R. Crockatt and S. Smith (eds), *The Cold War Past and Present*, London, Allen & Unwin, p. 63.

29 See Bevin's comments in Cabinet on 18 December 1947, CAB 128/10. The text of the new Fusion Agreement is reproduced in von Oppen, *Documents on Germany*, op. cit., pp. 268-75.

30 FO 371/64450.

31 Sir G. Jenkins, FO 371/64450.

32 Dalton, *High Tide*, op. cit., p. 269.

33 A Crawley (1973) *The Rise of Western Germany 1945-72*, London, Collins, p. 59.

34 The crisis in France was discussed at length in Cabinet Meeting 63 of 1947, which took place on 23 July, CAB 128/10.

35 CAB 128/12.

36 *Parliamentary Debates (Hansard)*, Fifth Series, Vol. 446, p. 398.

37 Elisabeth Barker (1983) *The British between the Superpowers 1945-1950*, London, Macmillan.

38 Bullock, *Ernest Bevin*, op. cit., p. 529.

39 FO 371/62555.

40 Quoted in Hogan, *The Marshall Plan*, op. cit., p. 113.

41 *Hansard*, Vol. 446, p. 402.

42 This line of argument is further explored in Stuart Croft (1988) 'British Policy towards Western Europe, 1947-9: The Best of Possible Worlds?', *International Affairs*, Vol. 64. Hogan argues that Bevin 'and other British leaders conceived of the middle kingdom as a self-supporting and equal partner in this larger alliance of Western states – a kingdom, moreover, that operated under British rather than American leadership', *The Marshall Plan*, op. cit., p. 118.

43 Cabinet Meeting 20, 8 March 1948, CAB 128/12.

44 FO 371/71851.

45 Roger Makins in a memorandum to Bevin, 8 September 1948, FO 371/71869. See M. Hogan, *The Marshall Plan*, op. cit., pp. 154-61.

46 Quoted in A. Bullock, *Ernest Bevin*, op. cit., p. 535.

47 FO 371/76569.

48 FO 371/70489.

49 CAB 21/1883. Statistical information on the airlift, 'Operation Plainfare', can be found in AIR 19/621.

50 Cabinet Meeting 44 (48) on 28 June, CAB 128/13.

51 FO 371/84084.

52 See M. Dockrill (1986) 'The Foreign Office, Anglo-American Relations and the Korean War', *International Affairs*, Vol. 62.

53 FO 800/517.

54 Dated 3 January 1951, FO 371/92067.
55 28 January 1950, FO 371/92067.
56 15 July 1950, FO 371/84089, quoted in Dockrill, 'Foreign Office, Anglo-American Relations and the Korean War', op. cit., p. 476.
57 See J. Young, *Britain, France and the Unity of Europe*, op. cit., pp. 127–8 and 143–4.
58 See Scott Newton (1985) 'The 1949 Sterling Crisis and British Policy Towards European Integration', *Review of International Studies*, Vol. 11, and Jan Melissen and Bert Zeeman (1987) 'Britain and Western Europe 1945–51: Opportunities lost?', *International Affairs*, Vol. 63, pp. 81–95.
59 A personal letter to Acheson, quoted in H. Pelling (1989) *Britain and the Marshall Plan*, London, Macmillan, p. 85.
60 There were major debates in the Foreign Office over German rearmament. See, for example, FO 371/85048; PREM 8/1429; FO 371/85054; and FO 371/85058.
61 William Mallet, Superintending General Secretary for the German Political Department, reporting a conversation with French Minister de Crouy Chanel, 26 October 1950, FO 371/85051.
62 Cabinet Meeting 29 of 1958, CAB 128/7.
63 Bevin to Sir Oliver Harvey, February 1951, WO 216/368.
64 FO 371/85667.
65 WO 216/368.

9 British perceptions of the European Defence Community

1 See, in particular, Edward Fursdon (1980) *The European Defence Community: A History*, London, Macmillan, Chapter 3.
2 Alfred Grosser (1980) *The Western Alliance*, London, Macmillan, p. 122.
3 C. Bertram (ed.) (1983) *Defence and Consensus*, London, Macmillan, p. 116.
4 D. Lerner and R. Aron (1957) *France Defeats EDC*, New York, Praeger, p. 13.
5 Ibid., p. ix.
6 C. Wilmot (1953) 'Britain's Strategic Relationship to Europe', *International Affairs*, pp. 409–17.
7 See G. Warner, 'The Labour Government and the Unity of Western Europe, 1945–51', in R. Ovendale (ed.) (1984) *The Foreign Policy of the British Labour Governments 1945–51*, Leicester, Leicester University Press, pp. 79–80.
8 Ibid.
9 *European Unity: A Statement by the National Executive Committee of the Labour Party*, London, Transport House, 1950.
10 Warner, 'The Labour Government', op. cit.
11 *The Union of Europe: Its Progress, Problems, Prospect, and Place in the Western World*, Strasbourg, Council of Europe, pp. 41 ff.
12 CAB 129/47 CP (51) 226, 22 October 1951.
13 *The Council of Europe Consultative Assembly, Ordinary Session, 1950 – Documents*.
14 Eisenhower Papers, 18 September 1954, quoted by Martin Gilbert (1988) *Winston S. Churchill*, Vol. 8, 1946–65. London, Heinemann, p. 1057.
15 D. D. Eisenhower (1963) *The White House Years – Mandate for Change, 1953–1956*, London, Heinemann, p. 246.
16 A. Eden (1960) *Memoirs – Full Circle*, London, Cassell, pp. 32 and 34. See also J. W. Young, 'German Rearmament and the European Defence Community', in J. W. Young (ed.) (1988) *The Foreign Policy of Churchill's Peacetime Administration, 1951–55*, Leicester, Leicester University Press, p. 102.
17 Wilmot, 'Britain's Strategic Relationship', op. cit.
18 See R. B. Manderson-Jones (1972) *The Special Relationship: Anglo-American Relations and Western European Unity 1947–1956*, London, Weidenfeld & Nicolson, Chapter 6.
19 K. Adenauer (1966) *Memoirs 1945–1953*, London, Weidenfeld & Nicolson, p. 348.
20 HC Debates, Vol. 495, 5th Series, Col. 820–1.
21 R. P. Stebbins (1953) *The United States in World Affairs 1953*, New York, Harper, p. 21.
22 D. Acheson (1969) *Present at the Creation*, New York, Norton, pp. 569–70.

NOTES 177

23 A. Bevan, B. Castle, T. Driberg, I. Mikardon and H. Wilson (1954) *It Need Not Happen: The Alternative to German Rearmament*, London, Tribune.
24 HC Debates, Vol. 515, 5th Series, Col. 883–98.
25 Manderson-Jones, *The Special Relationship*, op. cit., p. 118.
26 *Foreign Relations of the United States 1952–1954*, Vol. 5, p. 1799.
27 See P. Melandri, 'France and the Atlantic Alliance 1950–1953', in O. Riste (ed.) (1985) *Western Security*, Oslo, Universitetsforlaget, pp. 266–82.
28 Eden, *Memoirs*, op. cit., p. 166.
29 Cmnd. 9075.
30 See Manderson-Jones, *A Special Relationship*, op. cit., pp. 130–4 and D. C. Watt (1984) *Succeeding John Bull: America in Britain's Place, 1900–75*, Cambridge, Cambridge University Press.

10 Italy and the European Defence Community: 1950-54

1 On the link between the outbreak of the Korean war and a strengthening of the western European defence system see, among others, P. Melandri (1979) *L'alliance Atlantique*, Paris, Gallimard/Julliard, pp. 63–84; O. Riste (ed.) (1985) *Western Security: the Formative Years, European and Atlantic Defence 1947–1953*, Oslo, Norwegian University Press; L. S. Kaplan (1988) *NATO and the United States. The Enduring Alliance*, Boston, Mass., Twayne Publishers, pp. 33–51; W. LaFeber (1989) 'NATO and the Korean War: A Context', *Diplomatic History*, Vol. 13, pp. 461–77.
2 On west Germany's involvement in the Western defence system see N. Wiggershaus (1988) 'Zum Problem einer militarischen Integration West Deutschlands 1948-1950', in N. Wiggershaus and R. G. Foerster (eds), *Die Westlische Sicherheitsgemeinschaft 1948–1950*, Boppard am Rhein, Harald Boldt Verlag, pp. 311–41; E. R. May (1989) 'The American Commitment to Germany, 1949-1955', *Diplomatic History*, Vol. 13, pp. 431–60.
3 On French policy towards Germany during the postwar period see A. Grosser (1972) *La Quatrième République et sa politique extèrieure*, Paris, A. Colin, pp. 193–246; A. Grosser (1984) *Affaires Exterieures. La politique de la France 1944–1984*, Paris, Flammarion, pp. 49–54; M. Hillel (1983) *L'occupation Française en Allemagne 1945–1949*, Paris: Balland.
4 On Schuman's policy see R. Poidevin (1986) *Robert Schuman homme d'état 1886–1963*, Paris, Imprimerie Nationale, pp. 208–96. On Monnet's initiatives see J. Monnet (1976) *Memoires*, Paris, Fayard, pp. 313–434. For an evaluation of the Schuman Plan see A. Milward (1984) *The Reconstruction of Western Europe 1945–51*, London, Methuen, pp. 362–420, and K. Schwabe (ed.) (1988) *Die Anfänge des Schuman-Plans 1950/1951*, Baden-Baden, Nomos Verlag.
5 For an analysis of the events related to the European Defence Community see E. Fursdon (1980) *The European Defence Community. A History*, London, Macmillan.
6 On Italy's adherence to the Atlantic Pact see, M. Toscano, 'Appunti sui negoziati per la partecipazione dell'Italia al Patto Atlantico', in M. Toscano (ed.), (1963) *Pagine di storia diplomatica contemporanea, Vol. II, Origini e vicende della seconda guerra mondiale*, Milan, Giuffré, pp. 455–519; H. T. Smith (1983) 'The Fear of Subversion, the United States and the Inclusion of Italy in the Northern Atlantic Treaty', *Diplomatic History*, Vol. 7, pp. 139–55; P. Pastorelli (1987) *La politica estera italiana del dopoguerra*, Bologna, il Mulino, pp. 209–31; A. Varsori (1985) 'La scelta occidentale dell'Italia (1948-1949)', *Storia delle relazioni internazionali*, Vol. 1, pp. 95–159, and pp. 303–68; B. Vigezzi, 'La politica estera italiana e le premesse della scelta atlantica. Governo, diplomatici militarie le discussioni nell'estate 1948', in B. Vigezzi (ed.) (1987) *La dimensione atlantica e le relazioni internazionali nel dopoguerra (1947–1949)*, Milan, Jaca Book, pp. 1–189; O. Barie Gli Stati Uniti. L'Unione occidentale e l'inserimento dell'Italia nell' alleanza atlantica', in O. Barie (ed.) (1988) *L'Alleanza Occidentale*, Bologna, il Mulino, pp. 115–207.
7 On pacifism in Italy see G. Vecchio, *Movimenti pacifisti ed antiamericanismo in Italia*

(1948–1953), Florence, EUI Working Papers No. 86/249; G. Vecchio, 'Guerra fredda e rilancio del pacifismo in Italia', in O. Barie (ed.), *L'Alleanza*, op. cit., pp. 261–330.

8 On Communist and Socialist opposition to the Italian involvement in a Western military system see S. Galante (1973) *La politica del PCI e il Patto Atlantico*, Padova, Marsilio; D. Ardia (1976) *Il Partito Socialista e il Patto Atlantico*, Milano, Angeli. The attitude of the Italian political parties to the Atlantic alliance has been analysed in G. Di Capua (1971) *Come l'Italia aderi al Patto Atlantico*, Roma, EBE. See also G. Formigoni, 'Il mondo cattolico italiano e la 'scelta occidentale dopo le elezioni del 1948', in B. Vigezzi (ed.) *La dimensione*, pp. 191–237. Until late 1948 some sectors of the Catholic Church emphasized their preference for an Italian neutrality: see E. Di Nolfo (1988) 'La politica estera del Vaticano e l'Italia dal 1943 al 1948', and C. Meneguzzi Rostagni (1988) 'Il Vaticano e i rapporti est-ovest nel secondo dopoguerra1', *Storia delle relazioni internazionali*, Vol. 4, pp. 3–34 and 35–46.

9 For an example of British attitudes see Bevin's remarks in a conversation with French Foreign Minister Robert Schuman, Public Record Office (hereafter PRO), Foreign Office 371 (hereafter FO 371), Z 677/1074/72, memorandum of conversation, 13 January 1949. Transcripts of Crown-copyright records in the Public Record Office appear with the permission of the Controller of Her Majesty's Stationery Office.

10 On the attitude of the United States see, H. T. Smith, 'The Fear of Subversion', op. cit.; J. E. Miller (1986) *The United States and Italy 1940–1950. The Politics and Diplomacy of Stabilization*, Chapel Hill/London, University of North Carolina Press, p. 266 ff.; R. Quartararo (1986) *Italia e Stati Uniti gli anni difficili (1945–1952)*, Napoli, ESI, pp. 235–360.

11 On French-Italian relations during the postwar period see J. B. Duroselle and E. Serra (eds) (1988) *Italia e Francia 1946–1954*, Milan, Angeli, in particular the contribution by P. Guillen. See also P. Guillen 'La France, l'Italie et la defense de la Méditerranée (1947–1951)', in J. B. Duroselle and E. Serra (eds) (1990) *Italia, Francia, e Mediterraneo*, Milan, Angeli, pp. 15–24.

12 On Italy's misperception of the United States' attitude see A. Varsori (1986) 'Italian Diplomacy and Contrasting Perceptions of American Policy after World War II (1947–50)', *Storia Nordamericana*, Vol. 3, pp. 73–92.

13 For an analysis of Italy's postwar international role see in particular E. Di Nolfo, R. H. Rainero and B. Vigezzi (eds), *L'Italia e la politica di potenza in Europa 1945–50*, Milan, Marzorati.

14 On American plans for military aid see L. S. Kaplan, (1980) *A Community of Interests, NATO and the Military Assistance Program, 1948–1951*, Washington D.C., Office of the Secretary of Defense Historical Office. For Italy's case see L. Sebesta (1988) 'I programmi di aiuto militare nella politica americana per l'Europa. L'esperienza italiana 1948–1952', *Italia contemporanea*, No. 173, pp. 43–64.

15 See the remarks in I. Poggiolini (1985) 'Europeismo degasperiano e politica estera dell'Italia, un'ipotesi interpretativa (1947–1949)', *Storia delle relazioni internazionali*, Vol. 1, pp. 67–94.

16 Some interesting remarks about the Western critical view in Archivio Storico Ministero degli Affari Esteri (hereafter ASMAE), Ambasciata di Parigi (hereafter APA), b. 476, fasc. 1, teles. no. 2908/1583, A. Tarchiani (Washington) to Ministry of Foreign Affairs (MAE), March 1950, secret; fasc. 2, despatch, A. Tarchiani (Washington) to V. Zoppi (MAE), 11 April 1950; despatch no. 310/1527, P. Quaroni (Paris) to C. Sforza (MAE), 18 April 1950.

17 On Italy's attitude towards the Schuman Plan see in particular R. Ranieri, 'L'Italia e i negoziati sul Piano Schuman', in E. Di Nolfo, R. H. Rainero and B. Vigezzi (eds), *L'Italia*, op. cit., pp. 547–73; and R. Ranieri (1988) *L'espansione alla prova del negoziato. L'industria italiana e la Comunita del Carbone e dell'Acciaio*, 1945–1955. Ph. D. thesis, European University Institute, Florence.

18 An example of Italian fears in ASMAE, APA, b. 476, fasc. 3, report no. 641/3663, P. Quaroni (Paris) to C. Sforza (MAE), 14 August 1950; report no. 721/3838, P. Quaroni (Paris) to C. Sforza (MAE), 30 September, 1950.

19 See Zoppi's remarks to the French Ambassador in Rome, Fouques Duparc, in ASMAE,

APA, b. 463, fasc. 4, teles. no. Segr. Pol. P. A. 839/C (MAE) to various diplomatic representatives, 27 July, 1950, secret.

20 On the relations between Italy and Germany during the postwar period see P. Guillen (1987) 'L'Italie et le problème allemand', *Relations Internationales*, No. 51, pp. 269–87; L. Berti (1990) 'L'Italia e la Germania, l'atteggiamento della diplomazia Italiana dal 1950 al 1952', *Storia delle relazioni internazionali*, Vol. 6.

21 For the development of Italy's position see ASMAE, APA, b. 477, fasc. 1, tel. no. 700, MAE to Paris, 28.10.1950; tel. no. 756, MAE to Paris, 12 November 1950.

22 See the sources quoted in notes 11 and 17.

23 An interesting analysis of Italy's attitude to the Pleven Plan in Archives Ministere des Affaires Estrangeres (Paris) AMAE, Serie Z Europe 1949–55, sous-serie Italie, b. 30, Note Direction d'Europe, sous-Direction d'Europe Meridionale, 'Italie et rapports franco-italiens', 9 December 1950.

24 The records related to the French-Italian Conference in AMAE, Serie Z Europe 1949–55, sous-serie Italie, b. 31.

25 On the development of the Pleven Plan see E. Fursdon, *The European*, op. cit., pp. 50–103.

26 The wait-and-see attitude of the Italian delegation is confirmed in ASMAE. Fondo cassaforte (FC), b. 23, teles. no. 10/40, F. Cavalletti (Paris) to MAE, 2 June 1951. For a critical view of this policy see ASMAE, FC, b. 23, report no. 554, P. Quaroni (Paris) to A. De Gasperi (MAE), 2 August 1951, secret.

27 See E. Fursdon, *The European*, op. cit.

28 On the attitude of the Italian military see ASMAE, FC, b. 23. tel. no. 7476, P. Quaroni (Paris) to MAE, 15 June 1951, secret; report no. 429, P. Quaroni (Paris) to C. Sforza (MAE), 28 June 1951, secret.

29 As for the critical view of the 'rapport interimaire' see in particular ASMAE, FC, b. 23, report no. 2817, G. Malagodi (OEEC Paris) to A. De Gasperi e G. Pella, 28 July 1951, secret; and Movimento Federalista Europeo (Pavia) (MFE), Archivio Ivan Matteo Lombardo (AIML), lett. no. 1931, G. Malagodi (OEEC-Paris) to V. Zoppi (MAE), 2 June, 1951, confidential. Malagodi, a leading member of the Italian Liberal Party, headed the Italian delegation at the OEEC in Paris.

30 On the peace campaign against the Pleven Plan and the Atlantic alliance, vigorously led by the parties of the Left, see the interesting remarks in S. Galante (1988) *Il Partito comunista italiano e l'integrazione europea. Il decennio del rifiuto, 1947–1957*, Padova, Liviana, pp. 61–112.

31 As for the Trieste question and its influence on Italy's foreign and internal policy see J. B. Duroselle (1966) *Le conflit de Trieste 1943–1954*, Bruxelles, Editions de l'Institut de Sociologie de l'Universite Libre de Bruxelles; B. C. Novak (1970) *Trieste 1941–1954. The Ethnic, Political and Ideological Struggle*, Chicago, The University of Chicago Press; A. G. M. de Robertis (1983) *Le grandi potenze e il confine qiuliano 1941–47*, Bari, Fratelli Laterza; D. De Castro (1981) *La questione di Trieste. L'azione politica e diplomatica dell'Italia dall 1943 al 1954*, Trieste, LINT; G. Valdevit (1985) *La questione di Trieste 1941–1954. Politica internazionale e contesto locale*, Milan, Angeli. As for the attitude of the parties of the Right see S. Finotti (1988) 'Difesa occidentale e Patto atlantico, la scelta internazionale del MSI (1948–1952)', *Storia delle relazioni internazionali*, Vol. 4, pp. 85–124.

32 A general appraisal of Italy's attitude towards European integration in S. Pistone (1982) *L'Italia e l'unità Europea dalle premesse storiche all'elezione del Parlamento Europeo*, Torino, Loescher. See also the interesting remarks in R. Ranieri (1985) 'Europeismo e politica Europea, osservazioni sulla presenza Italiana in Europa occidentale dal 1947 al 1951', *Storia delle relazioni internazionali*, Vol. 1, pp. 161–82.

33 This document in A. Spinelli (1989) *Una strategia per gli Stati Uniti d'Europa*, Bologna, il Mulino, pp. 105–32. See also A. Spinelli (1989) *Diario Europeo 1948/1969*, Bologna, il Mulino, pp. 97–8.

34 On De Gasperi's policy see P. Pastorelli, *La politica*, op. cit. pp. 180–208.

35 Useful information about the role played by the Italian delegation at the Paris Conference in MFE, AIML op. cit.

36 An interesting evaluation about Italy's attitude towards European integration in PRO, FO 371, WT 10318/5, 'The Roman/Bonn rapprochement', memorandum by C. M. MacLehose, 18 June 1951. The Foreign Office official wrote: 'Since the war Italy has not been in a position to exercise much influence on her own account in international affairs, and has consequently been attracted by the idea, either of European federation, or in default of that of association with some other European country in collaboration with whom she could exercise a more decisive influence.'

37 For a thorough analysis of the treaty see E. Fursdon *The European*, op. cit., pp. 150–90.

38 On this important issue see the recent contribution, F. Romero (1989) 'L'integrazione dell'Italia in Europa negli anni Cinquanta, la questione dell'emigrazione', *Passato e Presente*, No. 20/21, pp. 75–105.

39 An evaluation of Italy's aims towards European integration, as well as of the link between the EPC project and economic cooperation in MFE, AIML, teles. no. 21/0023, MAE to 'Delegazione italiana nella Commissione per la Comunita europea', 6 January 1954, secret. Evidence of widespread Italian belief in the probable benefits of European integration is given by a minor episode. In October 1952 the French Consul in Genoa had a talk with the Italian Admiral Iannucci. The French diplomat reported on the conversation to the French Ambassador in Rome, 'Selon la règle il (Admiral Iannucci) se dit ardent partisan d'une union franco-italienne, ainsi que d'une Fédération européenne. Ne marchant pas ses mots il m'a tenu notamment ces propos, "Nous sommes d'autant plus fédéralistes en Italie que nous appartenons à un pays pauvre; si d'autres pays (il devait faire allusion notamment à l'Angleterre et meme aussi à la France) sont beaucoup moins ardents fédéralistes que nous, c'est probablement parce qu'ils sont plus riches."' See AMAE, Serie Z Europe 1949–55, sous-serie Italie, b. 33, report no. 279, the French Consul (Genoa) to Fouques Duparc (Rome) 21 November 1952.

40 See De Gasperi's evaluation in ASMAE, Direzione Generale Affari Politici DGAP, 1952, Italy, b. 165, tel. no. 6832/93/34, A. De Gasperi (MAE) to various diplomatic representatives, 13 July 1952, secret.

41 As an example of the difference of opinions between the French authorities and the Italian government over the issue of the EPC, see AMAE, Série Z Europe 1949–55, sous-série Généralités, b. 32, tel. various nos., Quai d'Orsay to various diplomatic representatives, 18 October 1952, reserve.

42 On the influence of the EDC issue on French policy, see among others G. Elgey (1968) *Histoire de la Quatrième République, Vol. II, La République des contradictions 1951–1954*, Paris, Fayard, pp. 1995–2340. For a more up-to-date interpretation see J. P. Rioux (1983) *La France de la Quatrième République, Vol. II, L'expansion et l'impuissance 1952–1958*, Paris, Editions du Seuil, pp. 18–29.

43 On the Additional Protocols see the records in AMAE, Serie Z Europe 1949–55, sous-série Généralités, b. 23, 24, 25.

44 For some remarks about Italy's reaction to the Additional Protocols see MFE, AIML, report no. 220, P. Quaroni (Paris) to A. De Gasperi (MAE), 13 February 1953; as well as teles. no. 21/0306 MAE to 'Delegazione italiana per la CED' (Paris), 22 January 1953.

45 ASMAE, FC, b. 25, teles. no. 21/0865, MAE to various diplomatic representatives, 3 March 1953.

46 On Italy's internal developments, see among others G. Mammarella (1974) L'Italia dalla caduta del fascismo ad oggi. Bologna, il Mulino, pp. 255–87; N. Kogan (1982) *Storia politica dell'Italia repubblicana*, Rome/Bari, Laterza, pp. 75–91.

47 See De Gasperi's position at the Conference of the Six held in Paris in May 1953, ASMAE, DGAP, 1953, Italy, b. 255, memorandum 'Appunto sulla riunione dei ministri della Comunita Europea' (Parigi, Quai d'Orsay, 12, 13 maggio 1953), drafted by M. Magistrati, 14 May 1953, strictly confidential.

48 As for American pressure on the Italian government, see as an example ASMAE, FC, b. 25, teles., F. Cavalletti (Luxemburg) to MAE, 3 March 1953, secret; teles. no. 21/1165, MAE to various diplomatic representatives, 25 July 1953, secret.

49 Some remarks about the difference of opinions between the United States and western

Europe in PRO, CAB 129/61, memorandum C(53)187, Foreign Ministers' Meeting in Washington. Policy towards the Soviet Union and Germany, 3 July 1953, secret.

50 See the sources quoted in note 46.

51 On Pella's policy towards the Trieste question, see in particular the contribution by De Castro and Valdevit.

52 For Pella's attitude towards the EDC and the EPC, see for example ASMAE, DGAP, 1953, Italy, b. 255, memorandum no. 21/3905, 'Appunto sulla riunione dei ministri degli Affari Esteri della Comunità Europea (l'Aja, 16–18 novembre 1953)', drafted by M. Magistrati, 30 November 1953, confidential.

53 See A. Canavero (1990) 'La politica estera di un ministro degli Interni. Scelba, Piccioni, Martino e la politica estera italiana 1954–1955', *Storia delle Relazioni Internazionali*, Vol. 6.

54 ASMAE, FC, b. 27, report no. 2151, A. Tarchiani (Washington) to A. Piccioni (MAE), 18 February 1954, secret.

55 ASMAE, DC, b. 26, report no. Ris. 0024, P. Quaroni (Paris) to V. Zoppi (MAE), 23 January 1954, secret.

56 A. Canavero, *La politica*, op. cit.

57 I. M. Wall (1989) *L'Influence Américaine sur la Politique Francaise 1945–1954*, Paris, Balland, pp. 395–448.

58 As for Mendès-France, see among others J. Lacouture (1981) *Pierre Mendès-France*, Paris, Editions du Seuil, pp. 225–393; F. Bedarida and J. P. Rioux (eds) (1985) *Pierre Mendès-France et le mendesisme*, Paris, Fayard; P. Mendès-France (1986) *Oeuvres Complètes, Vol. III, Gouverner c'est choisir 1954–1955*, Paris, Gallimard.

59 A portrait of Mendès-France in ASMAE, DGAP, 1954, France, memorandum, 19 June 1954. For Italy's fears about the neutralist influence on Mendès-France entourage see MFE, AIML, teles. no. 8/3340, 'Presidenza del Consiglio' to various diplomatic representatives, 5 May 1954.

60 On the attitude of the Italian delegation see ASMAE, DGAP, b. 331, memorandum 'Nota ufficiosa di commento sull'atteggiamento italiano alla Conferenza di Bruxelles 24 August 1954'. For an analysis of Italy's role during this period see A. Varsori (1988) 'L'azione diplomatica italiana dal fallimento della CED all'istituzione della UEO (1954–1955)', in *La France et l'Italie dans les annés cinquante*, Grenoble, Universite des Sciences Sociales-CRHIPA, pp. 63–94.

61 See among others E. Fursdon, *The European*, op. cit., p. 227; G. Soutou (1987) 'La France, l'Allemagne et les accords de Paris', *Relations Internationales*, No. 52, pp. 451–70; S. Dockrill, 'Britain and the Settlement of the West German Rearmament Question in 1954', in M. Dockrill and J. W. Young (eds) (1989) *British Foreign Policy: 1945–56*, London, Macmillan, pp. 149–72.

62 ASMAE, FC, b. 27, note, by C. A. Straneo, 27 August 1954, secret.

63 ASMAE, DGAP, b. 331, memorandum 'Circa la soluzione di ricambio', drafted by L. Benvenuti, 13 September 1954.

64 ASMAE, DGAP, b. 331, memorandum no. 21/2340, 'Verbale delle conversazioni anglo-italiane di Roma (Villa Madama, 14 September 1954)', secret.

65 For Italy's role see the records in ASMAE, DGAP, b. 331.

66 See, as an example, ASMAE, DGAP, b. 409, report no. 358, P. Quaroni (Paris) to G. Martino (MAE) 30 August 1955.

67 On these developments see E. Serra (ed.) (1989) *Il Rilancio dell' Europae i trattati di Roma. Actes du colloque de Rome, 25–28 mars 1987*, Bruxelles, Bruylant.

11 Attempting an unlikely union: the British Steel Industry and the European Coal and Steel Community 1950-54

1 Duncan Burn, (1961) *The Steel Industry 1939-1959 - A Study in Competition and Planning*, Cambridge, Cambridge University Press; for the rationale of his work see The London School of Economics and Political Science Archives – Papers and Correspondence of Duncan Burn (Burn Papers) 6/36, (111–2) Duncan Burn to Robert Shone, 1 February 1954.

2 Roger Bullen (1988) 'The British Government and the Schuman Plan: May 1950–March 1951', in K. Schwabe, (ed.) *Die Anfänge des Schuman Plans 1950/51 - The*

Beginnings of the Schuman Plan, Baden Baden, Nomos, pp. 199–210; and Roger Bullen (1986) Preface to *Documents on British Policy Overseas, Series II, Vol. 1, The Schuman Plan. The Council of Europe and Western European Integration. May 1950–December 1952*, London, HMSO, *DOBPO*, pp. ix–xxix.

3 *DOBPO*, op. cit., n.82.

4 Ibid., n.184.

5 On the structure of decision-making see Roger Bullen, Preface op. cit. pp. xiv–xv. The first WP was an emanation of the Franco-German Committee (FGC) which was comprised of the Treasury, Foreign Office (FO), Board of Trade (BoT), Ministry of Fuel and Power and the Ministry of Supply. In the WP a large part was also played by industrial representatives acting as experts. The WP was supervised and its conclusions examined by the relevant committee. After the winding-up of the FGC this role was taken by the Economic Steering Committee which in turn reported to the Economic Policy Committee. This last body presented their advice to the Cabinet.

6 See Richard Griffiths, 'The Schuman Plan negotiations: The Economic Clauses', and John Gillingham, 'Solving the Ruhr Problem: German Heavy Industry and the Schuman Plan', both in Schwabe (ed.), *Die Anfänge des Schuman Plans 1950/51*, op. cit., pp. 35–71 and 399–436.

7 *DOBPO*, n.109i.

8 *DOBPO*, n.308i; Alec Cairncross (ed.) (1989) *The Robert Hall Diaries: 1947–1953*, London, Unwin Hyman, pp. 112–13.

9 *DOBPO*, n.366.

10 *DOBPO*, n.334; Alan S. Milward (1984) *The Reconstruction of Western Europe 1945–1951*, London, Methuen, pp. 401–6.

11 *DOBPO*, n.112, n.128, n.132, n.334, n.342.

12 *DOBPO*, n.11G.

13 *DOBPO*, n.488.

14 *DOBPO*, n.456, n.461.

15 *DOBPO*, n.482.

16 *DOBPO*, n.506, n.512.

17 *DOBPO*, n.440. See Jean Monnet (1976) *Memoires*, Paris, Fayard, pp. 441–52.

18 See John W. Young (1988), 'The Schuman Plan and British Association' in John Young, (ed.) *The Foreign Policy of Churchill's Peacetime Administration: 1951–1957*, Leicester, Leicester University Press, pp. 119–20; and Max Beloff (1961) *New Dimensions in Foreign Policy – A Study in British Administrative Experience 1947–1959*, London, Allen & Unwin, pp. 91–2.

19 PRO, CAB (CAB) 134/1177 SPC (E) 53, Meetings and Papers; on the opinions inside the WP see PRO, FO (FO) 371, 105596/112. On the Foreign Office stance see John Young (1985) 'Churchill's No to Europe: the Rejection of European Union by Churchill's Postwar Government, 1951–2', *The Historical Journal*, Vol. 28, pp. 932–4.

20 See Duncan L. Burn (1940) *The Economic History of Steelmaking 1867–1939 – A Study in Competition*, London, Cambridge University Press; Bernard Elbaum (1986), 'The Steel Industry before World War I', in B. Elbaum and W. Lazonick, *The Decline of the British Economy*, Oxford, Oxford University Press, pp. 51–81; and Steven Tolliday 'Steel and Rationalization Policies, 1918–1950', in ibid., pp. 82–108.

21 Quoted in J. C. Carr and W. Taplin (1962) *History of the British Steel Industry*, Oxford, Oxford University Press, pp. 62 and 519.

22 Duncan Burn, *The Steel Industry*, op. cit., p. 129.

23 On the postwar assets of British steel see Duncan Burn, 'Steel', in D. Burn (ed.) (1958) *The Structure of British Industry – A Symposium*, Cambridge, Cambridge University Press, Vol. 1, Chapter 7, pp. 260–308; and John Vaizey (1974) *A History of British Steel*, London, Weidenfeld & Nicolson, Chapter 8.

24 CAB 134/1177 SPC (E) 53/3, 'The Common Market: Steel', note by the Ministry of Supply, 21-2-53.

25 CAB 134/1177 SPC (E) 53/2, 'Economic Consequences of a Coal and Steel Community', note by the Economic Section, 23-2-53.

26 CAB 134/1177 SPC (E) 53/6th meeting.

27 CAB 134/1177 SPC (E) 53/29, 'Report by a Working Party of Officials on the Economic Implications of an Association between the UK and the ECSC' 7-53.
28 Ibid.
29 CAB 134/1177 SPC (E) 53/15th meeting.
30 Ibid.
31 CAB 134/1177 SPC (E) 53/16th meeting.
32 CAB 134/885 ES 53/9th meeting and papers 21 and 22.
33 CAB 134/1177 SPC (E) 53/15th meeting.
34 CAB 134/1177 SPC (E) 53/14, 'A preliminary Steel Industry view on the Development of Association with the ECSC', BISF, 11-3-53.
35 As one committee member, Mr Laundrell explained: 'there was no large margin of profit that could be cut away and indeed . . . in recent years . . . profits had come largely from the export premium, which was now in danger of disappearing'. CAB 134/1177 SPC (E) 53/8th meeting. Also on the issue of steel exports, B. S. Keeling and A. E. G. Wright (1964) *The Development of the Modern British Steel Industry*, London, Longman, pp. 101–2.
36 CAB 134/1177 SPC (E) 53/12, BISF 'Problems in connection with the ECSC', 26-3-53.
37 CAB 134/1177 SPC (E) 53/19, BISF, 'A Preliminary Steel Industry View on the Development of Association with the European Coal and Steel Community', 11-5-53.
38 CAB 134/1177 SPC (E) 53/13th meeting; on Algerian ore see R. Ranieri, 'The Italian steel industry and the Schuman Plan Negotiations', in Schwabe (ed.) *Die Anfänge des Schuman Plans 1950/51*, op. cit., pp. 350–2.
39 CAB 134/1177 SPC (E) 53/14, BISF, 'Imperial Preference and Commonwealth Trade in Steel Products'.
40 CAB 134/1177 SPC (E) 53/24th meeting.
41 FO 371/111250/25; CAB 134/885 ES 53/9th meeting; CAB 134/888 ES 54/1st meeting.
42 CAB 134/1177 SPC (E) 54/1st and 2nd meetings.
43 CAB 128/7 CC 54/4 (2).
44 CAB 128/7 CC 54/27 (3).
45 For the views of the ISB see CAB 129/67 C 54/131.
46 CAB 134/1179 SPC (N) 54/1st and 2nd meetings.
47 CAB 134/1179 SPC (N) 54/6 'Association between the UK and the ECSC: possible arrangements related to the Iron and Steel Tariff' ISB, 29-4-54.
48 CAB 134/1179.
49 See note 45.
50 CAB 130/101 50.GEN 462/2nd meeting.
51 Burn, *The Steel Industry* op. cit., for the rationale of his work see The London School of Economics and Political Science Archives: Papers and Correspondence of Duncan Burn (Burn Papers) 6/36, (111–12) Duncan Burn to Robert Shone, 1 February 1954.
52 FO 371/105957/168, 'Letter by Monnet to Sir Cecil Weir' 24-12-53.
53 Record of discussion among the Six in Ministerie Van Buitenlandse Zaken, The Hague (MBZ), EGKS – 996.0 – Verenigd Konikrijk en de EGKS 1952-4 (32), 1-3-54, 'Onderhandelingen EGKS-Verenigd Koninkrijk'.
54 MBZ, 996.0, (n.32), ibid. Price differentials were estimated at between 10 per cent and 15 per cent: that is to say the Community price range was between 110 and 135, compared to 100 for Britain. The gap for rails and plates, however, was considerably wider.
55 Ibid.
56 For a comparison of fiscal systems see Burn, *The Steel Industry*, op. cit., pp. 431–2; and Burn Papers, 6/37 (43), Keeling to Burn, 11-3-60.
57 MBZ 996.0 (32), 5-4-1954, HA, 'Esquisse du contenu possible des negociation avec la Grande-Bretagne, compte-tenu des conversations avec les representants des pays membres'.
58 See John W. Young, 'The Schuman Plan and British Association', op. cit., pp. 127–30; and Richard Mayne (1970) *The Recovery of Europe – From Devastation to Unity*, London, Weidenfeld & Nicolson, pp. 210–17.

59 See William Diebold (1969) *The Schuman Plan - A Study in Economic Cooperation 1950-1959*, New York, Praeger, pp. 502-15.
60 See Luis Lister (1960) *Europe's Coal and Steel Community - An Experiment in Economic Union*, New York, Twentieth Century Fund, pp. 352-4.
61 See Burn, *The Steel Industry*, op. cit., pp. 565-8; Lister, *Europe's Coal & Steel Community*, op. cit., pp. 231-3.
62 For a good description of the ECSC pricing system, see British Iron and Steel Federation, 'Price Competition in the Schuman Community', *Monthly Statistical Bulletin*, Vol. 28, n.11, November 1953.
63 On the loss of competitiveness of the British industry, see Burn, *The Steel Industry* op. cit., p. 564; and for an emphasis on productivity differentials, see Sir Robert Shone 'Economic Development of the United Kingdom Steel Industry', paper delivered to the Royal Society of Arts on 22 March 1961, London.
64 See Burn, *The Steel Industry*, op. cit., pp. 303-4 and 307.

12 Resisting integration: aerospace national champions

1 'State' refers to nation-states.
2 Jacob Viner (1958) 'Power versus Plenty as Objectives of Foreign Policy in the Seventeenth and Eighteenth Centuries', in Jacob Viner (ed.) *The Long View and the Short: Studies in Economic Theory and Practice*, Glencoe, IL: The Free Press, p. 286.
3 Adam Smith specifically identified transportation systems - harbours, canals, roads - as infrastructures that should be provided by the government. See Charles P. Kindleberger (1978) 'Government and International Trade', *Princeton Essays in International Finance*, No. 129. Camden, NJ: International Finance Section, Princeton University.
4 Christer Jönsson (1981) 'Sphere of Flying: The Politics of International Aviation', *International Organization*, Vol. 35, No. 2, p. 281.
5 In most instances, one or two state-owned airlines constituted the 'national champion'. Even in the United States, where airlines were always privately owned, Pan American was supported as the US 'national champion' through the awarding of international airmail routes and other forms of support.
6 See B. Bluestone, P. Jordan and M. Sullivan (1981) *Aircraft Industry Dynamics: An Analysis of Competition, Capital and Labor*, Boston, MA: Auburn House Publishing Company, p. 170; Betsey Gidwitz (1980) *The Politics of International Air Transport*, Lexington, MA: Lexington Books; Vicki L. Golich (1989) *The Political Economy of International Air Safety: Design for Disaster?* London: Macmillan, Chapter 3; Keith Hayward (1986) *International Collaboration in Civil Aerospace*, New York: St Martin's Press, Chapter 5; David C. Mowery and Nathan Rosenberg (1982) 'The Commercial Aircraft Industry', in Richard R. Nelson (ed.) *Government and Technical Progress: A Cross-Industry Analysis*, New York: Pergamon Press, pp. 106-61; David C. Mowery and Nathan Rosenberg (1989) *Technology and the Pursuit of Economic Growth*, Cambridge, Cambridge University Press, Chapter 7.
7 'State élites' refers to those government officials who are influential in determining and implementing public policy.
8 See Golich, *The Political Economy of International Air Safety*, op. cit., Chapter 2.
9 Military aircraft were first used as 'a flying observation post'. In the early months of the First World War, 'pilots adhered to a code of chivalry that forbade trying to harm a fellow flyer, even if he was an enemy'. Eventually, rifles, followed by machine guns and other sophisticated weapons, were mounted onto the aircraft. See William Winter, William Byshyn and Hank Clark (1969) *Airplanes of the World, 1490-1969*, New York: Simon and Schuster, p. 49.
10 In 1936, while American aircraft manufacturers were developing the DC3 land plane that was to set the standard for the industry, the British were building flying boats for 'Empire' routes. See M. S. Hochmuth (1974) 'Aerospace', in Raymond Vernon (ed.), *Big Business and the State: Changing Relations in Western Europe*, Cambridge, MA: Harvard University Press, p. 159.

11 R. E. G. Davies (1964) *A History of the World's Airlines*, London: Oxford University Press, pp. 238–40 and 271–2.

12 From 1929 to 1954 the passenger-kilometres generated by the world's scheduled airlines increased at an average annual rate of 25 per cent. Hochmuth, 'Aerospace', op. cit., p. 154.

13 Keith Hayward (1983) *Government and British Civil Aerospace: A Case Study in Post-War Technology Policy*, Manchester, Manchester University Press, p. 1.

14 'Market size' refers to the number of aircraft sold rather than to geographic size.

15 'Germany' refers to the Federal Republic of Germany.

16 Hochmuth, 'Aerospace', op. cit., p. 150.

17 This was as effective as military procurement was in the United States because virtually all airlines in Europe were state-owned.

18 See Golich, *The Political Economy of International Air Safety*, op. cit., Chapter 3; Hayward, *Government and British Civil Aerospace*, op. cit.; Hayward, *International Collaboration in Civil Aerospace*, op. cit., p. 162.

19 Hayward, *Government and British Civil Aerospace*, op. cit., pp. 8–9.

20 Ibid.

21 Geoffrey Shepherd and François Duchene (1983) 'Introduction: Industrial Change and Intervention in Western Europe', in Geoffrey Shepherd, François Duchene and Christopher Saunder (eds) *Europe's Industries: Public and Private Strategies for Change*, Ithaca, NY: Cornell University Press, pp. 2 and 21.

22 Hayward, *Government and British Civil Aerospace*, op. cit., p. 4.

23 Ibid.

24 The Germans and the British developed jet-engine technology concurrently. The German Heinkel He 178 made the first jet flight on 27 August 1939 but the British Gloster Meteor, introduced in 1944, was the first jet aircraft to be operational, followed by the German Me 262. American manufacturers were not excited about jet transport until after the introduction of the British de Haviland Comet in 1949.

25 Government officials were concerned about foreign-exchange costs and 'that the Americans would deny British firms access to data which would help them in subsequent independent development'. Hayward, *Government and British Civil Aerospace*, op. cit., p. 17.

26 For an intriguing story about the evolution of the international commercial air-transport system, also associated with this insecurity, which emerged after the War, see Golich, *The Political Economy of International Air Safety*, op. cit., p. 25.

27 In 1943, the industry employed over one million people; by 1945, employment had fallen to 170,000.

28 Hayward, *Government and British Civil Aerospace*, op. cit., p. 13.

29 Ibid.

30 Ibid., p. 15.

31 Ibid., p. 16.

32 Namely, the 'stretched' version of the Douglas DC6 or Lockheed Constellation. De Haviland's Comet would have been a tremendous market success with its jet-engine technology, had it not been for serious structural failures that caused at least two fatal crashes. Before the surfacing of these problems, the Comet had penetrated the United States market with sales to Pan American.

33 Hayward, *Government and British Civil Aerospace*, op. cit., p. 17; Hochmuth, op. cit., 'Aerospace', p. 160.

34 By comparison, the United States had only five firms marketing only five basic aircraft; Hochmuth, 'Aerospace', op. cit., p. 160.

35 Quoted by Hayward, *Government and British Civil Aerospace*, op. cit., p. 31.

36 Ibid.

37 Ibid., p. 32. The Comet failure cost BOAC £7.8 million; delivery and technological problems with the Britannia cost £22.4 million.

38 Ibid.

39 For example, the VC10 was tailored to BOAC's Empire Route needs (primitive airports, etc.); the Trident was tailored for BEA but was eclipsed by B727. See Hayward, *Government and British Civil Aerospace*, op. cit., pp. 32–5.

40 Hochmuth, 'Aerospace', op. cit., p. 161. The Trident was developed by de Haviland Aircraft, which merged to become a part of the Hawker Siddeley Group in the early 1960s. Therefore, it is often referred to as the Hawker Siddeley Trident.

41 Hayward, *Government and British Civil Aerospace*, op. cit., p. 28.

42 Hochmuth, 'Aerospace', op. cit., p. 162.

43 Hayward, *Government and British Civil Aerospace*, op. cit., p. 36.

44 Hochmuth, 'Aerospace', op. cit., p. 164.

45 Mark A. Lorell (1980) *Multinational Development of Large Aircraft: The European Experience R-2596-DR&E*, Santa Monica, CA: Rand Corporation, p. 8.

46 As in Britain, this meant state-owned airlines were required to purchase French aircraft whenever possible and sometimes to the detriment of both airline and aircraft manufacturer. See Gidwitz, *The Politics of International Air Transport*, op. cit., p. 21; Golich, *The Political Economy of International Air Safety*, op. cit., p. 49.

47 Richard R. Nelson (1984) *High-Technology Policies: A Five-Nation Comparison*, Washington, D.C.: American Enterprise Institute for Public Policy Research, pp. 34 and 71.

48 While some obvious short-term inconveniences were associated with this requirement, such 'tight cooperation gave the French invaluable experience for the many subsequent joint ventures which required work to be parcelled out to different firms in different countries': Hochmuth, 'Aerospace', op. cit., p. 165.

49 Nelson, *High-Technology Policies*, op. cit., p. 33.

50 Ibid., p. 164.

51 The 1950s turbojet designed for short- and medium-range trips found a niche in the first generation jet market because the other jets – the Boeing 707, Douglas DC8 and de Haviland Comet – were designed for longer-range travel.

52 The Caravelle beat the BEA/Vickers Vanguard (the successor to the Viscount) into service and BEA was faced with the prospect of jet competition on the Continent. See Hayward, *Government and British Civil Aerospace*, op. cit., p. 21. The Caravelle was eventually surpassed by Boeing's 727 in the 1960s.

53 Lorell, *Multinational Development of Large Aircraft*, op. cit., p. 8.

54 This may be related to the controversial debate over the issue of technology transfer. States and corporations have sought to protect national security and trade secrets by controlling technology. Licenced production is one of the easiest ways to protect technology.

   The sense of inferiority European states felt *vis-à-vis* the United States may explain why the British were willing to share *their* technology with the French via licenced coproduction, but were unwilling to 'borrow' technology from the United States under similar conditions. There is more prestige associated with being the licensor than being the licencee. Similarly, once French policy-makers realized collaboration was imperative to industry survival, the British were a more desirable choice than the Americans.

55 Although the United States agreed, in 1953, to help fund the procurement project, in 1958, when the initial product – the Italian Fiat G91 – was available, only Germany agreed to buy it. In 1956, when officials called for the collaborative development of a maritime patrol aircraft – the Breguet 1150 Atlantic – fourteen NATO members participated in the planning stages, but only five agreed to help finance the project. Only two eventually decided to procure the aircraft.

56 Lorell, *Multinational Development of Large Aircraft*, op. cit., pp. 9–10.

57 Ibid., p. 13.

58 The Europeans 'have codeveloped an impressive array of tracked military vehicles, tactical missiles, helicopters, and aircraft since the 1950s. Because of the especially costly nature of the R&D programs, European codevelopment has emphasised the high technology aerospace sector': Ibid., p. 2.

59 Ibid., p. 6.

60 Alfred D. Chandler, Jr. and Herman Daems (eds) (1980) *Managerial Hierarchies: Comparative Perspectives on the Rise of the Modern Industrial Enterprise*, Cambridge, MA: Harvard University Press, Chapter 4.

61 See note 9.
62 Chandler and Daems, *Managerial Hierarchies*, op. cit., Chapter 3.
63 A. R. Weyl (1965) Fokker: *The Creative Years*, New York: Funk & Wagnalls, pp. 35–7 and 188. While working for the Kaiser, Fokker engineered many improvements in war-fighting aircraft. Germany's Junkers claims credit for the concurrent development of the first jet-engine capabilities. Germany's Hans von Ohain and Britain's Sir Frank Whittle simultaneously uncovered the secrets of jet-engined flight. The Heinkel He 178 had its first jet flight on 27 August 1939; Britain first introduced jet aircraft in 1944 with its Gloster Meteor, shortly followed by the German Me 262. See Jerome Lederer (1985) 'Highlights in the development of civilian aircraft', *Automotive Engineering* Vol. 88, No. 12, December, p. 41.
64 In 1911, Germany introduced the first passenger service in a dirigible with Count Zeppelin's Schwaben. Other firsts included all-metal plane design in 1910, all-metal planes used on a commercial scheduled route and the all-metal cantilevered monoplane in 1919. William Winter, *Airplanes of the World*, op. cit., p. 26; Don Middleton (1986) *Civil Aviation: A Design History*, London: Ian Allan, p. 13.
65 Winter, *Airplanes of the World*, op. cit., p. 78. Experimentation with tailless gliders eventually lead to the first rocket fighter, the Me 163 and eventually to the arrowhead-shaped fighting wing and delta airplane; ibid., p. 131.
66 For example, Fokker's factories in Holland and in Hungary, where Fokker aircraft were built under license, produced transports for Germany.
67 Ibid., p. 78.
68 Ibid., p. 182.
69 Ibid., p. 251.
70 Keith Hayward (1986) *International Collaboration in Civil Aerospace*, New York: St Martin's Press, p. 41.
71 Between 1955 and 1964, the most intensive period of German-French collaboration, Germany produced French aircraft under licence and codeveloped the Atlantic, Transall, Hot, Milan and Roland. The last three are tactical missiles. See Lorell, *Multinational Development of Large Aircraft*, op. cit., p. 6.
72 Anthony J. Lawler, 'Internationalisation of the Commercial Airframe Business', paper presented to the Air Transportation Research International Forum, Indianapolis, IN: 12 June 1985, p. 13.
73 The United Kingdom had been invited to Messina, but refused to attend.
74 Only the US, with its huge geographic and demographic market, could support domestic aircraft manufacturers. American airlines were reluctant to consider foreign aircraft unless there was no alternative. For example, the US sales of the BAC111 and Caravelle were made before the DC9 was launched. Initially, the F27 had no direct competitor. (Subsequently Convair 340s and 440s were successful competitors.) The F27 also had the advantage of being built under licence in the US by Fairchild. This was probably the first 'modern' move toward internationalization, as far as the US was concerned, on the civil side. The British jet Canberra bomber had been built for the USAF by the Glen L. Martin Company.
75 Hochmuth, 'Aerospace', op. cit., p. 158.
76 Arguably it was earlier, but in 1945 no other conclusion was viable whereas before the First and Second World Wars, the United States wanted to remain isolated from the system.
77 Shepherd, G. and F. Duchene, op. cit., p. 21.
78 Hochmuth, 'Aerospace', op. cit., p. 167.
79 Ibid., p. 168.
80 Ibid.
81 Chandler and Daems, *Managerial Hierarchies*, op. cit., Chapter 1.
82 This has been a repeated phenomenon in civil aviation in the manufacturing and service sectors. See Davies, *A History of the World's Airlines*, op. cit.; Golich, *The Political Economy of International Air Safety*, op. cit., Chapter 2.
83 In commercial-class-aircraft manufacturing, the European Joint Airworthiness Consortium is a good example of this phenomenon.

84 This is reminiscent of old functionalist and neo-functionalist literature, which very effectively explains some aspects of corporate-state behaviour in the aerospace industry.

13 The Council for Mutual Economic Assistance: 1949-57

1 Richard Vaughan (1976) *Post-War Integration in Europe*, London, Edward Arnold, pp. 132-3.
2 Albania also joined in 1949 but effectively ceased participating in the work of the organization after 1961, though it has not formally renounced membership. The German Democratic Republic joined in 1950 and the other member states in the 1960s.
3 János Szita (1974) *25 éves a KGST*, Budapest, Kosssuth Könyvkiadó, p. 10.
4 György Szelecki (1986) *Mit kell tudni a KGST-röl?* Budapest, Kossuth Könyvkiadö.
5 *The Collected Works of V. I. Lenin* (1975) Vol. 44. Budapest, Kossuth Könyvkiado, p. 299.
6 Szita, *25 éves a KGST*, op. cit., p. 37.

14 The political economy of international economic security: retrospect and prospect

1 E. H. Carr (1939) *The Twenty Years Crisis*, London, pp. 116-17.
2 J. Louis Halle (1967) *The Cold War as History*, New York, Harper & Row, p. 53; Edy Kaufman (1976) *The Superpowers and their Influence, the United States and the Soviet Union in Eastern Europe and Latin America*, London, Croom Helm; Klaus Knorr (1975) *The Power of Nations, the political economy of international relations*, New York, Basic Books; A. W. de Porte (1979) *Europe Between the Superpowers*, Newhaven, Yale University Press; John Sayer (1981) *Superpower Rivalry*, London, Arnold.
3 For accounts that emphasize the influence of United States perceptions and values in the development of trade régimes see F. V. Meyer (1978) *International Trade Policy*, London, Croom Helm, pp. 137-40; Robert Baldwin (1976) 'The political economy of post-war US trade policy', *The Bulletin*, No. 4, pp. 5-37; Robert Gilpin (1987) *The Political Economy of International·Relations*, Princeton, University Press. For a critique of the hegemonic theory of postwar economic stability, see R. O. Keohane (1980) 'Theory of hegemonic stability and change in international economic régimes', in Ole R. Holsti, R. M. Siverson and A. L. George, (eds) *Change in the International System*, Boulder, CO, Westview Press, pp. 131-62; Robert Keohane (1984) *After Hegemony, cooperation and discord in the World Economy*, Princeton, University Press.
4 See, for example, Dieter Senghaas (1985) *The European Experience: A Historical Critique of Development Theory*, Leamington Spa, Dover, Berg Publishers; Peter J. Katzenstein (1985) *Small States in World Markets: Industrial Policy in Europe*, Ithaca and London, Cornell University Press; Pekka Konsonen (1987) *Hyvuinvointivaltion haasteet ja pohjoismaisetr mallit*, Mantta, Vastpaino; Raimo Varynen (1988). 'Constraints and opportunities in the foreign policies of small states', in Bertel Heurlin and Christian Thune (eds) *Danmark och det Internationale System*, Poitiske Studien, Copenhagen.
5 For a fuller development of these arguments on the mediating role of international régimes and the limits of a 'nation centric' model of the international economy, see D. Willis 'International policy coordination, credibility and East European debt', paper presented at the International Conference of the European Association of Law and Economics, Rome 3 September 1990.
6 M. M. Kostecki (1978) *East-West Trade and the GATT System*, New York, St Martin's Press, pp. 2-4. Kostecki observes that the growing bipolarism in the late 1940s and early 1950s had the effect of placing the newly formed international economic régimes firmly in the 'West' in terms of their norms and rules, as well as the perception of the east European states and Soviet Union of the interests these represented.
7 Geopolitical considerations figured strongly in the arguments for economic manoeuvres to counter Soviet 'underground methods'. See, for example, United States Department of State *Foreign Relations of the United States 1946*, Vol. 6, pp. 698-9 and

706–8. The belief that the United States alone could take both military and economic action to counter the Soviet threat is redolent in both the private musings and public utterances of American diplomats and politicians in this period. See Dean Acheson (1969) *Present at the Creation: My Years in the State Department*, New York; A. Theoharis (1974) 'The politics of scholarship, liberalism, anti-Communism and McCarthyism', in Robert Griffiths and A. Theoharis (eds) *The Spectre: Original Essays on the Cold War and the Origins of McCarthyism*, New York.

8 Michael Mastanduno (1985) 'Strategies of economic containment: US trade relations with the Soviet Union', *World Politics*, Vol. 37, pp. 503–31; Michael Mastandundo (1983) 'In pursuit of closure, American East-West trade strategy, 1949–58', mimeo. Clinton, N.Y., Hamilton College; Robert Baldwin (1976) 'The political economy of postwar US trade policy', *The Bulletin*, No. 4, pp. 5–37.

9 Pitrim Sorokin writing in 1944 first developed a theory of 'natural' convergence of the economies of eastern and western Europe *in the absence* of military and ideological conflict. See P. Sorokin (1944) *Russia and the United States*, New York, Dulton; see also 'The mutual convergence of the United States and the USSR', *International Journal of Comparative Sociology*, September 1960. However, students have come to emphasize the restrictions on economic development resulting from military interests and a repression of economic nationalism. See, for example, A. Braun (1987) *The Warsaw Pact: Change and Modernisation in the Gorbachev Era*, Boulder, Col., Westview; R. Kolkowicz (1969) 'The Warsaw Pact, entangling alliance', *Journal of Soviet and East European Studies*, Vol. 70, No. 1, pp. 86–101.

10 Joseph Stalin (1955) *Economic Problems of Socialism in the USSR*, Moscow, Foreign Languages Publishing House. Stalin wrote of 'two parallel world markets . . . confronting each other'. The Stalinist thesis of parallel economic development has been rejected by a new generation of economists, particularly in Central Europe. See Imre Vajda and Mihaly Simai (eds) (1971) *Foreign Trade in a Planned Economy*, Cambridge, Cambridge University Press, p. 54. It has been convincingly argued by Andre Gunder Frank (1980) *Crisis In the World Economy*, London, Heinemann, Chapter 4, p. 183 that the autarchy of the Soviet Union in the Stalinist period, and Stalin's theory of 'parallel' economic systems was more a result of Western boycotts than internal volition.

11 For a survey of the empirical evidence on the impact of United States' perceptions of vulnerability in resources supplies on American strategic planning in the postwar period, see I. O. Lesser, *Resources and Strategy: Vital Materials in International Conflict 1600-Present*, Basingstoke, Macmillan. A classic study is that of D. Krasner (1978) *Defending the National Interest: Raw Materials' Investment and US Foreign Policy*, Princeton, Princeton University Press.

12 Valerie Assetto (1988) *The Soviet Bloc in the IMF and the IBRD*, Boulder and London, Westview Press, p. 74. Assetto argues that the ousting of Poland (a founding member of the IMF and World Bank) in 1950, and the withdrawal of Czechoslovakia in 1953–54 were more for ideological reasons than the economic grounds overtly stated. For details, see Assetto, ibid., pp. 75–92. See also Joseph Gold (1974) *Membership and Non-membership in the International Monetary Fund*, Washington, DC, IMF, pp. 129–30.

13 The problems of incorporation of the centrally planned economies in the world-trade system were recognized but not seen as representing insuperable barriers at the time. See Raymond F. Mickesell (1947) 'The role of the international monetary agreements in a world of planned economies', *Journal of Political Economy*, Vol. 55.

14 A draft of the White Plan in April 1942 contended that 'to exclude a country such as Russia would be an egregious error'. Cited J. Gold (1974) *Membership and Non-membership in the International Monetary Fund*, op. cit., pp. 129–30. While Soviet economists in the 1943–4 debate on international financial reconstruction remained divided over some aspects of the American White Plan, they appear in fact to have been more favourably inclined to the American neoliberal plan than the more interventionist version suggested by Keynes. For details see Assetto, *The Soviet Bloc*, op. cit., pp. 57–9; see also Marie Lavigne (1978) '*The International Monetary Fund and the Soviet Union*, Studien uber Wirtschaft und Systemvergleiche, Wiener Institut fur Internationale Wirtschaftsvergleiche, Vol. 9, Vienna, Springer Verlag, pp. 367–70.

15 Clair Wilcox (1949) 'The promise of the World Trade Charter', *Foreign Affairs*, Vol. 27, p. 495.
16 Robert Gilpin (1975) *US Power and the Multinational Corporation: the Political Economy of Foreign Direct Investment*, New York, Basic Books; Charles, P. Kindleberger (1973) *The World Depression*, Berkeley, University of California Press; D. Krasner (1976) 'State Power and the Structure of International Trade', *World Politics*, Vol. 28.
17 For propositions linking the openness of economic systems to a preponderance of power of nation-states as opposed to a classical balance of power, see A. F. K. Organski (1968) *World Politics*, (2nd edn.), New York, Knopf, pp. 338-76; George Modelski (1978) 'The long cycle of global politics and the nation state', *Comparative Studies in Society and History*, Vol. 20, pp. 214-35; Krasner, 'State Power', op. cit., pp. 317-47.
18 See Brian M. Russet and J. D. Sullivan (1971) 'Collective goods and international organisation', *International Organisation*, Vol. 25; John Gerard Ruggie (1972) 'Collective goods and future international collaboration', *American Political Science Review*, Vol. 66; Duncan Snidal (1979) 'Public goods, property rights and political organisation', *International Studies Quarterly*, Vol. 23, p. 544.
19 R. Vernon (1971) *Sovereignty at Bay, the Multinational Spread of US Enterprise*, London, Longman; Robert Gilpin (1975) *US Power and the Multinational Corporation*, op. cit., R. D. McKinlay and D. Mughan (1984) *Aid and Arms to the Third World, an Analysis of the Distribution and Impact of US Official Transfers*, London, Pinter.
20 See H. C. Wallich (1955) *Mainsprings of the German Revival*, New Haven, Yale University Press, pp. 355-7; Harold Zink (1957) *The United States in Germany, 1944-1955*, Toronto, van Nostrand, p. 263; Dale Clark (1948) 'Conflicts over planning at staff headquarters', in C. J. Freidrich and Associates, *American Experiences in Military Government in World War II*, New York, Rinehart, pp. 220-31; Lucious D. Clay (1950) *Decisions in Germany*, Garden City, NJ, Doubleday, pp. 260-1.
21 The prime goal of foreign policy was already defined in Truman's March 1947 speech and what came to be known as the 'Point Four' programme of development aid. See Robert H. Ferrell (1980) *The Autobiography of Harry S. Truman*, New York, W. W. Norton, p. 102. See also John Lewis Gaddis (1982) *Strategies of Containment*, New York; Melvin Gurtov (1974) *The United States Against the Third World: Anti-Nationalism and Intervention*, New York, p. 89. On United States aid to Social Democratic parties in Europe, see M. J. Hogan (1989) *The Marshall Plan, America, Britain and the Reconstruction of Western Europe 1947-1952*, Cambridge, Cambridge University Press. On the anti-Communist purges in Japan during the occupation, see Harry E. Wildes (1954) *Typhoon in Tokyo's New York*, London, Macmillan, pp. 269-316.
22 T. Balogh (1963) *Unequal Partners*, Oxford Blackwell, p. 11; Charles C. Maier (1977) 'The politics of productivity: foundations of American international economic policy after World War II', *International Organisation*, Vol. 31. For a view on the decisive impact of United States perceptions of the national interest in the reconstruction of the postwar international economic order along liberal lines, see Louis J. Halle, *The Cold War as History*, New York, Harper & Row, p. 53. See also R. Gardner (1956) *Sterling - Dollar Diplomacy*, Oxford, Clarendon Press; T. Balogh (1949) *The Dollar Crisis*, Oxford, Blackwell; C. P. Kindleberger (1950) *The Dollar Shortage*, Cambridge, MIT.
23 A conception of political hegemony in terms of comparative economic advantage is developed by Immanuel Wallerstein (1980) *The Modern World System*, New York, Academic Press, p. 38. Wallerstein defines hegemony as a situation in which a 'core state' produces goods so efficiently that it will be the prime beneficiery of a free-world market.
24 Albert, O. Hirschman (1980) *National Power and the Structure of Foreign Trade*, Berkeley, University of California Press, first published 1945; G. J. Ikenberry (1986) 'The irony of state strength, comparative responses to oil shocks in the 1970s', *International Organisation* Vol. 40 pp. 105-38.
25 A good example is the advocacy of the use of United States credits to support Tito's defiance of Stalin in Yugoslavia in 1949. See United States, Tariff Commission (1948) *Operation of Trade Agreements Program July 1934-April 1948, Part III Trade Agreements Concessions Granted by the US*, Washington D.C., GPO, p. 66.

26 Department of State Policy Statement, 1 September 1949, 711.00, p. 149. A theory of hegemonic predation has been applied in particular to intra-European and American most-favoured-nations treaties on tariff treatment in the 1930s. Of the 899 'concessions' granted by the United States between 1934 and 1939, only 258 were in manufactures. The majority were to small or weak countries supplying raw materials at low cost. *Foreign Relations of the United States 1949*, Vol. 5, Eastern Europe and the Soviet Union, Washington D.C., US Government Printing Office, p. 941.

27 See for examples of an essentially instrumental model of institutions such as the IMF, R. Parboni (1980) *The Dollar and its Rivals, Recession, Inflation and International Finance*, London, Verso, p. 50; Sidney Dell (1981) *On Being Grandmotherly: the Evolution of the IMF Conditionality*, Essays in International Finance No. 144, Princeton, Princeton University Press. For an early perception of the United States interests in European integration, see F. Hirschman (1945) *National Power and the Structure of Foreign Trade*, op. cit., see also F. V. Meyer (1978) *International Trade Policy*, London, Croom Helm, pp. 137–40.

28 Susan Strange (1982) 'Still an extraordinary power: America's role in a global monetary system', in R. E. Lombra and W. E. Witte (eds) *Political Economy of International and Domestic Monetary Relations*, Iowa, Iowa University Press/Ames; R. Triffin (1964) *The Evolution of the International Monetary System*, Princeton, Princeton University Press.

29 Parbonni, *The Dollar and its Rivals*, op. cit., p. 50.

30 See also Lionel Curtis (1945) *World War: its Cause and Cure*, London, Oxford University Press. A fascinating example of this convergence in intellectual thought on the need for a managed international economy is the response of Keynes to a brief to produce propaganda in favour of the free trade and the gold standard which he refused to do on the grounds that this would not have propaganda value. Keynes held, moreover, that once the War was over Britain would have to offer the world 'the same as what Dr Funk offers, except that we shall do it better and more honestly'. Cited Armand van Dormael (1978) *Bretton Woods, birth of a monetary system*, London, Macmillan, p. 7.

31 Ronald Steel (1988) *Walter Lippmann and the American Century*, Boston Mass., Little Brown.

32 US White House, Economic report of the President, January 1955 (52). Eisenhower, cited J. Gowa (1984) 'Subsidising American Exports abroad, pitfalls in the analysis of public and private power', *World Politics*, Vol. 37, p. 188.

33 Krasner *Defending the National Interest*, op. cit., suggests that the relative power position of the United States after the Second World War, coupled with the insulation of the executive from Congress on foreign-policy matters involving security issues, allowed central policy-makers to give priority to foreign-policy objectives over domestic economic considerations. He sees this as 'non-logical' behaviour potentially leading to misperceptions of the external situation, notably an exaggeration of the importance of the Communist element in foreign countries.

34 Armand van Dormael, *Bretton Woods*, op. cit., pp. 202–3. The dominant position of the United States in establishing the terms of the ITO and the IMF is beyond doubt. According to van Dormael, Harry Dexter and his staff had complete control over the organization of meetings, the scheduling of scripts, the rules of procedure and the drafting of all official documents including the daily minutes of the final act. White also headed a special committee that resolved ambiguities and elaborated operational details; he even 'prepared for inclusion in the final act a number of provisions that were never discussed or even brought up'.

35 This is an important observation, as these habits of respecting 'zones of economic interest' in the postwar period are an important part of the explanation for the emergent divisions in Europe and are generally overlooked in accounts that emphasize United States' economic interests. See Gyorgy Ranki (1983) *Economy and Foreign Policy, the struggle of the Great Powers for Hegemony in the Danube Valley, 1919–1939*, New York, Columbia University Press, p. 189. For an argument concerning the importance of Alliance indifference to eastern Europe, see R. L. Wolff (1974) *The*

Balkans in our Time, Cambridge, Mass., Harvard University Press, p. 249.

36 R. Parbonni, *The Dollar and its Rivals*, op. cit., cites the fact that the United States tolerated money devaluations that discriminated against American goods, op. cit., p. 49. Richard N. Gardner (1976) *Sterling-Dollar Diplomacy in Current Perspective*, New York, Columbia University Press, Chapters 6, 8, 14 and 17 establishes that typically over the last decade, a period when America's economic power has been reputedly in decline, America has generally sought to obtain full compensation for trade concessions with Europe and Japan, and has indeed resorted to protectionist barriers and bilateral agreements against the spirit of GATT.

37 Beverly Crawford and Stephanie Lenway (1985) 'Decision modes and international régime change, Western collaboration in East-West trade', *World Politics*, Vol. 37, pp. 375–402.

38 Mutual Assistance Act, US Code, 1951, 65 Stat 644, Chapter 575, Public Law 213, (US, Congress, 1951). This provided the basis, two years later, for the United States initiative in the formation of the COCOM, an international régime designed to coordinate and administer Western embargoes towards the Communist bloc.

39 K. S. Tomlinson (1985) 'United States Legislative framework for commercial relations with Eastern Europe', in *East European Economies, the Slow Growth in the 1980s*, Joint Economic Committee of the US Congress, October (US Congress); P. Hanson (1981) *Trade and Technology in Soviet Western Relations*, London, Macmillan.

40 M. Friedlander (ed.) (1990) *Foreign Trade in Eastern Europe and the Soviet Union*, Boulder, Col., Westview Press.

41 See G. Oblath and P. Pete, 'Mechanism and institutional systems of the Finnish-Soviet economic relations', in M. Friedlander (ed.) *Foreign Trade*, op. cit., pp. 117–28; Gabor Oblath and P. Pete (1986) 'The development, mechanism and institutional system of Finnish-Soviet Economic relations', *WIIW Forschungsberichte*, No. 111, Wien, pp. 1–69.

42 Eugene Staley (1935) *War and the Private Investor, a Study of the Relations of International Politics and International Private Investment*, Garden City, Doubleday. As Staley had observed as early as 1935 in arguments against mixing up commercial and political ambitions: 'those areas or ventures of most importance to diplomats, strategists and patriots, in which the presence of national capital would be serviceable to government's foreign policy, are the very ones least calculated to inspire enthusiasm in those who hold available funds'. Ibid., p. 273.

43 Robert Packenham (1973) *Liberal America and the Third World, Political Development Ideas in Foreign Aid and Social Science*, Princeton, Princeton University Press, p. 88.

44 Richard E. Caves (1982) *Multinational Enterprise and Economic Analysis*, Cambridge, Cambridge University Press, pp. 22 and 63.

45 President Eisenhower's letter to Vice-President Nixon, 1 May 1953. *Reciprocal Trade Agreement File*, Ann Whitman Series, Administration Series. Eisenhower library, 1953. Consider the following comment by Eisenhower in personal correspondence in 1953: 'through increasing international trade and stimulating in every practical way the flow of private investment abroad, we can strengthen the free world, including ourselves, in natural and healthy ways. By so doing, we can lessen and ultimately eliminate the heavy burden of foreign aid.' Ibid.

46 Burton I. Kaufman (1982) *Trade and Aid, Eisenhower's Foreign Policy, 1953–61*, Baltimore, Johns Hopkins Press, p. 46; cited Gowa, op. cit., 1984, p. 197.

47 According to Gowa, 'Subsidising American exports', op. cit., p. 199, this accounted in 1955 for less than one-third of 1 per cent of US GNP. By contrast, exports accounted for 3 per cent.

48 Robert H. Ferrell (ed.) (1981) *The Eisenhower Diaries*, New York and London, W. W. Norton, p. 310. Ferrell claims that with the exception of oil, the centrepiece of Krasner's study advancing such a strategic claim, there is only one mention of foreign investment in Eisenhower's diary entries.

49 According to Gowa's research on administration internal documents of the period the limited importance of FDI abroad 'paled in significance' against more pressing security concerns (e.g. the Soviet Union's explosion of the hydrogen bomb, 1954; the defeat of

the French at Dien Bien Phu, 1954; and the future of the Arbenz régime in Guatemala). Gowa, 'Subsidising American exports', op. cit., p. 196.

50 E. R. Barlow and Ira I. Wender (1955) *Foreign Investment and Taxation*, New Jersey, Prentice Hall, pp. 10–27 and 111.

51 While some tax concessions in support of American foreign direct investment were made in 1954 on the recommendation of the Committee of Ways and Means, this investment abroad was on the grounds of security.

52 See, for example, Alexander de Conde and W. R. Allen (1957) *Isolation and Security, Ideas and Interests in Twentieth Century American Foreign Policy*, Durnham, NC, Duke University Press; Ronald J. Caridi (1974) *Twentieth Century American Foreign Policy, Security and Self-interest*, Englewood Cliffs, NJ, Prentice Hall; C. F. Bergsten, T. Horst and T. H. Moran (1978) *American Multinationals and American Interests*, Washington D.C., Brookings; Theodore H. Moran (1973) 'Foreign expansion as an institutional necessity for US Corporate capitalism', *World Politics*, Vol. 25, pp. 369–86.

53 United States' strategic concerns look less unique and less successful in the field of foreign direct investment when compared with that of Japan, whose lack of native material resources is chronic by comparison. See Raymond Vernon (1983) *Two Hungry Giants, the United States and Japan in the Quest for Oil and Ores*, Cambridge, Harvard University Press.

54 The scale of Communist government acquisition of United States property which form the background to US foreign-policy concerns in this period were from the emerging Communist countries and were estimated in the region of $1 billion for Czechoslovakia, Rumania, Hungary, Poland, Bulgaria and Yugoslavia, and $46 million in China. US Congress, House Committee on Foreign Affairs (1963) *Expropriations of American-Owned Property by Foreign Governments in the Twentieth Century*, Washington D.C., Government Printing Office. One independent estimate puts American losses in eastern Europe at only $240 million. See Franklin Root (1968) 'The expropriation experience of American companies, what happened to 38 companies', *Business Horizons*, Vol. 111, April, pp. 69 and 71. For efforts to assess the total magnitude of expropriation, see R. S. Olson (1979) 'Expropriations and economic coercion in world politics', *Journal of Developing Areas*, Vol. 31, p. 247.

55 Bruce Martin Russet (1981) 'Security and the resources scramble, will 1984 be like 1914?', *International Affairs*, No. 58, pp. 241–58.

56 These divisions were reflected in intellectual opinion in this period, not simply aligned about an East-West ideological divide. Notable and opposed views on the role of economic security in international relations are those of Lionel Robbins (1939) *The Economic Base of Class Conflict*, London, pp. 112–19; and Friedrich A. Hayek (1944) *The Road to Serfdom*, London.

57 It is arguable that Sweden was, however, fairly unique in the way it developed a system of 'economic defence', originating in the 1930s wartime-contingency plans. See, for example, Ebba Dohlman (1989) *National Welfare and Economic Interdependence, the Case of Sweden's Foreign Trade Policy*, Clarendon, Oxford, esp. p. 37 and Chapter 1.

58 See Valerie Assetto *The Soviet Bloc*, op. cit., pp. 65–6. The Soviet Union's initial position in the Bretton Woods negotiations towards the Anglo-American initiative was in fact supportive, up until January 1946 when the Soviet Union announced that it 'did not deem it appropriate to join the (Bretton Woods) institutions . . . at this time'.

59 M. M. Kostecki (1978) *East-West Trade and the GATT System*, op. cit., pp. 1–2 and 48; Jozef van Brabant (1987) *The GATT and the Soviet Union – a plea for reform*, Working Paper Series No. 6, New York, United Nations Department of International Economic and Social Affairs, pp. 6–7 and 14; William R. Kaylor (1984) *The Twentieth Century World – an International History*, Oxford University Press, p. 274.

60 Henry Pelling (1989) *Britain and the Marshall Plan*, Basingstoke, Macmillan.

61 P. J. Taylor (1990) *Britain and the Cold War: 1945 as geopolitical transition*, London, Pinter.

62 Bruce Russet (1970) *What Price Vigilance? The Burdens of National Defense*, New Haven, Conn., Yale University Press; Bruce Martin Russet (1975) 'America's Retreat from World Power status', *Political Science Quarterly*, Vol. 90, pp. 1–21; Walter

Goldstein (1981) 'The opportunity costs of acting as a superpower, US military strategies in the 1980s', *Journal of Peace Research*, Vol. 18, pp. 241–60.

63 The rationale for Soviet refusal to join the IMF and IBRD is set out in Valerie Assetto *The Soviet Bloc*, op. cit., p. 64–5. See also Joyce Kolko and Charles H. Lipson (1974) *America and the Crisis of World Capitalism*, Boston, Beacon Press, pp. 396 and 416; C. Randal Henning (1987) *Macroeconomic Diplomacy in the 1980s*, London, Croom Helm, pp. 48–52.

64 Robert Triffin (1960) *Gold and the Dollar Crisis*, New Haven, Yale University Press.

65 R. O. Keohane (1971) 'The big influence of small allies', *Foreign Policy* No. 2, Spring, pp. 161–82; R. W. Cox and H. K. Jacobson (1973) 'The anatomy of influence' in R. W. Cox et. al. (eds) *The Anatomy of Influence*, New Haven, Yale University Press, p. 428; C. J. Bartlett (1974) *The Rise and Fall of Pax America, United States Foreign Policy in the Twentieth Century*, London, Elek.

66 Ragnar Nurske (1944) *International Currency Experience, Lessons of the Inter-war Period*, League of Nations, Washington D.C., Economic, Financial and Transit Department, Chapter 4. Nurske stressed the shift in opinion in favour of multilateralism, while other writers saw the centrally planned economies as posing no insuperable barriers to multilateralism. See Herbert Feis (1947) 'The conflict over trade ideologies', *Foreign Affairs*, Vol. 25; Raymond F. Mikesell (1947) 'The role of international monetary agreements in a world of planned economies', *Journal of Political Economy*, Vol. 55.

67 James R. March (1966) 'The power of power', in David Eaton (ed.), *Varieties of Political Theory*, Englewood Cliffs, N. J. Prentice Hall, Vol. 1, pp. 50–4. A 'basic forces' model assumed that actors exert all their force within a system and that choice is the 'direct resultant' of these powers. For a critique of such a model in the context of international economic régimes, see R. O. Keohane (1982) 'Theory of hegemonic stability', in Ray Lombra and Bill Witte (eds) *The Political Economy of International and Domestic Monetary Relations*, Iowa, Iowa State University Press/Ames, pp. 131–62.

68 Whitman, for example, argues that the IMF was not an instrument of American policy interests, but, on the contrary, largely due to the strength of the US dollar, was drawn into a largely *passive* role in the exchange-rate adjustment process (up to the formal termination of the Bretton Woods system in 1971) while bearing most of the adjustment costs. See also Marina von Neumann Whitman (1979) *Reflections of Interdependence, Issues for Economic Theory and United States Policy*, Pittsburgh, University of Pittsburgh Press, p. 224.

69 This is neatly captured by Adolf Berle in 1943, when he foresaw that US-British collaboration would have to 'free the British people of their fear that they might have to subordinate their international social policy, and to assure the United States that a share of its production was not claimable by tender of a new "trick" currency'. Cited van Dormael, *Bretton Woods*, op. cit., p. 103.

70 R. N. L. Cooper (1975) 'Prolegomenta to the choice of an international monetary system', *International Organisation*, Vol. 29. The Anglo-American 'Joint Statement of Principles' signed before the Bretton Woods agreement erected a 'double screen' to secure domestic economies against strictures of balance of payments – short-term assistance to finance payment deficits on current accounts through the IMF. The aim was to correct fundamental disequilibrium while leaving national governments with the freedom to maintain capital controls. Cooper, ibid., p. 85.

71 J. Ruggie (1982) 'International régimes, transactions and change: embedded liberalism in the postwar economic order', *International Organisation*, Vol. 36, pp. 374–416. Ruggie argues that these amounted to 'a shared common purpose, intergovernmental collaboration to facilitate balance-of-payments equilibrium, in an international environment of multilateralism and a domestic context of full employment'. Ibid., p. 211. The distinction between 'embedded' and 'disembedded' economic orders was made by Karl Polanyi in 1944, in (1957) *The Great Transformation*; see also his (1957) *Trade and Markets in Early Empires*, Glencoe, Ill, Free Press.

72 Horsfield, *The IMF*, op. cit., p. 228.

73 For accounts of the establishment of the IMF see Fred. L. Block (1977) *The Origins of International Economic Disorder*, Berkeley, University of California Press, Chapter 5.

74 Stuart Corbridge (1988) 'The asymmetry of interdependence: the United States and the geopolitics of international financial relations', *Studies in Comparative International Development*. Corbridge argues that 'the principal character and dynamics of the postwar international economic order have been determined by the geopolitical strategies – and economic imperatives – of the United States'.

75 For a survey of this literature see P. Guerreri and P. C. Padoan (1987) 'The political economy approach to international cooperation, a critical survey', *Economic Notes*, Vol. 2; and, for the relevance to the process of East-West financial integration, D. Willis (1990) 'Financial market liberalization and the efficiency of capital transfer mechanisms, East-West-South Perspectives, Part I', paper presented at the 1st International Conference of EACES, Verona, 27–29 September 1990 (forthcoming).

76 An example of the conflict between the old 'state élite' struggles for control over markets and the logic of transnational authority in some areas of commerce is provided by Vicki Golich's study of transnational collaboration in the aerospace industry, this volume, Chapter 12.

77 A contrary position has been argued by Stanley Hoffman (ed.) (1987) *Contemporary Theory in International Relations*, Westview, Conn., Greenwood. He observes that 'One of the crucial features and paradoxes of politics today is that whereas internal politics are conditioned and affected by world problems more than ever before, the foreign policies of nations remains largely dictated by the domestic experiences and by the nation's image of itself.'

78 Jacques Attali (1977) 'L'acception des règles de l'economie mondiale est irreversible', *La Parole et l'Outil*, Paris. Attali argues that economic integration since the Second World War is so far advanced that the establishment of a pure Socialist state is no longer feasible.

79 Gunnar Alder-Karlsson, *Western Economic Warfare*, op. cit.; Alan S. Milward (1977) *War, Economy and Society 1939–45*, London, Allen Lane, Chapter 9 on Economic Warfare.

80 Staley, *War and the Private Investor*, op. cit., 'International friction has been a good deal more frequent and dangerous where private investment has been pressed into service as instruments, tools, of a larger political purpose which the instruments themselves did not originate' (xv–xvl). Thus, 'It would be a mistake . . . to imply that a clear-cut distinction can be made between . . . the use of private capital as a tool of diplomacy and . . . the use of diplomacy as a tool of private capital. The foreign policies of states and the foreign investments of their citizens mutually influence and condition each other.' p. 358.

81 On the problems of Soviet military control, see J. Simon (1984) *Warsaw Pact Forces, Problems of Command and Control*, Boulder, Col., Westview.

82 See, for example, Garret Hardin (1968) 'The tragedy of the Commons', *Science*, Vol. 162, 1243–8, p. 129. The pure economic logic of cooperation assuming individual rational behaviour in economic theory has generally run counter to this optimism, suggesting that collaboration will tend to produce suboptimal outcomes. The alternative view favoured by the present author is more in the tradition of Locke: that the existence of conflict will tend to produce a demand for a 'final arbiter', and an interest of rational agents in conforming to 'fair' and mutually agreed principles in governing future behaviour. See also Thomas Schelling (1960) *The Strategy of Conflict*, Cambridge, Harvard University Press, Chapter 4: Towards a theory of interdependent decision.

Index